Marketing in the 21st Century

MARKETING IN THE 21ST CENTURY

New World Marketing
Volume 1

Timothy J. Wilkinson and
Andrew R. Thomas
Volume Editors

Bruce D. Keillor, General Editor

Praeger Perspectives

Westport, Connecticut
London

Library of Congress Cataloging-in-Publication Data

Marketing in the 21st century / Bruce D. Keillor, general editor.
    p. cm.
    Includes bibliographical references and index.
    ISBN-13: 978–0–275–99275–0 (set : alk. paper)
    ISBN-13: 978-0–275–99276–7 (vol 1 : alk. paper)
    ISBN-13: 978-0–275–99277–4 (vol 2 : alk. paper)
    ISBN-13: 978-0–275–99278–1 (vol 3 : alk. paper)
    ISBN-13: 978-0–275–99279–8 (vol 4 : alk. paper)

  1. Marketing. I. Keillor, Bruce David.
    HF5415.M2194 2007
    658.8—dc22   2007016533

British Library Cataloguing in Publication Data is available.

Library of Congress Catalog Card Number: 2007016533
ISBN-13: 978-0–275–99275–0 (set)
ISBN-13: 978-0–275–99276–7 (vol. 1)
ISBN-13: 978-0–275–99277–4 (vol. 2)
ISBN-13: 978-0–275–99278–1 (vol. 3)
ISBN-13: 978-0–275–99279–8 (vol. 4)

First published in 2007

Praeger Publishers, 88 Post Road West, Westport, CT 06881
An imprint of Greenwood Publishing Group, Inc.
www.praeger.com

Printed in the United States of America

The paper used in this book complies with the
Permanent Paper Standard issued by the National
Information Standards Organization (Z39.48–1984).

10 9 8 7 6 5 4 3 2 1

CONTENTS

SET INTRODUCTION

It is my privilege to introduce this four-volume set, *Marketing in the 21st Century*. Given the myriad changes that have taken place in the area of marketing over the past several years, and the increasingly dynamic nature of marketing as a business discipline, the publication of these volumes is particularly relevant and timely. Each volume deals with an aspect of marketing that is both a fundamental component of marketing in this new century as well as one that requires new perspectives as the marketplace continues to evolve.

The set addresses four of the most compelling areas of marketing, each of which is changing the foundation of how academics and businesspeople approach the marketing tasks necessary for understanding and succeeding in the changing business environment. These areas are global marketing, direct marketing, firm-customer interactions, and marketing communications. By using recognized experts as authors—both academic and business practitioners—the volumes have been specifically compiled to include not just basic academic research, but to speak to business people in terms of how they can translate the information contained in each chapter into long-term success for their firm or organization.

Volume 1, *New World Marketing*, edited by Timothy J. Wilkinson and Andrew R. Thomas, deals with the salient aspects of the global marketplace. More specifically, it focuses on the realities of the 21st-century global market and then moves into how to identify emerging markets of opportunity, operate in these markets successfully from the perspective of the customer, and develop global strategies that are grounded in the concept of constant improvement through the use of value-added strategies. Authors of numerous books and articles related to international marketing, with extensive experience in executive education in international/global marketing, the editors are uniquely qualified to create a cutting-edge volume in their area of expertise.

In Volume 2, *Interactive and Multi-Channel Marketing,* edited by William J. Hauser and Dale M. Lewison, the focus shifts toward the various mechanisms through which firms and organizations can establish a means for direct interaction with their customers, whether individual consumers or other businesses. Using a two-step approach, Volume 2 discusses in great depth issues related to understanding the various direct-marketing options and then moves on to the application of these options to maximize results. As Director and Associate Director, respectively, of the Taylor Institute for Direct Marketing at The University of Akron, the leading institute worldwide for direct marketing, the editors have the ability to draw on the knowledge of the "best and brightest" in this rapidly emerging and influential area of marketing.

Volume 3, *Company and Customer Relations,* edited by Linda M. Orr and Jon M. Hawes, tackles the challenges of not only establishing and maintaining a functioning relationship between company and customer, but also how to sell successfully in the 21st century. Along the way, they deal with thorny issues such as when to disengage customers and where technology fits into what are, typically, personal interactions. Dr. Hawes is a well-recognized expert in building and maintaining customer trust, while Dr. Orr has a wide range of business and academic experience in organizational learning. This combination of perspectives has resulted in a volume that deals head-on with issues of immediate concern for any business organization.

Finally, Volume 4, *Integrated Marketing Communication,* edited by Deborah L. Owens and Douglas R. Hausknecht, addresses the various means of creating a basis for communication between company and customer that goes well beyond the traditional approaches of advertising, public relations, and sales promotion. The volume begins by considering how the new age customer "thinks" in the context of consumer behavior and then segues into methods to construct an interactive communication platform. Both editors are widely recognized in business and academic circles as experts in the field of marketing communication. They are also known for their ability to view traditional marketing communication tools "outside of the box." The result is a volume that puts a truly fresh perspective on communicating with customers.

Each of the volumes in the set presents the most advanced thinking in their respective areas. Collectively, the set is the definitive collection of the necessary new paradigms for marketing success in the 21st century. It has been my pleasure to work with the volume editors, as well as with many of the chapter authors, in bringing this collection to you. I am convinced that, regardless of your area of interest in the field of marketing, you will find *Marketing in the 21st Century* an invaluable and timeless resource.

Bruce D. Keillor, General Editor

Part I

WORLD MARKETING STRATEGY

CHAPTER 1

THE NEW GLOBAL MARKETING REALITIES

Gary A. Knight

Today, business operates in a fiercely competitive, borderless world in which customers access products and services from everywhere, and their expectations regarding value and quality have grown apace. Increasingly, international marketing capabilities honed on global experience are minimal requirements to participate in the global marketplace. Spectacular growth in technology, a consequent revolution in the telecommunications industry, and a broad-based spread of e-commerce have shifted the ways organizations manage themselves. The emergence of an inextricably linked international marketplace for goods, services, capital, and investment contributes to complexity and competition in a global market that is growing in magnitude and scope.

Perhaps the most important trend of the last few decades is globalization, which reflects the growing interconnectedness of national economies and interdependence of consumers, producers, suppliers, and governments in different countries. It reflects the production and marketing of products and brands worldwide by firms located across the globe. Combined with declining trade barriers and the increasing ease with which international business takes place, the activities of these firms are leading to gradual integration of the economies of most nations in the world.

Globalization is a revolution in progress, the central story line of the 21st century, with major consequences within as well as between nations. Globalization is a powerful and positive force that stimulates economic growth, creates jobs, raises incomes, expands both choice and competition, improves product quality, and lowers prices. The fact that virtually all the world's nations willingly participate in some form of international free trade is evidence that they see it as being in their own best interests. Indeed, it is a lack of trade, investment, and freedom that keeps the world's poorest economies in poverty and environmental degradation.

Business leaders must confront the key future challenges of international marketing. In this chapter, I review key trends and realities that confront the contemporary international marketer. Let us first review the critical role of information and communications technologies.

INFORMATION AND COMMUNICATIONS TECHNOLOGIES

While globalization makes going global an imperative, advances in information and communications technologies (ICTs) provide the means for taking business operations abroad. ICTs make the cost of international operations affordable for all types of companies, explaining why so many small and medium enterprises have entered the international arena. Figure 1.1 shows how global communications costs have plummeted to almost zero. Meanwhile, the number of Internet users has grown dramatically.

Communications technology is critical. It took five months for Spain's Queen Isabella to learn about Columbus's voyage, two weeks for Europe to learn of President Lincoln's assassination, and 1.5 seconds for the world to witness the collapse of New York's World Trade Center. The most profound technological advances have occurred in the area of communications, especially telecommunications, satellites, optical fiber, wireless technology, and, of course, the Internet. These developments are revolutionary and similar in their effects to the commercialization of the printing press in Europe in the 15th century. The resultant widespread dissemination of information and knowledge gave rise to a giant leap in human activity.[1]

More than 500 million people worldwide already have access to the Internet. It has become the information backbone of the global economy, allowing for voice, data, and real-time video communication, as well as facilitating cross-border business transactions. A wide range of goods and services—from auto parts to bank loans—are marketed online. South Korea, where Internet access is nearly 100 percent, is leading the way. South Korea's broadband networks for home use are much faster than European and U.S. systems. Korean schoolchildren use their cell phones to get homework from their teachers and play games online with gamers worldwide. Adults use their phones to pay bills, do banking, buy lottery tickets, and check traffic conditions. South Korea is becoming the dominant global player in high-tech industries such as mobile communications, digital robotics, and various software categories.[2]

Widespread diffusion of the Internet and e-mail make company internationalization extremely cost-effective. The Internet provides cheap and ready access to information and opens up the global marketplace to companies that would normally not have the resources to do international business, including countless

Figure 1.1
Falling Communication and Information Costs Facilitate International Marketing

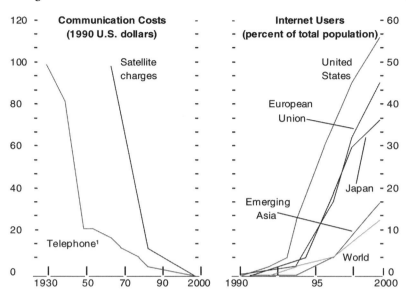

[1]Cost of a three-minute phone call from New York to London.
Source: IMF (2005), *World Economic Outlook,* Washington, DC: International Monetary Fund.

small and medium enterprises and born-global firms. Such companies often succeed by entering "virtual alliances" with partners in key markets and locations overseas. The Internet has fostered an ongoing revolution in the way firms acquire and use information vital to conducting international market research. Search engines, databases, reference guides, and countless government and private support systems assist managers to maximize knowledge and skills for international business success.

The Internet also facilitates international marketing activities, particularly by smaller firms. By establishing a Web site, even tiny companies take the first step in becoming multinational firms. Today many firms leverage the Internet to engage in direct marketing, the selling of goods or services directly to end users, bypassing traditional intermediaries. Some direct marketers engage in catalog sales, in which catalogs of the firm's offerings are mailed to potential customers. For instance, Eddie Bauer does a thriving catalog business with customers in Asia, Europe, and North America. More and more firms use the Internet to provide detailed product information and the means for foreigners to purchase offerings. Some are entirely Internet based, with no retail stores at all, such as Amazon.com. On the other hand, more than one-third of traditional retailers (for example, Kohl's, Tesco, Wal-Mart, and Zellers) now employ some type of Internet-based marketing.[3]

The Internet also facilitates consolidation and increased efficiency of the global supply chain and international distribution channels. It facilitates efficient outsourcing, which allows firms to concentrate on their core competencies. With real-time information sharing, manufacturers and distributors optimize cross-national communications and consequent international operations. Small and medium enterprises (SMEs) benefit through the ability to project the image of being larger firms, cut international operations costs, and provide products through virtual warehouses. The time from ordering to receipt can be greatly reduced, allowing smaller firms to compete internationally.

But while many direct marketers have flourished on the Internet, others have floundered. Skillful supply-chain management based on brick-and-mortar facilities still provides the backbone for global sales. However, the Internet holds great promise, and its role in direct international marketing will likely increase over time.

GLOBALIZATION

Globalization is of course a key international marketing reality. Cross-national merchandise trade has increased dramatically since the 1980s. By the early 2000s, the total of merchandise exports and imports represented more than 40 percent of world gross domestic product (GDP). Globalization and technological ad-
vances permit more and more firms to target billions of consumers and industrial buyers worldwide. Highly international firms source input goods from suppliers worldwide and sell their products and services in hundreds of foreign markets. Growth in world trade is presenting a much greater choice in products and services to consumers worldwide. The competitive and value-adding activities of globally active firms are pushing down prices and contributing to higher living standards worldwide.[4]

The most salient feature of globalization is growing integration and interdependence of national economies. Global companies devise extensive multi-country operations via investments aimed at production and marketing activities. The aggregate activities of these firms give rise to economic integration.

Globalization also means convergence of buyer lifestyles and needs. Today people in Tokyo, New York, and Paris can buy the same household goods, clothing, automobiles, and consumer electronics. The same pattern is observable in industrial markets as well, where the raw materials, parts, and components that professional buyers source from suppliers worldwide are increasingly standardized, that is, similar or uniform in design. As income levels rise, demand preferences are converging for both industrial and consumer goods and services. More than 90 percent of the movies shown in Canada are made abroad, primarily in the United States. The movie market in Europe and Japan is dominated by popular Hollywood films. Media contribute to the homogenization of world consumer preferences, in part by emphasizing a particular lifestyle dominated by the United States. Increasingly, this trend is spreading to the developing countries as well. Converging tastes and global production platforms facilitate the launch and marketing of highly standardized products to buyers around the world.

Intense global competition is forcing firms to reduce the costs of production and marketing. Global corporations strive to drive down prices via economies of scale and by standardizing what they sell. Today, globalization of markets is transforming the world into a global village, where companies undertake international marketing activities in a giant global marketplace. In their own way, globalization and technological advances are resulting in the "death of distance."[5] That is, the geographic and, to some extent, the cultural distance that separate nations are shrinking.

THE RISE OF TERRORISM

One of the negative manifestations of globalization is the rise of global terrorism. Terrorism is the threat or actual use of force or violence to attain a political goal via fear or intimidation. Large-scale terrorist attacks have proven capable of stimulating declines in the global economy. Terrorism is similar to natural disasters, wars, political crises, and other "supply chain shocks" that occasionally threaten international firms. The main threat of terrorism and other shocks results from *indirect* effects. These include the decline in buyer demand, unpredictable global supply chain shifts or interruptions, and government policies and laws enacted to deal with terrorism. Such outcomes decrease revenues, increase costs, and generally increase the complexity of international marketing. Among all the business functions, sales, marketing, and the global supply chain are among the most affected.[6]

Perhaps the greatest threat from terrorism is the resultant psychological response leading to substantial declines in consumption and other shifts in peoples' behavior. For instance, following the September 11, 2001, attacks, there emerged a short-term flight from the dollar, and Swiss banks recorded a sharp increase in inquiries about their special accounts for foreigners. The indirect effects of terrorism can also trigger shortages of externally sourced critical inputs, especially for multinational firms—be it due to production or to delivery constraints. Attempts to recoup decreasing sales via increased advertising and other promotional activities lead to unplanned expenses. The cost of protecting against such events will increase as insurance providers raise premiums to account for increased risk.

But managers can take proactive steps to deal with indirect effects. Emphasizing strong brands and superior product quality helps companies deal more effectively with declines in buyer demand following disasters. Marketing communications and public relations are potentially important "recovery marketing" tools to help maintain demand. Regular scanning and forecasting about emergent business conditions are critical for firms that rely heavily on foreign-sourced input goods. Global supply chains benefit from "scenario planning," in which specific strategies and tactics are developed around possible terrorism-related scenarios.

Managers may need to consider the potential role of terrorism when evaluating foreign countries, both as markets and as potential sites for foreign direct investment (FDI). The issue of terrorism will be progressively more used as a segmentation variable in the evaluation and selection of markets. This is bad news for those countries and regions that experience regular or particularly severe terrorism. Colombia and India are especially vulnerable, followed by countries in the Middle East, Latin America, and Asia. Terrorism is most likely to occur in those regions where it has tended to occur historically, that is, in non-Western or less-developed countries. These areas will also tend to be most vulnerable to economic and consumption downturns in the wake of terrorist events.

As firms face increasing regulations, policies, and other imperfections imposed by national and supranational governments, distribution and logistics are particularly affected. Shipments are delayed and shortages occur. Thus, some firms will tend to produce more essential inputs themselves, as opposed to buying them from suppliers. Or they will acquire needed inputs from a broader range of suppliers, from sources located in a broader range of locations, or from sources that are more familiar in order to reduce their vulnerability. For example, Compaq, a brand of Hewlett-Packard (HP), before its acquisition by HP, established secondary suppliers for all of its critical input components. The firm owned assembly operations in various locations worldwide. Management could quickly shift production from one locale to another in the event of a crisis. Jabil Circuit, a manufacturer of high-tech electronics, requires suppliers to be able to boost deliveries by 25 percent with a week's notice, and by 100 percent with four weeks' notice.[7]

Some firms will increase their inventories of essential inputs as a cushion against terrorism's effects. Inventory stocks are more vulnerable the greater the firm relies on international supply sources. Careful supply chain management is critical to ensure a proper balance between customer service and the inventory costs of growing safety stocks.[8]

EMERGING MARKETS

One of the most exciting new realities for international marketers is the rise of emerging markets. These fast-growth, modernizing countries are responsible for much of the explosion in world trade and investment over the past two decades.

The *Economist* (www.economist.com) tracks the progress of emerging markets, including countries such as China, India, South Korea, Thailand, Argentina, Brazil, Chile, Mexico, South Africa, Turkey, the Czech Republic, Hungary, Poland, and Russia. In the mid-2000s, the top 25 emerging market countries together sustained average annual GDP growth rates of nearly 7 percent. They have been growing much faster than those of the advanced economies, which suggests that several emerging markets will join the group of wealthy nations in the not-too-distant future. Most importantly, they have engaged in substantial privatization, modernization, and industrialization. Significantly, they have growing middle classes that can afford to participate in the market for a broad variety of goods and services.

China and India together represent about one-third of the world's population. China is the biggest emerging market, and its role in international business is rapidly expanding. With a population of 1.3 billion people (one-fifth of the world total), China is the world's second largest economy in purchasing-power parity terms. The Chinese economy continues to grow at the astonishing annual rate of nearly 10 percent. During the past decade, the number of Global 500 firms headquartered in China has risen from 3 to 15 and will expand further. Leading exemplars include Shanghai Automotive Industry Corporation (China's top automaker), Sinopec (a large oil company), and Shanghai Baosteel Group Corporation (a steel manufacturer).

Emerging markets are increasingly important target markets, that is, buyers of goods and services. They enjoy strong growth rates and prospects for market expansion. Accelerating demand growth will soon make the 25 emerging markets larger and more attractive than the countries of Europe and Japan combined. Consumer expectations are rising as local governments open markets to international competition. Infrastructural investments are improving the climate for business. These trends greatly improve the prospects for global business success, especially among multinational corporations that collaborate closely with local intermediaries. Instead of dismissing emerging markets, international marketers now see them as important target markets. Despite widespread poverty, most have high-income segments that represent attractive markets. For instance, China has some 300 million consumers and India has roughly 200 million consumers with significant purchasing power. Roughly one-quarter of Mexico's 100 million people enjoy affluence equivalent to many in the United States.

Emerging markets are excellent targets for sales of raw materials, parts, machinery, and other industrial goods used in the manufacture of finished goods. Most specialize in particular industries that create focused product demand, such as the textile machinery industry in India. They also house a range of niche markets.

Finally, governments and state enterprises are major target markets for sales of, especially, infrastructure-related goods and services. The government and industrial segments are promising targets for capital equipment, machinery, power transmission equipment, transportation equipment, high-technology products, and other goods typically needed by countries in the middle stage of development.

But multinational corporations (MNCs) must be mindful of risks in emerging markets. Legal frameworks are often inadequate, existing laws are insufficiently enforced, or judicial systems may be slow, corrupt, or subject to manipulation. Intellectual property protections for new technologies, brand names, logos, and manufacturing processes are often inadequate. Piracy and other intellectual property violations are commonplace in some emerging markets. Political instability is an important, potentially inhibiting factor. Protectionism may take the form of special loans, subsidies, or tax incentives for homegrown firms, and high market entry barriers for foreign competitors. Infrastructure is often inferior in emerging markets in areas such as energy systems, transportation, and communications.

Many emerging markets are characterized by family conglomerates (FCs), large, highly diversified holding companies that have been around for some time. FCs are dominant players in emerging economies such as South Korea where they are known as *chaebols,* India where they are called business houses, Mexico where they are termed *groupos,* Turkey where they are known as *holding companies,* and various other Asian and Latin American countries. Many are well-known international firms—Daewoo, Hyundai, Koç, Reliance, San Miguel, Samsung, Tata Group—that seek partnerships with foreign firms because of the opportunity to gain new technical know-how, strong brands, and intellectual property.

CHINA AND INDIA AS SOURCING PLATFORMS

Along with the growth of emerging markets, China and India are playing a growing role in international trade. Offshoring (also known as "global sourcing") is a key new reality. It reflects the tendency of firms to establish value-adding operations in advantageous locations abroad. Offshoring offers economies of scale, access to specialist knowledge, and the ability to subcontract critical organizational processes. China and India have grown in popularity as offshoring destinations because their cost of labor is substantially lower than that in the advanced world, and because they possess large pools of knowledge workers. For example, the cost of hiring a software code writer in India is typically one-fifth of that in the United States.[9]

Information and communications technology mean that the output of design and research jobs can be transferred around the globe at the touch of a button. For example, Massachusetts General Hospital has its CT scans and X rays interpreted by radiologists in India. At present about 40 percent of world software is written in India. Information technology firms, from Intel to Microsoft Corporation, are moving their programming activities to Bangalore, India.

The lower costs of upstream activities that MNCs enjoy by offshoring are passed on to consumers. This translates into lower prices at JCPenney, Marks & Spencer, Wal-Mart, and other firms that outsource extensively from the developing world. Lower prices across a whole range of retailers and other businesses provide for much higher standards of living by allowing people to keep more of their money.[10]

INTERNATIONAL SERVICES MARKETING

A critical but often overlooked reality is the growing international marketing of services. Services are deeds, performances, or efforts performed directly by people working in banks, hotels, airlines, construction companies, repair shops, retailers, and countless other firms in the services sector. The production of services represents about 80 percent of U.S. GDP and two-thirds or more of the annual GDP in nearly all other developed countries. Thus, services are extraordinarily important in the world economy and global trade. In the United States and several European countries, travel and tourism are now the number one source of revenue from foreigners. Because services have become the biggest part of the economy of nearly all countries, global trade in services is growing dramatically. In recent years services trade has been growing faster than products trade. In total, world exports of commercial services (that is, excluding government services) amounted to nearly $1.6 trillion in 2002, about 20 percent of total world trade.

But most services cannot be exported and are normally offered abroad by establishing "brick-and-mortar" facilities via FDI.[11] Banks often expand internationally by forming strategic alliances with foreign correspondent banks. They use multibank alliances to provide automatic teller machine access in many locations for their clients. Partly because services comprise nearly 70 percent of GDP in developed nations and approximately 50 percent of GDP in most other countries, the internationalization of services is growing rapidly. Indeed, in recent years internationalization of services has been growing faster than that of products.

FDI in services has grown enormously in recent years. Among the reasons for this trend is the innovative application of product design and engineering, advanced production processes, marketing and distribution, customization, outsourcing, and globalization strategies as critical factors to the international success of manufacturing firms. Finance, telecommunications, insurance, transportation, distribution, and information services are the focal key support activities that underpin international trade and facilitate international marketing activities.[12]

But marketing services abroad is challenging. While the cost of establishing services operations abroad tends to be less capital-intensive than for products-producing firms, operating services firms internationally can be costly. This results in part because services production does not benefit to the same degree as products production from economies of scale. To serve customers, the service MNC must establish a full-service operation in each location where it operates, so it must replicate the existing structure in each affiliate. This presents challenges for finding qualified personnel to staff each operation, to maintain quality control, and to standardize services cross-nationally.

Knowledge is important to all firms, but particularly to services providers. A key issue for these firms internationally, therefore, is protecting critical knowledge that provides the basis for the firm's competitive advantages. Much knowledge in services firms is relatively tacit and is therefore embedded in the firms' personnel. Knowledge that is transferred via more traditional means—manuals, training programs, and various telecommunications vehicles—is harder to protect. Internationally, services firms that rely heavily on such knowledge, particularly in countries with weak intellectual property laws, are relatively vulnerable.[13]

A key knowledge-related source of competitive advantage is often relationships with customers. This knowledge includes knowledge of key individuals and historical knowledge of the relationship as it has evolved over time. Robert Grosse suggests that this type of knowledge can be protected if it is retained within multi-person teams, as opposed to individual employees. In this way, if an employee leaves, the knowledge still remains with the team. The international marketing of services implies a strong role for customer relationship management.

BORN GLOBALS AND INTERNATIONAL SMES

Another new reality is the rise of the international small and medium enterprises (defined here as firms with less than 500 employees). SMEs make up over 95 percent of all companies and create about 50 percent of the total value added worldwide. They have far fewer financial, human, and tangible resources than the large multinational corporations that have traditionally plied the waters of global trade. Historically, international business was beyond the reach of most SMEs. However, technological advances and globalization have created a business environment in which young, smaller firms can market their offerings around the world. As a result, companies that internationalize at or near their founding, *born-global firms,* have sprung up rapidly.[14]

Despite the scarce resources that characterize most SMEs, born-global managers see the world as their marketplace, from or near the firm's inception. The period from domestic establishment to initial foreign market entry is often three or fewer years. By internationalizing as early and as rapidly as they do, they develop a "borderless" corporate culture. Born globals typically target their products and services to a dozen or more countries. Smaller size confers much flexibility for succeeding abroad. Born globals usually internationalize via exporting and leverage relationships with strong foreign distributors who provide key local advantages related not only to downstream international business activities, but also gathering market intelligence, forging links with key foreign contacts, deepening relations within extant markets, and cultivating new buyer segments.[15]

These young entrepreneurial firms internationalize early for various reasons. Management may perceive big demand for the firm's products abroad—"export pull." Management may possess a strong international orientation, pushing the organization into foreign markets—"export push." Occasionally the firm specializes in a particular product category for which demand in the home market is too small, pushing management to seek growth abroad. Often born globals enjoy relationships with foreign facilitators and customers who pave the way for international expansion.[16]

The emergence of born globals has given rise to the field of *international entrepreneurship*. Entrepreneurship is the process of creating or seizing opportunities and pursuing them even in the face of limited company resources. Management at entrepreneurial firms is typically innovative, proactive, and risk seeking. When a firm exhibits these characteristics in cross-border business, it is engaged in international entrepreneurship.[17] International entrepreneurship involves the firm in new and innovative activities in the pursuit of business activities across national borders. Managers with an entrepreneurial orientation have an obsession for opportunity. They are comfortable dealing with uncertainty and have the flexibility to make course changes to company strategies as the need arises. In international business, entrepreneurial managers are creative, innovative, have a strong feel for the firm's business environment, and are ready to pursue new opportunities. They are capable of anticipating the future. Such behaviors can be found in any company, but today they are particularly salient in born globals and other smaller international firms.[18]

International entrepreneurship is an exciting trend because it implies that *any* firm, regardless of size, age, or resource base, can participate actively in global markets. The traditional view of the large multinational corporation as the dominant player in international business is evolving. Youth and lack of experience, as well as limited financial resources, are no longer major impediments to the large-scale internationalization and global success of the firm. Countless SMEs are internationalizing at or near their founding and are succeeding in international markets. Younger, smaller firms are playing a substantially greater role in international marketing than ever before.

COLLABORATIVE APPROACHES

Collaborative ventures have been around for many years, but they continue to contribute much to firms' international marketing performances. While collaboration can take place at similar or different levels of the value chain, most ventures focus on research and development (R&D), production, or marketing. Collaboration makes possible the achievement of projects that exceed the capabilities of the individual enterprise. Groups of firms sometimes form strategic alliances to accomplish large-scale goals such as development of new technologies, or the construction of major projects, such as building power plants. They draw on a range of complementary technologies, accessible only from other firms, to innovate and develop new products. The advantages of collaboration help explain why the volume of such partnerships has grown substantially in the last few decades.[19]

Firms are more likely to collaborate if, relative to other international entry modes, collaboration reduces the partners' *transaction costs,* that is, the general costs of doing business. Firms also enter collaborative arrangements for strategic reasons. That is, they transact internationally by whichever mode helps them achieve strategic objectives, leading to long-term profit maximization. Consistent with *organizational learning theory,* firms may also collaborate in order to share organizationally embedded knowledge or technology that is not easily conveyed in written or explicit form.[20]

Royal Philips Electronics and AT&T formed a joint venture to develop central office switching devices for the telecommunications industry. Nabisco entered a joint venture with a Japanese firm, Yamazaki, to market its snack products in Japan. The host country partner contributes knowledge of the local language and culture, market navigation know-how, and useful connections to the host country government. Western firms often seek joint ventures to access markets in Asia. The partnership allows the foreign firm to access key market knowledge and gain immediate access to a distribution system and customers.

Project-based, nonequity alliances are increasingly common in international business. They involve pooling resources and capabilities among firms in order to pursue a well-defined project in a finite period. Once the venture bears fruit, the partners may shift their approaches and compete in more traditional ways.

For example, IBM and NTT Communications formed a strategic partnership for a limited period. Under the arrangement, IBM provides outsourcing services to NTT, Japan's dominant telecommunications carrier, and in turn, NTT provides outsourcing services and contacts for computer services sales to customers in Japan.[21] Companies also increasingly form consortia, large-scale partnerships that involve more than two firms for handling very large projects. For example, The Boeing Company, Fuji, Kawasaki, and Mitsubishi joined forces to design and manufacture major components of the Boeing 767 aircraft.

A firm enters a collaborative venture when it ascertains that a necessary link in its value chain is somehow weak or inadequate. If this is the case, it then chooses a partner that can replace the function of the weak link. In this way, the firm can meet its growth and other strategic objectives faster or more effectively. More specifically, firms enter collaborative arrangements in order to gain access to new markets or opportunities, reduce the costs and risks of international business, gain access to knowledge or other assets, create synergies for innovative activities, placate government authorities or access protected markets, and prevent or reduce competition.[22]

About half of all collaborative ventures fail within their first five years of operation. The majority fall short of partners' expectations.[23] International ventures are especially problematic because in addition to involving complex business issues, they also entail the additional burden of dealing across culture and language, as well as differences in political, legal, and economic systems.[24]

International collaborative ventures sometimes break down due to cultural differences. The partners may never arrive at a common set of values and organizational routines. The undertaking is especially complex when the parties are from very distinct cultures. For example, European and North American firms face considerable challenges in managing joint ventures with partners in China. Another challenge in international collaborations is the risk of creating a competitor. Collaboration takes place between firms that are current or potential competitors. Accordingly, the partners must walk the line between cooperation and competition. For example, for several years, Volkswagen (VW) and General Motors Corporation (GM) succeeded in China by partnering with the Chinese firm Shanghai Automotive Industry Corporation (SAIC). The Western firms transferred much technology and know-how to the Chinese partner. Having learned much from VW and GM, SAIC is now poised to become a major player in the global automobile industry and a competitor to its old partners.[25]

CONTEMPORARY APPROACHES TO INTERNATIONAL MARKETING

Market Orientation

In order to respond optimally to differing conditions abroad, contemporary firms develop a market orientation. Having a market orientation means that the firm attempts to ascertain the needs and wants of the buyers in a market and then creates products and services that specifically fit those needs and wants. It is realized by conducting market research to ascertain market characteristics and the needs of buyers, by disseminating the research findings throughout the firm, and by responding to the findings by creating products and services that specifically address buyer needs and wants. Typically, a strong market orientation translates into substantial adaptation of products and services to suit the needs and tastes of foreign customers.

For example, when targeting China and other Asian markets, dairy producer New Zealand Milk adds ginger and papaya flavoring to its milk products to suit the tastes of people in Asia.[26] When Procter & Gamble introduced Oil of Olay skin moisturizer in Taiwan, it reformulated the product to suit the preferences of Taiwanese women after market research revealed that they prefer less moisturizer.[27] Hollywood movies must be dubbed or translated into the language of target markets. Packaged foods in Europe are often labeled in four different languages.

Customer Relationship Management (CRM)

International firms also increasingly strive to develop strong relations with their foreign customers via CRM. It involves collecting, storing, and analyzing customer data to develop and maintain two-way communication between the firm and its key customers. By leveraging information technology, international firms like Credit Suisse and HP identify their most valuable buyers and then tailor product and service offerings to closely match their needs. In this way, the firm develops "customer equity."[28] The ultimate goal is to maximize value propositions to the firm's most important customers so they remain customers indefinitely. For most firms, keeping good customers is more profitable than finding new customers.

Global Marketing Strategy

When the firm extensively standardizes a product for foreign markets, it is following a global strategy. It involves creating a relatively standardized marketing mix, targeted to all countries or, at a minimum, major world regions. It is based on identifying and targeting cross-cultural similarities. The firm applies the same or similar approach or content for one or more elements of the marketing mix across as many markets as possible. Citibank, Nestlé, HP, and Xerox Corporation are examples of MNCs that use global strategy to great success.

The viability of global marketing strategy varies across industries and product categories. For example, commodities, industrial, and high-technology products lend themselves to a global approach, while many consumer goods require greater adaptation. Procter & Gamble applies a global strategy for its international marketing of disposable diapers, a commodity. But its line of laundry detergents is more adapted to local markets, because cleaning methods and washing machines vary significantly across countries.

Product Innovation

Product innovation is also critically important to the success of international firms. Many product innovations originate from firsthand knowledge of dealing with the needs of individual foreign markets. Various new ideas about how to improve products emerge from dealing in the extreme conditions often found abroad. Some MNCs have globalized R&D by locating development laboratories in different countries and then coordinating R&D activities to leverage the technical resources of the firm's worldwide operations.

R&D intensity, that is, total R&D expenditures as a percentage of total sales, has increased in many industries such as chemicals, electronics, pharmaceuticals, and medical equipment. This has resulted because firms increasingly recognize that technology is a major source of global competitive advantage. Innovative processes are needed to develop global products and stay abreast of growing global competitive pressures. The growth of information and communications technologies facilitate low-cost coordination of global R&D activities. More than 12 percent of total R&D spending is performed by firms' foreign affiliates (www.oecd.org). One disadvantage of performing R&D activities abroad, however, is the risk of dissipating proprietary knowledge to foreign partners or competitors, particularly in countries with lax intellectual property laws.

The ability to innovate depends on the availability of knowledge workers and university graduates trained in the sciences and high-technology areas. Accordingly, countries such as Australia, Canada, Finland, France, Germany, India, Japan, South Korea, the United Kingdom, and the United States enjoy particular advantages in innovation and the development of new technologies. Many firms leverage links with universities. For instance, Rolls-Royce co-opts research with academic technology centers, such as Loughborough University in the United Kingdom, to develop new technologies for the firm's jet engines.

Innovation leads to new product development. Before 1980, product development and design was a sequential process, usually based in a single country. Engineers and marketing people agreed on a set of technical specifications, and a product was developed and sent to the factory for manufacturing. However, because the product was developed in a single national environment, it required substantial adaptation for selling abroad.

Global Products

Today, many more firms develop global products, which are adapted for world markets from scratch. The primary impetus is to capture economies of scale in R&D, product development, production, and marketing. Growth in R&D parallels the emergence of demanding global customers with increasingly similar needs and tastes. Procter & Gamble (P&G) developed Pringles potato chips as a standardized global product. Worldwide it is produced and promoted as one product, one process, one package, and one marketing campaign. The savings for P&G have been enormous.[29]

Global firms increasingly employ cross-national teams from the firm's major subsidiaries and functional areas to design new products. The team approach requires substantial cross-national coordination, but when skillfully managed, it results in products that are both cost-effective and relatively customized to individual markets. It reduces development time and costs. Companies make their suppliers partners in the design process to optimize sourcing and production. Product development is no longer a sequential process; rather, design and development occur simultaneously, and all major players are co-opted from the beginning.[30]

For developing global products, the team leverages computer-aided design, which facilitates three-dimensional design on compatible computer systems that accommodate contributions by design team members from around the world. Sophisticated software allows the team to pilot various configurations of the product at virtually no cost. Rapid prototyping means that new designs can be quickly tested on global customers and modified based on resulting market research. Savings result from a single, unified design effort.[31] The Boeing 777 was developed by design teams composed of members from Europe, Japan, and the United States. The jet was broken down into tail, fuselage, wings, and other modular sections. Each section was designed and developed by a global team.

In developing global products, leading MNCs focus on the commonalities among countries rather than the differences.[32] The team develops a basic product or product platform into which variations for individual markets can be incorporated inexpensively. Development of a basic product platform appropriate for all markets allows the firm to capture economies of scale for producing most of the product. For example, personal computers are now designed so that the expensive hardware is virtually the same everywhere, but the software is changed to accommodate local languages. While the basic computers that Dell sells worldwide are essentially identical, the letters on its keyboards and the languages used in its software are unique to countries or major regions. Roughly speaking, the balance is about 80/20. That is, about 80 percent of each Dell computer sold worldwide is identical, and about 20 percent is adapted for each local market as a function of differing languages.

Many products are designed using modular architecture, a collection of standardized components and subsystems that can be rapidly assembled in various configurations to suit the needs of individual markets. For example, global cars like the Ford Mondeo or the Honda Accord are designed around a standardized platform to which modular components, parts, and features are added to suit specific needs and tastes.

Global Branding

The worldwide standardization of positioning, advertising strategies, personality, look, and feel characterize a global brand. Management seeks to achieve a clear and consistent identity with its target market regardless of geographic location.

Developing and maintaining a global brand name is the most effective way to build global recognition and maximize the international marketing program.[33] For example, the Eveready Battery Company consolidated its various national brand names—such as Ucar, Wonder, and Mazda—into one global name, Energizer, in order to build a consistent image and global brand name. While most brands are conceived on a national level and then internationalized, the best approach is to build a global brand from scratch. Several firms have done this, choosing brand names and images that can be easily recognized and pronounced worldwide. An example is Japan's Sony Corporation.[34]

Strong global brands have the following attributes:

- Brand development is based on understanding customers via market research; managers understand the brand's meaning for each target audience.
- The brand delivers the benefits that customers seek. It is based on a targeted and compelling concept that provides superior value, a solid "value proposition."
- The brand is both consistent and relevant.
- The firm employs a full range of marketing communications activities to deliver the desired customer experience and build brand equity.
- Brand equity is continuously monitored.
- The firm commits sufficient financial and other support to maintain the brand over time.[35]

The most successful brands are positioned around a strong psychological proposition. For example, research revealed that consumers in China value products that give them a sense of "well-being," "self-indulgence," and "harmony." Volkswagen and Vidal Sassoon attempt to incorporate these values into their brands when marketing to the Chinese.[36]

THE MANAGERIAL IMPERATIVE FOR INTERNATIONAL MARKETERS

The centers of economic activity are shifting profoundly. Today, Asia (excluding Japan) accounts for 13 percent of world GDP, while Western Europe accounts for more than 30 percent. Within the next 20 years the two will nearly converge. In the coming years, the United States will continue to dominate much of international trade, but China and India will become the most important new international players in the near term. Partly due to the rise of China and India, the consumer landscape will change and expand substantially. Almost a billion new consumers will enter the global marketplace by 2015 as economic growth in emerging markets pushes them beyond the threshold level of $5,000 in annual household income—a point when people begin to spend on discretionary goods. Through 2015, consumer spending power in emerging markets will increase from \$4 trillion to more than \$9 trillion—almost the present spending power of Western Europe. The elderly market segment will balloon, and firms will need to develop products and services for this key market. In the United States, the Hispanic population will expand dramatically.[37]

Technological connectivity is transforming the way people live and interact. We are still at the early stage of this revolution. Firms are learning how to make the best use of information technology in designing processes and in developing and accessing knowledge. New developments in fields such as biotechnology, laser technology, and nanotechnology are moving well beyond the realm of products and services. More transformational than the technology itself is the shift in the behavior that it enables. Increasingly, people work not just globally but also instantaneously. They are forming communities and relationships in new ways. More than 2 billion people now use cell phones. They send 9 trillion e-mails a year and enter a billion Google searches a day. For perhaps the first time in history, geography is not the primary constraint on the limits of international marketing and other global activities.[38]

A purely domestic focus is no longer viable for most firms, particularly product manufacturers. In order to remain competitive, domestic management must develop a greater understanding and knowledge of international marketing. Managers must adopt a global rather than a local focus. The most sophisticated firms will deliberately seek a simultaneous presence in all of the world's major trading regions. A global approach is critical to gain and maintain a competitive advantage and ensure long-term performance. Companies must locate their value-chain activities in those countries and in markets where they can derive maximal competitive advantages.

Having a global presence is not limited to large MNCs. Smaller firms are also increasingly global, often pursuing global niche strategies by targeting specialized foreign markets. Trade liberalization implies greater competitive rivalry from global firms. In order to meet globalization's growing competitive challenges, companies are increasing the level of their offshore investment and overseas sourcing. Suppliers are following their internationalizing customers abroad.

Managers must strike some ideal balance between global control of the organization and decentralized decision making at the level of individual countries. This implies striking the right balance in standardizing and adapting products, services, and marketing itself. Managers must leverage technology, especially in information and communications, to manage their international marketing activities. To achieve economies of scale, companies will emphasize standardization of products and marketing and centralization of production activities in fewer locations. By the same token, global competition pressures firms to be entrepreneurial and flexible in their pursuits of new or latent opportunities and the resolution of current problems and future threats.

NOTES

1. *Economist* (1999), "The Net Imperative: A Survey of Business and the Internet," June 26, pp. B5–B7.

2. *Fortune* (2004), "Broadband Wonderland," September 20, pp. 191–198.

3. *Economist* (2005), "Clicks, Bricks and Bargains," December 3, pp. 57–58.

4. Friedman, Thomas L. (2005), "It's a Flat World, After All," *The New York Times Magazine,* April 3, pp. 33–37.

5. *Economist* (1995), "The Death of Distance: A Survey of Telecommunications," September 30.

6. Czinkota, Michael, Gary Knight, and Peter Liesch (2004), "Terrorism and International Business: Conceptual Foundations," in *Terrorism and the International Business Environment: The Security-Business Nexus,* ed. Gabriele Suder. Cheltenham, England: Edward Elgar.

7. Sheffi, Y. (2005), *The Resilient Enterprise,* Cambridge, MA: MIT Press, p. 47.

8. Czinkota, M., and G.A. Knight (2005), "Managing the Terrorist Threat," *European Business Forum,* 20 (Winter): 42–45.

9. *Economist* (2004), "A World of Work: A Survey of Outsourcing," November 13, special section.

10. Bhagwati, Jagdish, Arvind Panagariya, and T. Srinivasan (2004), "The Muddles over Outsourcing," *Journal of Economic Perspectives,* Fall.

11. Erramilli, M.K., and C.P. Rao (1993), "Service Firms' International Entry-Mode Choice: A Modified Transaction-Cost Analysis Approach," *Journal of Marketing,* 57(7) (July): 19–38.

12. Feketekuty, G. (1999), "Keynote Address: A Framework for Global Trade in Services," in *Proceedings of the Services 2000,* ed. I.T. Administration. Washington, DC: U.S. Department of Commerce.

13. Grosse, Robert (2000), "Knowledge Creation and Transfer in Global Service Firms," in *Globalization of Services,* ed. Y. Aharoni and L. Nachum. London: Routledge, pp. 217–232.

14. Knight, Gary (2000), "Entrepreneurship and Marketing Strategy: The SME under Globalization," *Journal of International Marketing* 8(2): 12–32.

15. Knight, Gary A., and S. Tamer Cavusgil (2004), "Innovation, Organizational Capabilities, and the Born-Global Firm," *Journal of International Business Studies* 35(2): 124–141.

16. Knight and Cavusgil, 2004.

17. McDougall, Patricia, and Benjamin Oviatt (2000), "International Entrepreneurship: The Intersection of Two Research Paths," *Academy of Management Journal* 43(5): 902–906.

18. Knight and Cavusgil, 2004.

19. Kotabe, Masaaki, Hildy Teegen, Preet Aulakh, Maria Cecilia Coutinho de Arruda, Roberto Santillan-Salgado, and Walter Greene, "Strategic Alliances in Emerging Latin America: A View from Brazilian, Chilean, and Mexican Companies," *Journal of World Business,* 35(2): 114–132.

20. Kogut, Bruce (1988), "Joint Ventures: Theoretical and Empirical Perspectives," *Strategic Management Journal,* 9, pp. 319–332.

21. Guth, Robert (2000), "IBM Announces Deal with Japan's NTT," *Wall Street Journal,* November 1, p. 23.

22. Terpstra, Vern, and Bernard Simonin, "Strategic Alliances in the Triad," *Journal of International Marketing* 1(1): 4–25.

23. Doz, Yves (1996), "The Evolution of Cooperation in Strategic Alliances: Initial Conditions or Learning Processes," *Strategic Management Journal,* 17 (Summer): 55–85.

24. Hoon-Halbauer, Sing Keow (1999), "Managing Relationships within Sino-Foreign Joint Ventures," *Journal of World Business,* 34(4): 334–370.

25. Taylor III, Alex (2004), "Shanghai Auto Wants to be the World's Next Great Car Company," *Fortune,* October 4, pp. 103–110.

26. Prystay, Cris (2005), "Milk Industry's Pitch in Asia: Try the Ginger or Rose Flavor," *Wall Street Journal,* August 9, p. B1.

27. Calantone, Roger, S. Tamer Cavusgil, Jeffrey Schmidt, and Geon-Cheol Shin (2004), "Internationalization and the Dynamics of Product Adaptation—An Empirical Investigation," *Journal of Product Innovation Management,* 21, pp. 185–198.

28. Lemon, Katherine, Roland Rust, and Valarie Zeithaml (2001), "What Drives Customer Equity," *Marketing Management,* 10(1), pp. 20–26.

29. Galbraith, Jay (2000), *Designing the Global Corporation,* San Francisco: Jossey-Bass.

30. Galbraith, 2000.

31. Galbraith, 2000.

32. Yip, George, (2003), *Total Global Strategy II,* Upper Saddle River, NJ: Prentice Hall.

33. Aaker, David A. (1991), *Managing Brand Equity,* New York: The Free Press.

34. Yip, 2003.

35. Gregory, James, and Jack Wiechmann (2002), *Branding across Borders,* Chicago: McGraw-Hill.

36. Lee, Gilbert, and Nic Hall (2004), "Brand Strategy Briefing: The 15 Global Hot Buttons," *Brand Strategy,* June, p. 58.

37. Brooke, Simon (2006), "Out with the Old, In with the Old," *Financial Times,* March 16.

38. *Financial Times,* 2006.

Part II

EMERGING MARKETS

CHAPTER 2

EMERGING MARKETS

Masaaki (Mike) Kotabe

Country competitiveness is neither fixed nor stable. The dominant feature of the global economy is the rapid change in the relative status of various countries' economic output. In 1830, China and India alone accounted for about 60 percent of the manufactured output of the world. By 1913, the share of the world manufacturing output produced by the 20 or so countries that are today known as the rich industrial economies increased by 50 percent, from 30 percent in 1830 to almost 80 percent in 1913.[1] In the 1980s, the U.S. economy was characterized as "floundering" or even "declining," and many pundits predicted that Asia, led by Japan, would become the leading regional economy in the 21st century. Then the 1997–1999 Asian financial crisis changed the economic milieu of the world. Since the September 11, 2001, terrorist attacks, the U.S. economy has grown faster than any other developed countries at an annual rate of 3–4 percent. However, even the U.S. economic growth rate pales in comparison to China and India, two leading emerging economic powers in the last decade or so. China and India have grown at an annual rate of 7–10 percent and 4–7 percent, respectively, since the dawn of the 21st century.[2] Obviously, a decade is a long time in the ever-changing world economy, and, indeed, no single country has sustained its economic performance continuously.

EMERGING MARKETS

In much of the 20th century, large economies and large trading partners were located mostly in the Triad Regions of the world; North America, Western Europe, and Japan collectively produced about 80 percent of the world's gross domestic product (GDP) with 20 percent of the world's population.[3] However, in the next 10 to 20 years, the greatest commercial opportunities are expected to be found increasingly in 11 Big Emerging Markets (BEMs)—the Chinese Economic Area (including China, the Hong Kong region, and Taiwan), India, Commonwealth of Independent States (Russia, Central Asia, and the Caucasus states), South Korea, Mexico, Brazil, Argentina, South Africa, Central European countries,[4] Turkey, and the Association of Southeast Asian Nations (including Indonesia, Brunei, Malaysia, Singapore, Thailand, the Philippines and Vietnam). An increasing number of competitors are also expected to originate from those emerging economies.

For instance, in the past 20 years, China's real annual GDP growth rate has averaged 9.5 percent a year, while India's has been 5.7 percent, compared to the average 3 percent GDP growth in the United States. Accordingly, an increasing number of competitors are also expected to originate from those emerging economies. According to a trade report published by the World Trade Organization in 2005,[5] the world's nine largest exporting countries accounted for almost half of the world trade in 2004: namely, Germany ($915 billion), the United States ($619 billion), China ($593 billion), Japan ($565 billion), France ($451 billion), Britain ($346 billion), Italy ($346 billion), Canada ($322 billion), and Mexico ($189 billion). A few notable recent changes attest to the globalization of the markets. First, Germany overtook the United States as the largest exporting country for the first time. Second, China surged to become the third largest exporting country, surpassing Japan. Third, Mexico has emerged as one of the major exporting countries. Clearly, the milieu of the world economy has changed significantly.

As a result, over the next two decades, the markets that hold the greatest potential for dramatic increases in U.S. exports are not the traditional trading partners in Europe and Japan, which now account for the overwhelming bulk of the international trade of the United States, but they will be those 11 BEMs listed above. Already there are signs that in the future the biggest trade headache for the United States may not be Japan, but China and India. China's trade surplus with the United States ballooned from $86 billion in 2000 to $162 billion in 2004; it had already surpassed Japan's trade surplus position with the United States by 2000.[6] India has increasingly become a hotbed as a source of information technology (IT), communications, software development, and call centers, particularly for many U.S. multinationals. Russia is extremely rich in natural resources, including oil and natural gas, which are dwindling in the rest of the world, has gradually warmed up to international commerce, and will potentially become a major trading nation. As these three leading emerging economies, among others, are likely to reshape the nature of international business in the next decade, the profiles of these countries will be highlighted here. (See Table 2.1 for a country profile summary.)

Table 2.1
Country Profile in 2005

	China	India	Russia
Population	1,306 million	1,080 million	143 million
Population Growth Rate	0.58 percent	1.4 percent	−0.37 percent
GDP in current U.S.$	$1,909.7 billion	$746.1 billion	$772.1 billion
GDP in current U.S.$ based on purchasing power parity	$8.09 trillion	$3.60 trillion	$1.59 trillion
GDP per capita based on purchasing power parity	$6,193	$3,315	$11,209
GDP real growth rate	9.1 percent	6.2 percent	6.7 percent
Inflation rate	3.0 percent	3.9 percent	12.8 percent
Current account balance	$115.6 billion	−$13.5 billion	$101.8 billion
Current account balance/GDP	6.1 percent	−1.8 percent	13.2 percent

Sources: Compiled from International Monetary Fund statistics and U.S. Central Intelligence Agency, *The World Factbook 2005,* http://www.odci.gov/cia/publications/factbook/index.html.

CHINA

Economy

The People's Republic of China (China) was founded in 1949 by the Chinese Communist Party. Starting in 1978, China's president introduced economic reforms to the country. Since then, China's leaders have pursued economic liberalization and sustainable economic growth alongside enduring communist political control. As a new member of the World Trade Organization (WTO) effective in 2001, China has become one of the world's emerging giants, along with India, Brazil, and Russia. Unlike other emerging economies, China has recently received much attention due to its greater participation in the global economy. China has a population of 1.3 billion people with its nominal GDP of U.S.$1.9 trillion in 2005. However, according to the purchasing power parity-adjusted estimate, China's real purchasing power could now exceed U.S.$8 trillion, while Japan's purchasing power is estimated at around U.S. $4 trillion. The United States, as the largest economy, stands at a total purchasing power of about $12 trillion. In other words, in terms of real purchasing power, China could now rank as the second-largest economy in the world after the United States.

However, China's purchasing power is not distributed evenly throughout the country. It is mainly concentrated in major cities, such as Shanghai, Beijing, Shenzhen, and Dalian. Consumers from the top ten cities account for only

4 percent of the total population, but represent 22.6 percent of the total purchasing power. One phenomenon in China is the increasing income inequality. Generally a large part of China's growing income has been represented by a small share of the population living in coastal areas. In China, two-thirds of the population of 1.3 billion live in the countryside or in rural areas without rural retirement pension and unemployment benefits. The impact of foreign direct investment (FDI) on the country's economic development has been recognized; however, most of it flows to the locations around the coastal areas with the inland experiencing little impact. Even today, nearly 30 million Chinese people live below the poverty line, and the gap between China's richest and poorest is one of the widest in Asia. Even the Chinese central government realized that raising living standards of the rural poor is essential to maintain the social stability of the country. With growing economic development, the income gap widens from region to region. As a result, people in developed areas, such as the east coast, gained higher income than those in developing and underdeveloped areas (inland China), thus making the income disparity between coastal and inland, urban and rural areas, and within regions more obvious.

Industry

There were no private companies back in the 1970s. During the 1980s, the structure of China's industry changed fundamentally. After two decades of reform and privatization, roughly only one-third of China's economy is still controlled by the government through state-owned enterprises (SOEs). But they are concentrated in key sectors like defense and utilities. Although many of the biggest SOEs have publicly quoted subsidiaries on international stock markets, the government retains ultimate ownership. For example, the top 190 or so SOEs are directly controlled by the State Assets Supervision and Administration Commission, which was set up in 2003 to restructure these often moribund firms. Unlike the Japanese government whose officials coordinated their domestic development before launching foreign expansion, Chinese firms are not guided by one single, controlling legislative body. Nevertheless, a study by the Organisation for Economic Cooperation and Development found that, in 2003, private companies in China accounted for 63 percent of business-sector output, which represents 94 percent of the GDP. China has been developing formidable capabilities in technology production, and the entire nation is embracing a great leap forward in modern technology. Some automobile, steel, and telecommunication companies have reported revenue growth in excess of 30 percent.

For example, Haier Group, China's leading manufacturer of home appliances, has built a commanding domestic market share of 20–70 percent for most home appliances, with offices in more than 100 countries and overseas revenues of over $1 billion. Recently, the company attempted to make a bid for Maytag

Corporation to further extend its competitive advantage to foreign countries. Similarly, Whirlpool Corporation, a leading U.S. manufacturer of home appliances, has to face competition from Haier and Guangdong Kelon, two major Chinese competitors, whose technology is nearly as good as Whirlpool's, but with lower prices and better distribution channels. By 1997, Whirlpool had to close down its refrigerator and air-conditioner plants and devote the microwave factory to exports. Now Whirlpool's only surviving washing-machine factory makes appliances under contract for Kelon, under Kelon's own brand—a reversal of the usual hierarchy between Western and Chinese firms. It also happened to Ericsson, Lucent Technologies, and other equipment makers to accept the reality of losing ground to China's domestic telecoms firms such as Huawei.

It is important to note that China is on its way to becoming the world's largest Internet community. It is estimated by the Central Intelligence Agency that in 2004, China had 94 million Internet users. Fueling this tremendous growth of the Internet are younger consumers with a thirst for fun, knowledge, and communication with the outside world. The Internet facilitates prepurchase information searches, product comparisons, and sharing product experience with others. Chinese youths are becoming more pragmatic, educated, and cosmopolitan. eBay, for example, is adding about 1 million users per quarter, totaling 11.6 million registered users during three years' investment in China. In 2004, the e-commerce business in China entered a golden period, with the transaction volume of online trading reaching 21.86 billion yuan (U.S.$2.64 billion). Among the 94 million Internet users, more than 40 million people conducted transactions on the Internet in 2004. Without a doubt, with a population of 1.3 billion, the Chinese market is inviting online businesses to achieve great prospects for years to come.

China is also challenged by its troublesome banking system, the lack of a transparent legal system, corruption, the risk of social and political conflicts, and severe environmental pollution. One major issue international managers must manage in the growing market is corruption. According to the University of Passau's calculation of the Corruption Perceptions Index (CPI) 2004, the corruption issue has cost productivity losses of a whopping $4 trillion in those countries, which is roughly 12 percent of the world's GDP. China is still one of the countries (ranked 77 out of 146 countries, with 146th being the most corrupt) that has a higher CPI score. Accordingly, China's relatively high corruption discourages FDI by a significant amount. Moreover, inexplicit regulatory burdens in China would be another important impediment that discourages investors from venturing into the promising market. After all, it is not easy to understand different legislative bodies, namely, the central government, provincial, and municipal governments.

Besides corruption and other factors, China's lack of intellectual property protection and weak enforcement of contracts are troublesome. Some domestic companies in China have to fight with counterfeit goods, let alone famous Western companies. The majority of counterfeit products are sold from mobile stores, so it is difficult for local government to track down those illegal activities. Procter & Gamble reckons that 10–15 percent of its revenues in China are lost each year to counterfeit products. Furthermore, poor telecommunications, inadequate infrastructure, and the vast size of the country compound the intellectual property right investigators' problems. Unfortunately, China is by far the world's leading producer of counterfeit goods—from upscale designer-brand clothing, to pirated films and books, to imitation consumer electronics and aircraft parts. It is estimated that at least $16 billion worth of goods sold each year in China are counterfeit products. The illegal market costs legitimate companies in America and elsewhere billions of dollars in lost sales annually. Most Chinese buy pirated products, such as software, motion pictures, and music CDs because they are a lot cheaper than their legitimate counterparts. For instance, pirated Microsoft Office software may cost as little as $1 on the black market, whereas it may cost roughly the monthly income of most middle-class Chinese if bought from legitimate companies. It seems that only those companies that are willing to bring their price closer to the black market price or offer differentiated services would secure the big market in the long run.

Market

In general, business in China has taken off, but it is quite different from how business is conducted in the West. Companies must meet the challenge of serving hard-to-reach, price-sensitive consumers who typically have more stringent requirements than their counterparts in the developed world. On the one hand, China has roughly 10 percent of the population, or 10–13 million consumers who prefer luxury goods. Most of those consumers who prefer luxury brands are entrepreneurs and young professionals working for multinational firms with much higher salaries than the majority of people. With higher education and higher purchasing power, the young generations are brand and status conscious and consider luxury goods as personal achievements and high social status. As stated earlier, they live in major cities on the country's eastern coast, where luxury brands are considered prominent logos for the high-income clientele. Many luxury brands such as Armani, Prada, and Louis Vuitton have been introduced to the east coast of China in recent years, and business has been booming. According to Louis Vuitton, China is its fourth-largest market in terms of sales worldwide. No wonder many high-end firms label Chinese shoppers as the "new Japanese": a potentially huge group of status-conscious, increasingly wealthy people hungry for brands and fanatical about spending.

On the other hand, with an average GDP per capita (based on purchasing power parity) of $6,200 in 2005, a majority of Chinese consumers are extremely price sensitive. Therefore, to attract both the status conscious and highly price-sensitive consumers, many domestic and foreign companies are readjusting their marketing strategies based on demand predictions. General Motors Corporation (GM), for example, has an extremely well-developed range of brands and cars to target different market segments. To lure China's newly rich consumers, the company offers $75,000+ Cadillac SRX sport-utility vehicles and $55,000 CTS sedans. A $30,000 Buick Regal is positioned to the cost-conscious entrepreneurs who want a prestigious car. Moreover, the $15,000–$20,000 Buick Excelle is offered to mid-level consumers. As for young urban consumers eager to have their first car, the company promotes minicar, hatchback, and other models ranging from $5,700 to $12,000. To sell to the three-fourths of China's population in the country, GM offers the Wuling, which goes for $4,000–$6,500 to the countryside consumers. In 2004, 25 percent of GM's profit came from the China market, and the percentage is expected to grow in the future. Now GM counts its sustainable growth in China as a critical factor for the company's development in the global market. Statistics from the China Ministry of Commerce revealed that over 5 million cars were sold in the Chinese market in 2004 and the country boasted 27.1 million cars at the end of the year, making it the third largest auto market in the world. Apparently, understanding that China is not a homogeneous market is imperative to win different customer segments.

After all, China is a country with a population of 1.3 billion people, with 56 ethnic groups that speak more than 100 dialects. Accordingly, what people prefer to have differs greatly from north to south, east to west, rich to poor, young to old, and city to country. Procter & Gamble (P&G), for instance, has won over inland consumers with a relatively inexpensive detergent called Tide Clean White, while promoting the more expensive brand Tide Triple Action to city consumers. Differentiated marketing strategies are developed to meet the desires and needs of people from all over the country. P&G introduced a 320-gram bag of Tide Clean White for 23¢, compared with 33¢ for 350 grams of Tide Triple Action. Clean White does not offer such benefits as stain removal and fragrance and contains less advanced cleaning enzymes, but it costs less to make and, according to P&G, outperforms every other brand at that price level. With no doubt, the tiered pricing initiative helps the company compete against cheaper local brands while protecting the value of its global brands. Moreover, in order to reach China's urban consumers, P&G has sponsored a popular reality TV show called *Absolute Challenge,* which has featured contestants competing to win a product representative position for multinational companies. To reach the inland consumers, P&G has blanketed village kiosks and corner shops with advertising materials emphasizing the value offered by Tide Clean White and other low-end products.

What P&G and other multinational companies learned in China is that it is no longer enough simply catering to big cities. Although it was once good enough for companies to focus on such major metropolitan areas as Beijing and Shanghai, more and more companies are trying to offer differentiated products tailored to different segments of the population in exchange for market share. Take Wahaha, the largest domestic beverage producer, for example. The company has successfully developed distribution channels not only in urban but also rural areas. The company not only actively sponsors prime time TV programs to target the urban population, but also paints the company's logo on village walls to reach the mass rural population. Like P&G, many multinational companies find distribution to rural Chinese areas a huge challenge. Motorola, for example, found that in China's lower-tier cities, the young people not only look at the value of the cell phone, but also tend to be very individualistic. As a result, the company has to design its least expensive phones with MP3 downloading and customized ringtone capabilities when promoting to the lower-tier market segment. Today the company is capable of getting the right handsets to each location, with a bigger supply of cheaper phones in rural areas and snazzier ones in cities. Since it entered China in 1987, Motorola has witnessed substantial growth both in major metropolitan areas and the countryside largely credited to the everlasting demand of mobile phones.

Today, multinationals are competing with local companies for more discerning Chinese consumers. More products now available on the domestic market are similar. Consequently, consumers are more likely to be attracted by low prices or promotions rather than brand reputation and product quality. In the automobile industry, most consumers prefer affordable small cars and are most likely to purchase cars priced under $12,000. One popular Chinese automaker, Chery, priced its QQ model between $5,500 and $7,500 in China. Xiali, another aggressive domestic automaker, priced its cars at similarly affordable prices. Foreign automakers, such as Honda Motor Co., GM, and Volkswagen, face the reality that although the Chinese market is lucrative with a growing demand, they cannot compete with the Chinese automakers' competitive prices to attract price-conscious Chinese consumers. It turns out that some foreign automakers have to compromise profits for sales volume in the growing market.

China is a brutal place when it comes to competition. Take mobile phones as another example. The China market is inviting to domestic and foreign companies by having 3.3 million mobile phone subscribers in the first seven months for a total of 368 million. In 2004, the country's shops offered over 700 kinds of mobile phones produced by over 30 companies. Foreign makers of mobile phones face fierce competition from domestic manufacturers, which tend to use price (low cost) as their main differentiator. In such a volatile environment, market shares can be transformed seemingly overnight. Many foreign giants have found it increasingly difficult to generate profits in China's market. Like the dairy industry, especially the liquid-milk sector, the market is dogged by price wars and dominated by local brands—foreign companies like Groupe Danone, Kraft, and

Friesland Coberco have quit dairy production in China. Some foreign companies find it difficult to sell their products, especially when they look similar to competitors', as their marketing and pricing strategies do not cater to Chinese consumers. Accordingly, only those companies that develop core technology, with advanced management and marketing expertise, excel in the volatile market. To mitigate marketing disadvantages, many multinational companies have had to buy their way into the Chinese market by taking an equity interest in leading domestic companies or forming joint ventures with established local brands. They agreed to offer their capital and technology expertise in exchange for market penetration in China.

Apparently, multinational firms cannot simply assume that they have first-mover advantages to enter the promising Chinese market in return for brand recognition and established distribution channels with prominent market share. It seems that price-conscious consumers are far more unpredictable than expected, as are the bureaucratic issues companies have to deal with at different administrative levels. It may not be that promising for firms, and, consequently, firms have to consider China as a long-term investment, longer than expected to achieve positive cash flows.

Moreover, some foreign companies found it difficult to exit their investments in China. A successful exit not only requires selling or liquidating the foreign investor's stake in the venture in a tax-efficient manner from both a China and a foreign tax perspective, but also navigating through a potentially difficult path of administrative procedures through China's foreign exchange controls in order to repatriate capital. Just as entering an investment in China, exiting an investment also requires careful planning. In achieving the optimal result, foreign investors should give due attention to exit planning as part of the evaluation process undertaken before the investment is made.[7]

INDIA

Economy

India gained independence in 1947 after two centuries of British colonial rule. Now India is the second most populous country (with 1 billion people) in the world behind China. With a nominal GDP of U.S.$746 billion in 2005, India has the world's tenth largest economy. India's real GDP grew by an average of 5.6 percent a year in the 1980s, and in more recent years, India's real GDP growth achieved 8.5 percent, 6.9 percent, and 6.7 percent, respectively, from 2003 to 2005. India's trade has been growing fast with its two-way trade amounting to $150 billion in 2005. India's foreign direct investment inflow amounted to $3.4 billion during the same time. Information technology and IT-enabled services output has grown rapidly largely owning to India's reputation and cost advantages in these sectors. In its own way, India has climbed the economic ladder and has become the world's key process outsourcing center. Roughly 40 percent of Fortune 500 companies are estimated to have outsourced services from India. Meanwhile, its software exports amounted to $7.6 billion in 2001–2002. All of these factors indicate that technical and process outsourcing will continue to be a key component of India's mainstream economy.

India's key exporting commodities include gems, jewelry, cotton, fabric, and pharmaceutical and petroleum products. Its key trading partners for exports are the United States, the United Arab Emirates, and the United Kingdom. In particular, the United States accounts for 22 percent of India's total merchandise exports. It is estimated that almost 200 of the blue-chip firms on the Fortune 500 list outsource at least some of their software requirements to India software ventures. The United States, the European Union (EU), and China are its major partners for imports. Imports from the EU account for 22 percent of the total. India's trade deficit rose to an estimated $22.7 billion in 2004 from $8.9 billion in 2003. Although exports performed strongly, rising by 13.5 percent to $67.3 billion, imports soared by 32 percent to $90 billion in this period.

India has a two-tier economy, with cutting-edge and globally competitive knowledge-driven service sectors that employ the brightest of the middle classes, on the one hand, and a large agricultural sector that employs the majority of the vast and poorly educated population, on the other. With a reputation for low-quality products, India's manufacturing sector has traditionally been underdeveloped. Currently the agricultural sector represents 20 percent of the GDP, services 53 percent, and manufacturing 27 percent. Apparently, the services area is the most dynamic growth sector, particularly the software industry.

India's rigid labor laws are the main obstacle to an increased role for manufacturing. A large proportion of heavy industry is still publicly owned. After liberalization, India has gradually reduced its policy on anti-export bias, and more resources have been moved into labor-intensive industries. Historically, a policy of import substitution in the decades after independence encouraged the development of a broad industrial base, but a lack of competition contributed to poor product quality and inefficiencies in production. Several sectors have now been opened up to foreign participation under India's liberalizing reform program.

In the early 1990s, India started economic reforms, but they have been slow and patchy when compared to other fast-growing, emerging economies. Economic development has been spread unevenly across states. Nevertheless, India has a large number of highly qualified professionals, as well as several internationally established industrial groups. Gradually, the country has become a prodigious exporter of its remote services, ranging from skilled software coders, accentless call-center representatives, long-distance salespeople, invisible insurance clerks, medical-record transcribers, and patient number crunchers. Aiming to become the back office for the world's banks, India wants to climb up the value chain by offering more sophisticated services to foreign companies.

Industry

India's software industry has been growing at 50 percent annually. According to a study by McKinsey & Company, India's software and service industry's output will rise to $87 billion in 2008, of which $50 billion will be exported. Two-thirds of the increase is projected to generate from new growth opportunities in IT-enabled services, including call-center operations, transcription, and design and engineering services. It is estimated that roughly 2.2 million will be employed in the software and IT-related industries. India is on its way to becoming a major exporter of software services based on its large workforce of well-educated people skilled in English and engineering. Moreover, India is revealing strength in skill-intensive tradable services, ranging from software development, IT-enabled services, product/project engineering and design to biotechnology, pharmaceuticals, media, entertainment, and health care. Many world-famous companies are building their research and development centers in clusters like Bangalore and Hyderabad. Thus, India's international competitiveness and opportunities present for multinational corporations (MNCs) will differ from those emerging economies such as China that are manufacturing powerhouses. Rapid technological change in IT industries indicates that India is not locked into lower-level manufacturing activities, but could move up the value chain to export value-deepening services, such as consulting and project management, research and development, among others.

India has also attracted many IT-enabled projects from financial firms and other service sectors. GE Capital International Services, for example, employs more than 13,000 people in India in various departments including finance, accounting, and remote marketing. Similarly, Citigroup Inc.'s e-Serve has employed more than 3,000 people in Mumbai and Chennai. What MNCs are doing today is transferring more complex processes to India. Consequently, many investment banks, accountants, and consulting firms are outsourcing their work to India-based subcontractors.

As in other emerging economies, some Indian government restrictions become barriers for foreign investors to overcome. One example is Press Note 18, which requires any investor with previous or existing joint ventures or technology agreements to seek approval from the Foreign Investment Promotion Board for fresh direct investments in the same or related field. Applicants must prove that the new proposal will not jeopardize the interest of the existing joint venture or technology partners. Press Note 18 is intended to protect the interests of shareholders, public financial institutions, and workers. Government officials have been reluctant to abandon the guideline because they consider their domestic industry not strong enough to face direct competition from foreign firms in selected sectors. Under the guidelines, Suzuki Motor Corporation has to include Maruti Udyog, its existing joint venture, in its plans to make new investments for a car assembly plant and a diesel engine plant. According to Suzuki, Indian governmental regulations have become a tool of the Indian partners to demand unrealistic and opportunistic exit valuations or to create more barriers for foreign competitors.

It is imperative for multinational companies to assess the political power of their domestic competitors before committing to a significant investment in India. After all, even though India's legal systems are relatively impartial, free, and fair, they are notoriously slow. Disputes often take decades to be resolved and, as a result, many foreign companies build in clauses allowing for international arbitration of disputes. What makes it worse is the regulatory system, which is not immune from policy reversals due to pressures from vested interests and interministry rivalries. Fortunately, in recent years, more transparent regulatory systems are being introduced in previously under-regulated sectors.

Still, tariff and nontariff barriers continue to be used in the country to protect domestic industry. India's removal of its remaining import quotas in April 2001 was expected to lead to a surge in imports. However, this did not happen because the government compensated by introducing high tariffs on some products. Customs duties on agricultural goods were raised, and the total duty on secondhand cars is now more than 180 percent. Well-connected companies or lobby groups have consistently been able to counteract many of India's WTO liberalization measures. In general, foreign companies should assess the political power of their domestic competitors before proceeding with a significant investment.

Like investing in other developing countries, international managers must deal with corruption in India. In 2004, India ranked 90th out of 146 countries (with 146 being the most corrupt) in an international corruption evaluation. Even though India's intellectual property protection is far better than China's, its weak legal regime has ambiguous rules toward patent products. GlaxoSmithKline (GSK), one of the world's biggest drug firms, for instance, has long aspired to do more drug development in India. However, what the company combats in India is those companies that specialize in making copycat drugs and then selling them cheaply to India's vast domestic market. Recently, GSK was quite disappointed to find out that even under the new legislation and patent regulations of the WTO, the Indian government still ignored the need to protect patent products so that domestic firms can make or market the same drug using the data released with the product.

Market

Having been attracted by its vast market potential, many MNCs have made longer than expected commitments to market expansion in India. For example, The Coca-Cola Company is one company that tried for decades to enter the promising market. Initially, the company was India's leading soft-drink producer. In 1977, the company was ordered by a new government to dilute its stake in its Indian unit and turn over Coke's secret formula. As a result, Coca-Cola had to decide to exit the market. Later on, when the Indian government began to attract foreign investment, Coca-Cola returned in 1993. Even though the company quickly gained a lead in the market by buying up famous local brands, it has spent millions of dollars to fight legal and legislative battles all across India, in particular, dealing with nongovernmental organization campaigns. Basically the company was accused of stealing water, poisoning land, and selling drinks laced with dangerous pesticides. Moreover, the company suffered financially due to its lack of understanding that affordable prices are essential to win the hearts of Indian consumers. Unlike Unilever, an Anglo-Dutch consumer-goods conglomerate, which successfully adopted the low-margin/high-volume business model for India, Coca-Cola raised prices on certain products only to accept a failed market. In 2004, Coca-Cola reintroduced its 200-milliliter bottles and reduced prices to Rs5 (just under 11¢) to secure its market in India.

Although consumers in emerging markets are much more affluent than they were a decade ago, they are not affluent by Western standards. In India, the top tier consists of a small number of consumers (2 million) who are willing to accept Western brands and can afford them. Tier two has a much larger group of people (60 million), but is less attracted to international brands. The massive group, tier three (the rest of the population) in the economy, is more loyal to local customs, habits, and often to local brands than otherwise. The market pyramid in India can well explain why U.S. automakers failed to penetrate the emerging markets in the last decade. For example, Ford's recent introduction of Escort, priced at more than $21,000, falls into the luxury segment. Remember that in India the most popular car, the Maruti Suzuki, sells for only $10,000 or less. Apparently, Ford has ignored tier two of the pyramid with its market positioning. No wonder despite almost a decade in India, Ford and GM still lag far behind some competitors that came to India at about the same time. Today, GM and Ford are small players in India's car market with a meager 3 percent market share. Their Korean competitor, Hyundai, has snatched a 17-percent market share by selling its tiny Santro. It seems that U.S. automakers are trying to bring their existing products and marketing strategies to India without properly accounting for the country's market pyramids. Many companies, therefore, become high-end niche players. In India, only 7 million people have purchasing power greater than U.S. $20,000 dollars. No wonder when Revlon, Inc. introduced its beauty products in India, only the top tier could afford the Revlon brand. Many companies, such as Ford and GM, have learned that in order to survive the fierce competition, affordable prices tailored to local tastes and needs are crucial. After all, in India, roughly 63 million of the population have the purchasing power between $10,000 and $20,000. Although the fast-growing, emerging market will make a significant contribution to their future performance of worldwide businesses, MNCs will have to reconfigure their resource bases, readjust their cost structures, redesign their product-development processes, and challenge their assumptions about existing business models.

In India, the median household income is about $480; however, the private savings rate is an impressive 24 percent. Most people are worried about their social-security system, so frugality has deep historical roots in the country. For example, although India is the world's largest market for razor blades, it is not a market for disposable shavers. Less than 1 percent of the blades bought in cities are attached to plastic handles. The logic is simple. People cannot stand the waste of throwing away the razor blades. Similarly, sanitary-napkin manufacturers face the same dilemma when entering the 1-billion population country. What companies found is that most Indian women recycle old cotton sheets. As a result, less than 2 percent of all Indian women and just 23 percent of adult urban women use sanitary napkins. Generally speaking, Indian consumers are very sensitive about the price/quality equation, which greatly provides low-cost local competitors the edge in the fast-growing market. MNCs cannot duplicate their success business models in other developed countries to the Indian market. They have to learn to turn these price-sensitivity characteristics to their advantage by offering customers good prices along with global standards.

In the past decade, many companies learned that family-sized quantities are not easy to promote in India, whether they are detergents, shampoos, or tea leaves. On the contrary, small packs give consumers the satisfaction of using branded products at low costs and are more affordable to the lower-income group and the rural masses. Now MNCs try to promote products such as detergents, shampoos, ready-to-eat food products, tea, coffee, nail polish, toothpaste, among other things with small-quantity packages. Surprisingly, the small packaged products make up 20–30 percent of the market share. What multinational companies gradually learned in India is that small-package size is more efficient to target the urban, semiurban, and rural markets by targeting consumers from the middle class and the lower class. Companies, domestic or international, dealing in the fast-moving consumer-goods industry or durables have recognized the fact that price is the greatest determinant of perceived value for the India consumers and are enjoying the success story with "small consumption-small price tag" logic.

Coca-Cola, as mentioned earlier, has reintroduced its 200-milliliter cola bottles with an impressive Rs5 (11¢) price tag. The low-price strategy is very rewarding for the company, as it accounted for half of the revenues of the cola products. To secure its market share, Coca-Cola also introduced its returnable 200-milliliter glass bottle with the same price range. The efforts have paid off, and 80 percent of new sales now come from the rural markets. Similarly, Nestlé's offer of Chocostick with an Rs2 (4¢) price tag has achieved remarkable success.

Nestlé has not only secured the market with small packs of products, but it has also successfully localized products and appeased price-conscious housewives. To win the hearts of the price-sensitive consumers, Nestlé has created an Indian-style instant coffee, Sunrise, which is blended with chicory to produce a strong and familiar flavor to Indian consumers at an affordable price. The company also promotes a mint flavored with the local betel nut, as well as mixes for traditional Indian desserts. More than half of Nestlé's products sold in India cost less than 70¢. One example is that when Nestlé cut the price of its Maggi noodles from 19¢ to 14¢, sales volume tripled. Increasingly, MNCs realize that in order to be competitive with pricing, localization in India is a must. Today, many automakers have learned to rely on Asian sources for price and suitability of components to meet the demand of the price-sensitive consumers.

It is also imperative for MNCs to reconsider their branding strategy in India. Coca-Cola, for example, has overvalued the pull of its brand among the tier-two consumers. The company had originally based its advertising strategy on its worldwide image, only to later accept the failed market. Now the company is positioning itself by using local heroes in its advertising and also promoting the local cola brand—Thums Up. Coca-Cola purchased Thums Up in 1993, but yet took years to realize the importance of localized branding in terms of attracting local consumers. Many companies, such as Hindustan Lever Limited (HLL) and PepsiCo, have developed effective brand operations and thus achieved huge success. Branding in India is more complex than many companies would expect, largely due to the complexity and variances of culture and people across the Indian subcontinent. When MNCs do not have enough knowledge about the end users and fail to effectively segment the market into accessible groups, they find it difficult to increase their market share with their already established global-branding strategies.

Multinational companies gradually realized that India's consumption boom has been fueled with price wars for everything, whether it is cars or shampoo products. For instance, HLL, the Indian subsidiary of consumer-goods giant Unilever, and rival Procter & Gamble have long been locked in a bitter price war. Following rival Unilever's huge lead by developing an Avon-style direct sales force, P&G is countering with its own van sales program to reach rural areas. P&G has also followed Unilever by introducing low-cost, single-use sachets of its laundry detergent brands. The two famous MNCs are trying to capture the largest segment of the market. Similarly, with the dramatic increase of cell phone subscriptions in the past five years, there are fierce competitions among phone companies, both from domestic and international manufacturers. Subsequently, to grasp a market share of the emerging economy, MNCs have been discounting their products to maintain a stable market share. Some auto companies have decreased their prices about 20 percent to secure their leading market position. Moreover, it may also take longer than expected for MNCs to generate profits in India. For example,

Johnson & Johnson, one of the most successful consumer products multinationals, had been in India for decades before it realized profits. Johnson & Johnson entered India some 35 years ago, but its turnover of $50 million is only equivalent to its sales in Malaysia, home to just 19 million people. Many new entrants must sit tight through years of losses before they make profits. It seems that consumption of consumable and luxury products is much less than expected in this country of more than 1 billion people.

Without a doubt, India has caught the world's attention in terms of fostering genuine entrepreneurship in some industries by favoring domestic over foreign investment. Some IT firms, such as Infosys Technologies Limited, Wipro Technologies, and Tata Consultancy Services, are now among the world's best. Outside the IT industry, unfortunately, many firms still retain bad habits and feuding that often afflict family firms. To enter the vast emerging market, MNCs must realize that the country's economy and industrialization are far from homogeneous or uniform. Consequently, MNCs should think strategically and selectively about which states or regions to enter, rather than India as a whole. Further, MNCs should establish and maintain informal ties with all important political parties, given the fact that political power changes hands rapidly in India both at the federal and state levels. Eventually, many MNCs found it beneficial to set up joint ventures with a native partner for assistance in precisely such delicate situations when tact or diplomacy and public relations savvy are needed.

Currently, foreign investment in some sectors of the Indian economy—such as insurance and the media—is limited to a minority stake. In the retail sector, it is banned altogether. Companies such as McDonald's Corporation of the United States and Italy's Benetton Group have opened in the subcontinent, but usually through franchising agreements in which Indian partners dominate and make most key decisions. That may explain why investors have not found India, which received $4 billion in FDI in 2004, as attractive as the Chinese market. Nonetheless, as the world's second-most-populous country, the Indian government has become more accommodating to foreign investment, and there is an abundance of growth potential for foreign companies.[8]

RUSSIA

Economy

With a population of 143 million people and a current GDP of $772 billion (or $1.59 trillion in purchasing power parity) in 2005, Russia is one of the largest markets in the world. Many MNCs have come to Russia since 1986 when Soviet President Mikhail Gorbachev encouraged foreign investors to seek joint ventures with Soviet partners. Since the financial crisis of 1998, the country has experienced six straight years of growth, averaging 6.5 percent annually thanks largely to rising oil prices. To date Russia is considered the next economic superpower of the world. Foreign direct investment hit a record high of $9.4 billion in 2004, with a 39-percent increase from the previous year. Shifting to a market economy, Russia presents many opportunities for foreign companies. Russia has also improved its international financial position since the 1998 financial crisis, as witnessed by its foreign debt reduced from 90 percent of the GDP to around 28 percent in 2005. However, the country's economy largely depends on oil, natural gas, metals, and timber representing more than 80 percent of exports, leaving the country vulnerable to swings in world commodity prices. High oil prices are expected to put strong upward pressure on the real exchange rate, undermining the cost competitiveness of the industrial sector and dampening growth in the medium term. Accordingly, Russia must rejuvenate its manufacturing sector if the country is to achieve broad-based economic growth. At the present, the country's per-capita purchasing power is about 35 percent of the developed EU level and 25 percent of that of the United States.

Russia's improved competitiveness and higher oil prices greatly facilitated its dramatic turnaround in the external current account, from a deficit of around half of 1 percent of the GDP in 1998 to a surplus of 12 percent of the GDP in 1999. This surplus increased further during 2000 to an estimated 17 percent of the GDP. In spite of its recent economic upturn, the Russian economy is facing some serious problems. One of the most significant is the continued impact of corruption in both the public and private sectors. The country also suffers from a weak banking system, a poor business climate that discourages both domestic and foreign investors, and widespread lack of trust in institutions. Even though reforms of the tax regime and the newly established political and economic stability have improved the investment climate, the country still needs to improve its enforcement and implementation of policies to reduce operational risks for businesses. For foreign investors, investing in Russia still requires a long-term commitment and patient cultivation. Hence, it is imperative for MNCs to fully understand local rules and regulations before they locate their operations and further align their expertise with local partners.

Industry

Despite these problems, FDI inflows have picked up strongly, as have other forms of capital inflow. FDI inflows had averaged $3 billion annually during 1998–2002 and then picked up remarkably to $8 billion in 2003 and $11.7 billion in 2004. Many of the large-scale investments were concentrated in the natural resources sector, that is, oil and gas. Meanwhile, retail and fast-growing consumer-goods sectors have also attracted many foreign companies. Largely due to the country's high tariff on foreign imports, many firms are motivated to build plants in Russia. In the past, Russia's attractions of market size, abundant natural resources, and a cheap and relatively skilled workforce had been more than offset by serious deficiencies of the institutional environment. Recent political and economic reforms have greatly enhanced the country's investment situation. One example is that the government initiated a new law on foreign investment, passed in 1999 and amended later, on guarantees of national treatment, repatriation of profits, and compensation in the case of nationalization.

Despite its continuous growth in FDI inflows since 2003, the country's FDI remains below potential given its obvious attractions. After all, Russia is home to one-third of the world's gas reserves, around 8 percent of proven oil reserves, a skilled and low-cost workforce, and an underdeveloped but fast-growing consumer market of 143 million people. In other words, its economic growth still lags behind the country's potential, especially compared to other emerging econo-mies, such as China's $50 billion FDI inflows during the same period. Russia's cumulative FDI inflows are one of the lowest among all 27 countries of the tran-sition region, and one-fifth of the average penetration ratio in East-Central Europe.

For foreign investors, one of its major barriers to enter the country is its overall complexity of institutional environment. On the one hand, there has been politi-cal and macroeconomic stabilization in recent years, and the business environ-ment has improved. On the other hand, the country's overall business environment remains difficult and unpredictable. Recent campaigns against the Yukos Oil Company highlighted institutional deficiencies, which demonstrates that property rights still ultimately depend on the will of the state. The concentra-tion of economic power in a few massive conglomerates impedes competition in an economy. Although the government is trying to reduce the regulatory burden on business, policy implementation will continue to be hindered by an inefficient and cumbersome bureaucracy.

According to a recent corruption report, Russia's corruption perceptions index (2004) ranked 90th out of 146 countries (146 is rated as the most corrupted country). The government's control of corruption is much lower than that of China and India. Corruption also occurs at all levels of the government. The country's high levels of official corruption, a crumbling legal system, and inad-equate laws covering the enforcement of property rights combine to discourage foreign and domestic investment.

Accordingly, the inefficient controls of bureaucracy compound the issue of investment uncertainty. Investors in the natural resource and metals sectors, in particular, are facing considerable uncertainty as Russia defines which assets it considers strategic and thus open to foreign majority control. Many foreign com-panies form alliances to gain access to government and local inputs, instead of considering Greenfield investments and acquisitions. Although the Russian government has urged legislation to clarify the situation and delineate which areas will be subject to restricted access, government policy remains confusing and uncertain.

Nevertheless, a recent survey indicates that foreign investment in Russia on average yields higher returns than investment in China or India. Many foreign companies have developed the skills and local knowledge to navigate the Russian business environment. Although corruption tops the list of foreign investors' concerns, it does not appear to be an insuperable barrier to doing business in Russia. Hence, many businesses were satisfied with their business success in Russia and planned to expand their investments in the country.

Despite the continuing problems of the business environment and the regulatory uncertainty affecting the natural resources sector, macroeconomic fundamentals remain strong and market opportunities are inviting. When compared to other emerging economies, such as China's and India's, Russia has yet to diversify its industrial performance beyond the oil, gas, and minerals sector. Nevertheless, the country's growth of both consumer spending and domestic investment has been incredible. Judging from last year's economic data, consumer consumption and fixed investment represent 5.8 percent and 2.8 percent, respectively, of its 7.1-percent GDP growth. The fixed investment by domestic businesses in Russia is much smaller than its counterparts. For instance, Russian businesses invested 17 percent of the GDP in themselves last year, compared with 20 percent from Latin America and 50 percent from Chinese businesses.

Market

Nevertheless, in recent years the general economic improvement in Russia has led to increased consumer spending and demand for consumable products. One of the driving forces for increased consumer spending has been the growing Russian middle class, especially in Moscow. One has to notice that Russia has the third largest number of billionaires on *Forbes Magazine*'s list of richest people, after the United States and Germany. Growth of consumer expenditure has also benefited from the impact on real disposable incomes of continuing utilities and housing subsidies.

Imported goods made heavy inroads into the Russian market throughout most of the 1990s. Until the 1998 financial crisis, imported goods were stimulated by real appreciation of the ruble and the advertising-enhanced power of Western brand names. In the wake of the 1998 ruble devaluation, many of these imports were crowded out of the market, which in turn helped in reviving domestic production across the full range of consumer-goods industries. Since 2000, with the help of recovery in incomes and renewed ruble appreciation, consumers have been moving back to consume foreign brands for many categories.

Apparently, the new free market offers Russian consumers options and alternatives that were unavailable during the Soviet era. With the liberalized market,

Russian consumers have more choices to select between domestic and imported products. Although most consumers may prefer certain domestic brands, such as chocolates and vodka, to foreign brands, Russian products, in general, cannot compete with Western and Asian imports because their product quality standards have been lower than these foreign counterparts' standards. Consequently, consumers prefer global brands in automobiles and high-technology products, whereas local brands succeed in the food and beverage industries.

Like other emerging economies, Russia has extremely wide income disparities. According to the government official data, the richest 10 percent of the population receive around 30 percent of the national income, whereas the poorest 10 percent receive only 2 percent. The richest 10 percent also have incomes that are nearly 15 times higher than the poorest 10 percent. It is not surprising that Forbes recently announced that there are more billionaires living in Moscow than in New York (33 compared to 31).

Currently, young Russian consumers represent more than 20 percent of the population (age 5–18). Some 5 percent of Russia's high-income earners are under age 20, making $500 per month or more. MNCs, such as Reebok International Ltd., Nike, Inc., and The Coca-Cola Company have targeted Russian teens with aggressive advertising. Unlike teenagers in China who prefer to buy products from U.S., European, and Japanese companies, Russian teenagers love both domestic and foreign products as long as product quality meets their expectations. That is to say, they buy Western products simply because products are better, not because of the country of origin. Moreover, MNCs learned that companies cannot judge Russian young generations with Western standards. Russian youth are yearning for self-expression, yet they like to be dressed in the same style. Russian young consumers also demonstrated polarized consumption styles —namely, the New Soviets and the New Cosmopolitans. Both segments are eager to try new things, but New Soviets are deeply rooted in the past, thus are more "Russian," and accept new ideas only that make them comfortable. New Cosmopolitans, on the other hand, are more experienced, better educated, emotionally stronger, and more ready to accept new things. To grab the hearts of young consumers, properly understanding their unique characteristics is crucial. After all, the youth market is worth battling for even though it is as fickle as the Western one.

It is imperative for MNCs to carefully examine their advertising strategy in Russia. Toyota Motor Corporation has learned the hard way the importance of carefully selecting an advertising agency and further controlling the marketing campaign. To launch its $50,000–$100,000 Lexus model to the Russian rich, the company decided to advertise the car along with the opening of the sci-fi U.S. film *Minority Report*. Toyota hired a local advertising agency to design a strategy to send out invitations. The advertising company designed a threatening invitation letter, saying "you are under suspicion" to match the theme of the marketing campaign. The attendance was impressive, with three-quarters showing up to the film, but the public-relations effect was unfavorable. The ad company received worried phone calls from the security services of 40 of the targeted companies. Obviously, even some local and global ad agencies are readily available in Russia; foreign companies need to pay close attention to the conduct of marketing campaigns.

In general, Russian consumers are much more suspicious of marketing campaigns and are less responsive to TV and outdoor advertising; a friend's recommendation (word of mouth) works better. As a result, foreign investors have to rethink appropriate marketing techniques to penetrate the Russian market. Eastman Kodak Company, for instance, allocated 20–30 percent of its annual budget to promotions and advertising campaigns. It also promotes its brand name by organizing and sponsoring various public events. To date, Kodak has gradually established consumer acceptance through open and frequent communications with its consumers. Reebok, a manufacturer and distributor of footwear and other clothing products, successfully created public good will by donating $50,000 worth of products to public schools and the Russian Olympic team. Accordingly, Kodak and Reebok have made successful market entries in Russia.

Like those in other emerging economies, MNCs found that consumers in Russia are not highly loyal to brands. As in India, they found in Russia that small packaged products offer consumers the satisfaction of using branded products at low costs and are more affordable to the mass population. Unilever followed that logic with small packed Brooke Bond, Lipton, and Beseda teas. The company also introduced trial sachets of its Sunsilk shampoos. Similarly, to penetrate the vast market, Eastman Kodak Company increased diversification by offering new lines specifically for local demand. Kodak introduced a number of inexpensive products that the average Russian could generally afford. So far the company's most successful product launched in Russia was "Kodak Color Plus." The film was not on the cutting edge of consumer-imaging technology like Kodak Gold film, but was a well-balanced, good-quality, inexpensive product with a total cost of approximately $1 per roll. The introduction of Kodak Color Plus in Russia strengthened the company's competitiveness in the price-sensitive market.

To target those consumers who do not display a preference for foreign brands, foreign companies have tried to promote their products by emphasizing local roots. Mars Incorporated, the U.S. sweets giant, has presented itself as a semi-Russian company since 1996. The company has strongly established itself by advertising the extent of its local production in its marketing campaigns. Although all categories of consumer-goods imports have witnessed a plunge in market share in Russia, Mars brand management has won many consumers and become one of the country's top five sellers.

Many foreign companies entering the Russian market in the 1990s learned to be extremely cautious about their capital investment. The financial crisis demonstrated how crucial it is for companies to quickly pull corporate funds out of the sinking economy. Some foreign investors still prefer minimum capital investment to stay away from potential disadvantages. One important note is that in the short term there may be a difference in approach between established and potential new investors, with the latter being more sensitive to recent developments. Most companies that are already in place, by contrast, seem to be gearing up for more investments. General global conditions for FDI also appear favorable after several relatively lean years. Recently, Toyota Motor Corporation announced its $140-million investment to build an automobile manufacturing plant in St. Petersburg. A week earlier, LG Electronics unveiled plans to build a $100-million plant, making flat-screen televisions, refrigerators, washing machines, and audio equipment. In 2004, Alcoa of the United States acquired two fabricating facilities. The Coca-Cola Company also acquired Russia's largest juice maker for an estimated $600 million. More interestingly, a Germany company BASF has entered the gas field by taking a 50-percent-minus-one-share stake. FDI reached a record $11.7 billion in 2004, up from $8 billion in 2003; inflows in the first quarter of this year already amounted to $5.4 billion.

All in all, Russia's rapidly growing consumer market and further economic opening resulting from WTO accession will make Russia comparatively attractive for foreign companies. Although the country has gradually enhanced its competitive position, in the long run, Russia needs institutional and structural reforms to effectively utilize its human capital and develop other manufacturing sectors to sustain its competitiveness.[9]

SUMMARY

Various forces are responsible for the increased integration. Major emerging economies have begun to reshape the nature of international trade and investment. Growth in international trade continuously outpaces the rise in national outputs. Transportation and communications are becoming faster, cheaper, and more widely accessible. The nature of value-adding activities is changing in the advanced countries from manufacturing to services and information manipulation. Such changes are a result of and are a force behind the rapid advancement in telecommunications and computers. Even developing nations, regardless of their political colors, have realized the importance of telecommunications and electronic commerce and are attempting to improve their infrastructure. The capital markets of the world are already integrated for all practical purposes, and this integration affects exchange rates, interest rates, investments, employment, and growth across the world. Multinational corporations have truly become the global operations in name and spirit that they were envisaged to be. Even smaller companies are leapfrogging the gradual expansion pattern of traditional multinational companies by adopting e-commerce that has no national boundaries. In short, to repeat an old maxim, the world is becoming a global village. When Karl Marx said in 1848 that the world was becoming a smaller place, he could not have imagined how small it truly has become.

NOTES

1. Paul Bairoch, "International Industrialization Levels from 1750 to 1980," *Journal of European Economic History* 11 (1982), pp. 36–54.

2. United Nations Conference on Trade and Development, *Trade and Development Report 2005*, Geneva: United Nations.

3. Lowell Bryan, *Race for the World: Strategies to Build a Great Global Firm*, Boston: Harvard Business School Press, 1999.

4. Central European countries are Poland, Czech Republic, Slovakia, Slovenia, Hungary, Estonia, Latvia, Lithuania, Romania, and Bulgaria. See an excellent article, "The Rise of Central Europe," *Business Week*, December 12, 2005, pp. 50–56.

5. *World Trade Report 2005: Exploring the Link between Trade, Standards, and the WTO*, Geneva, World Trade Organization, 2005.

6. "U.S. Presses China on Goods Piracy," *Wall Street Journal*, May 2, 2005, www.wsj.com

7. Useful sources on China follow: "The Other Side of China's Success Story," *Financial Times*, January 19, 2003; "The Struggle of the Champions," *Economist*, January 6, 2005; "U.S. Presses China on Goods Piracy," *Wall Street Journal*, May 2, 2005, www.wsj.com; "The Myth of China Inc.," *Economist*, September 1, 2005; "The Frugal Giant," *Economist*, September 22, 2005; and "A Billion Tough Sells," *Business Week*, March 20, 2006, pp. 44–45.

8. Useful sources on India follow: "Marketing Gurus Say: In India, Think Cheap, Lose the Cold Cereal," *Wall Street Journal*, October 11, 1996; Devesh Kapur and Ravi Ramamurti, "India's Emerging Competitive Advantage in Services," *Academy of Management Executive* 15(2), 2001, pp. 20–32; C.K. Prahalad and Kenneth Lieberthal, "The End of Corporate Imperialism," *Harvard Business Review* 81(8), 2003, pp. 109–17; Jayashree Dubey and Rajni Patel, "Small Wonders of the Indian Market," *Journal of Consumer Behaviour* 4(2), 2004, pp. 145–151; and "The Great Divide," *Economist*, March 3, 2005.

9. Useful sources on Russia follow: "Young and Restless," *Business Russia*, Economist Intelligence Unit, 1998, pp. 4–5; "Brand Aid," *Country Monitor*, Economist Intelligence Unit, 1999, p. 3; "Suspicious Behavior," *Business Russia*, Economist Intelligence Unit, 2002, p. 5; Gary Anders and Danila Usachev, "Strategic Elements of Eastman Kodak's Successful Market Entry in Russia," *Thunderbird International Business Review* 45 (March/April 2003), pp. 171–183; Khanna Tarun, Krishna G. Palepu, and Jayant Sinha, "Strategies That Fit Emerging Markets," *Harvard Business Review* 83(6), 2005, pp. 63–76; and "Russia: Shoppers Gone Wild," *Business Week*, February 20, 2006.

CHAPTER 3

TACKLING CONSUMERS IN CENTRAL AND EASTERN EUROPE

Gerhard A. Wührer and Dana-Nicoleta Lascu

Gone are the days when Communist authorities relegated consumers' needs to the lowly "light industry" category, when consumer desires were mostly ignored by all but the black market and the luxury market targeting exclusively the hard currency of Western consumers. Gone too are the euphoric early 1990s, when shopping established itself as the new opium of the masses, with consumers giving free reign to their appetites for long-coveted Western goods. Central and Eastern Europe (CEE) have changed dramatically, and so have Central and Eastern European consumers.

To understand CEE consumers, a background is in order. Central and Eastern Europe, also referred to as Eastern Europe, or the former Eastern Bloc, constitute a market of about 385 million consumers—5 million more than Western Europe—who are educated and demanding.[1] The CEE encompasses the European countries that were, until the end of the Cold War, part of the former Soviet Empire. These countries are also commonly included in other ad hoc categories, such as Southeastern Europe/Balkans, Central Europe, and Northern Europe. For example, Poland, the Czech Republic, Slovakia, Hungary, Slovenia, and Croatia are often considered part of Central Europe rather than Eastern Europe; in this self-reference, the respective countries hint to their past as part of Mitteleuropa, a cultural and political center for many centuries in European history. Similarly, the Baltic states of Estonia, Latvia, and Lithuania are categorized as Northern European states. But, as regions are merely social constructs, these terms vary depending on the focus of deliberations. For the purpose of this chapter, the following countries are referred to jointly as the CEE: Albania, Belarus, Bosnia-Herzegovina, Bulgaria, Croatia, Czech Republic, Estonia, Hungary,

Latvia, Lithuania, Macedonia, Moldova, Montenegro, Poland, Romania, Russia, Serbia, Slovakia, Slovenia, and the Ukraine.

CENTRAL AND EASTERN EUROPE IN TRANSITION

Until 1989, the CEE was a virtually untapped market, accounting for 15 percent of the world gross national product, a market characterized by centralized state control, totalitarian rule, and consumer isolation from world markets.[2] Many Central and Eastern European markets are now struggling to escape the damaging vestiges of Communism that have dominated their recent history. Many of the CEE countries—Poland, the Czech Republic, Hungary, and Romania, for instance—have a pre-Communist history of successful capitalism that makes them very different from the rest of the CEE countries. Capitalist enterprise in these countries created sophisticated consumer societies; however, with decades of totalitarian anti-consumerism, consumer memories dating to that period had practically fully eroded by 1989.

Subsequent to the fall of Communism in 1989, the CEE has become one of the primary growth markets for multinationals; automakers, such as Ford Motor Company, Toyota Motor Corporation, Renault, Peugeot, Volkswagen, and Daewoo, are intensifying their production and distribution in the region, as are most of the leading consumer product companies in Western Europe, the United States, Japan, and other emerging markets such as China and Turkey. To offer an example, U.S. exports to the Central and Eastern European emerging markets are at the double-digit level, with Lithuania leading the list, followed by Russia, the Ukraine, Poland, and Romania.[3] The CEE countries have established themselves as growth markets for imported goods, with Russia as the most prominent and promising growth market, as Table 3.1 illustrates.

Overall, Central and Eastern European countries have generated an annual growth rate in the range of 3.4–6 percent per year from 1999 to 2005. The average growth rate for Southeastern Europe and the Commonwealth of Independent States (CIS), 5.8 percent, exceeds that of any other economic region so far, including China.[4] Table 3.2 offers an account of total merchandise imports in each of the CEE countries discussed in this chapter.

Behind these promising figures was a long and arduous economic process, with the CEE countries transitioning to a market economy, some at a more rapid pace than others; the countries that were the first to join the European Union in 2004 have made the most remarkable advances, with Poland, Hungary, and the Czech Republic leading the pack. Less progress is noted for the former Soviet republics, such as Belarus, Moldova, Russia, and the Ukraine, and the countries that have experienced civil war and internal turmoil in the past decades, such as Albania and the former Yugoslav republics.

Table 3.1
World Output Growth^a 1990–2005 (percentage change from previous years)

Region/Country^b	1990–2000^c	1999	2000	2001	2002	2003	2004^d	2005^e
World	2.7	2.9	4.0	1.3	1.8	2.5	3.8	3.0
Developed countries	2.4	2.7	3.5	1.0	1.3	1.7	3.0	2.3
Japan	1.4	0.1	2.8	0.4	−0.3	1.4	2.5	1.6
United States	3.4	4.1	3.8	0.3	2.4	3.0	4.4	3.5
European Union (EU)	2.1	2.9	3.6	1.7	1.1	0.9	2.1	1.5
EU–15	2.1	2.9	3.5	1.6	1.0	0.8	2.0	1.4
Euro area	2.0	2.6	3.5	1.6	0.9	0.5	1.8	1.2
France	1.7	3.2	3.8	2.1	1.2	0.5	2.1	1.5
Germany	1.6	2.0	2.9	0.9	0.2	−0.1	1.0	0.8
Italy	1.6	1.7	3.0	1.8	0.4	0.3	1.0	−0.4
United Kingdom	2.7	2.8	3.8	2.1	1.7	2.2	3.1	2.0
Southeast Europe and CIS	−4.3	3.4	8.1	5.6	4.9	6.9	7.5	6.0
Developing countries	4.8	3.5	5.4	2.4	3.5	4.7	6.4	5.4
Developing countries, excluding China	4.0	3.0	5.0	1.5	2.7	3.9	5.7	4.6

^a·Calculations are based on the gross domestic product (GDP) in constant market prices based on 1995 dollars.
^b·Region and country groups correspond to those defined in the *UNCTAD Handbook of Statistics 2004.*
^c·Average.
^d·Preliminary estimates.
^e·Forecast.
Sources: United Nations Conference on Trade and Development (UNCTAD) secretariat calculations, based on *UNCTAD Handbook of Statistics 2004;* United Nations Department of Economic and Social Affairs (UN/DESA), Development Policy and Planning Office, Project Link estimates; National Unit [Economist Intelligence Unit (EIU)], Country Forecast, various issues; and Organisation for Economic Co-operation and Development, Economic Outlook No. 77.

CENTRAL AND EASTERN EUROPEAN CONSUMERS

The fall of Communism in the 1980s led to a shopping revolution: consumers spent much of their income on the new Western brands that entered the market. However, this shopping frenzy did not last long, as consumers were left with an income that could barely cover the costs of necessities.[5] The desire to shop quickly

Table 3.2
Total Merchandise Imports (Units: U.S.$million) in CEE Countries

Country	1995	2000	2003	2004	2005
Albania	714	1,090	1,864	2,309	2,614
Belarus	5,564	8,646	11,558	16,491	16,699
Bosnia and Herzegovina	N/A	N/A	N/A	N/A	N/A
Bulgaria	5,661	6,505	10,902	14,467	18,181
Czech Republic	26,385	33,852	53,801	71,619	76,554
Estonia	2,400	4,236	6,480	8,336	10,109
Hungary	15,377	31,955	47,602	59,637	65,296
Latvia	1,818	3,184	5,242	7,048	8,537
Lithuania	3,013	5,219	9,668	12,386	15,449
Macedonia	1,719	2,094	2,306	2,932	3,228
Moldova	841	776	1,403	1,773	N/A
Poland	29,050	48,940	68,004	87,909	100,903
Romania	10,278	13,055	24,003	32,664	40,463
Russian Federation	68,863	49,125	83,677	107,120	137,833
Slovakia	9,225	13,412	23,760	30,469	36,123
Slovenia	9,492	10,116	13,853	17,571	19,532
Ukraine	15,484	13,956	23,020	28,997	36,141

Source: IMF, *International Financial Statistics,* www.europaworld.com/comparative-statistics, 2006.

ceded to feelings of insecurity and frequent expressions of dissatisfaction with post-Communist life; consumers in the CEE today frequently express confusion about the state of things. On the one hand, they are nostalgic for the old days where they were guaranteed safety, and they are often hopeless about what the future might bring.[6] On the other, they are becoming astute and demanding shoppers, readily enjoying the higher quality and the variety of products that a free market offers. Consumers have spent now almost two decades in a process of reeducation, learning about consumption and also about restraint. They have also learned about and responded to the elements of the marketing mix—product, price, promotion, and distribution. In the next section, the chapter addresses the developments that CEE consumers have experienced with regard to each of the elements of the marketing mix.

Product and Brand Issues

In the product category, consumers have made noteworthy leaps in understanding the concept of branding. During Communism, consumers had an understanding of products and branding only at their most basic levels. The concept of branding and differentiation was a novel idea, and products were judged solely on basic features and benefits rather than on brand-related considerations.[7] This original understanding has carried over into the consumers' current relationship to the brand and branding; consumers in Central and Eastern Europe are more interested in what the products can deliver than in brand personality and brand values, as the idea of the brand as a more intangible, conceptual, or emotional idea appears to still resonate on deaf ears.[8]

This may also account for the success of private labels in the CEE, especially in the case of established Western supermarkets and hypermarkets. For instance, in Hungary and the Czech Republic, locals flock to shops like Tesco, Cora, and Auchan to purchase private label brands.[9] In these stores, shelves are lined with international brand names that are located side-by-side with locally manufactured private label brands that retail for a third of the price or even less. For example, at Tesco, pan-European brands such as Barilla pasta sells for three times the amount of the Tesco pasta brand. Hungary, Poland, and the Czech Republic have posted the highest private label growth rates, with an average growth rate in private label sales of nearly 50 percent, and with Poland experiencing a staggering 115-percent growth, and the Czech Republic and Hungary each experiencing a growth rate of 44 percent.[10] This trend will very likely take hold in many of the other CEE countries, as these retailers make inroads into their marketplaces.

Memories of drab state-manufactured products—shampoo that looked like toothpaste and toothpaste that looked like soap—are quickly fading, and Central and Eastern Europe are quickly becoming a fertile region for brand building. For example, high involvement brands such as skin care, hair care, and beauty care are developing an understanding of the aesthetic ideals coveted by this market and appropriately serving the market.[11] In the cosmetics industry, consumer expenditure is high. Russian women, on average, spend more than $300 a month on cosmetics when the average monthly salary is slightly over $2,000; in fact, Russia spends 1.3 percent of its GDP on cosmetics and toiletries in a market that is the fastest growing in the world.[12]

The brand's country of origin is an important consideration in this region. Western products are typically perceived as superior to local, regional, and other emerging-market offerings. Western brands such as Sony and IKEA have a strong draw with consumers in Central and Eastern Europe. In the cosmetics industry in particular, consumers have a high awareness of and are very receptive to imported brands, as all things Western are coveted; Max Factor International, L'Oréal, and Revlon, Inc. are all entering the market along with prestige beauty and fashion brands, as direct-sales companies Mary Kay Inc. and Avon Products, Inc. continue to grow.[13]

Packaging is often used to connote Western provenance, and it is quickly acquiring importance. Companies find that they have to provide sophisticated primary and secondary packaging, which includes heavy glass jars and bottles, overwraps, and premium materials, all connoting affluence—in fact, when consumers disapprove of the design, they refer to the packaging as Soviet-like.[14]

However, in spite of the fact that local brands are generally perceived as inferior to Western offerings, consumers continue to have a strong national pride that often creates an ambivalence toward foreign products. Research to date[15] has broadly documented consumer ethnocentrism—the perception that buying foreign products is morally wrong[16]—for Central and Eastern European consumers. This bias exists even for products originating in other emerging markets. In an example MOL Hungarian Oil and Gas Company Limited bought a Croat company Slovnaft and branded it under its own Hungarian name, only to find that consumers were unwilling to purchase its offering under the new brand name.[17] Numerous CEE brands are becoming quite popular; for example, the Tisza-branded trainers and sports equipment are quickly achieving cult status with Hungarian consumers.[18]

A noteworthy illustration of adaptation is offered by the entry strategy of the Turkish Efes brewery in the Russian market. In order to position the new beer in accordance with traditional Russian values, Efes labeled the brand "Stary Melnik" meaning "Old Miller" in English. The brand draws heavily upon local craftsmanship and skills. The product introduction was a carefully studied, deliberate process, the result of dedicated market research.[19] The brand identified its own place in the market as a local premium segment and has defined the rules of the game for the new entrants in the Russian market ever since. Stary Melnik is now considered a local brand, which is exported to Kazakhstan and the Ukraine; it is also exported to countries such as Israel and Greece, where Russian consumers constitute substantial minorities.

With regard to food marketing, product preferences are country specific in the CEE. In this region, distinctive cuisines and strong traditions are the norm, and the CEE food market is becoming a discerning one; firms found that they succeed only when they focus on local consumer needs, same as they do in the West, rather than persuading CEE consumers to consume the firm's traditional offerings.[20] Examples of products successfully adapted to the local market are the French company Groupe Danone's chocolate-covered pretzels and the U.S. Frito-Lay, Inc.'s butter and parsley crisps.[21] Bakery products are especially in demand in these markets, and foreign investments in bakery manufacturing have fared well. Promising ventures serving bakery consumers target (a) Romania, where food accounts for over 50 percent of household expenditures, and bakery products account for 25 percent of all household expenditures; (b) Russia, where premium products, such as specialty breads, buns, rolls, and waffles are in high demand; and (c) Poland, where an agricultural economy is a good source of flour and fruit, and where British firms such as Inter Link Foods invested into Cukiernia Mistrza Jana, a Polish cookies and cakes company.[22]

Fashion preferences are country specific as well. With the gradual acquisition of Western values, consumers in this region have become more individualistic and are thus more likely to express themselves through fashion. Consumers in the countries that joined the European Union in the first wave, particularly those in Hungary, Poland, and the Czech Republic, appear to rank higher on individualism and on fashion consciousness.[23] Similarly, men appear to be at least as fashion conscious as women, if not more so.[24] To serve these markets, many Western retailers and manufacturers are present in the capital cities, resorts, and other large cities in the CEE. Among them, especially prominent are Germany's Stefanel, Sweden's Hennes & Mauritz, Spain's Zara, Italy's Benetton Group, and many others.

Distribution and Consumers

Shopping venues and shopping experiences differ greatly in the markets of Central and Eastern Europe. Products such as cosmetics and toiletries are sold in some markets at department stores, in pharmacies, in salons, or even at roadside vendors and freestanding kiosks.[25] For example, in Hungary, cosmetics products are available in open-air markets, drugstores (for example, Azúr, Drogerie Markt, and Rossman), discount stores, and specialty boutiques (for example, Nature Blue and Clinique), and from multilevel direct marketing firms (for example, Avon and Oriflame Cosmetics).[26] In fact, multinational companies (for example, Unilever, Procter & Gamble, and L'Oréal) and retailers marketing health, beauty, and fashion products perceived the "new" Hungarian consumer as having the money and time to care about appearance; consequently, consumers there are now confronted with thousands of products.[27]

Scrambled merchandising is the norm, with kiosks selling premium scotch, used blue jeans, warm bread, and tram tickets, all in the same establishment. The flea market concept is interpreted many times over into unique environments. One such example is Ukraine's Seven Kilometer Market, sprawling over 170 acres (for comparison, the largest mall in the United States, the Mall of America in Bloomington, Minnesota, covers 96 acres). It is located on the airport road outside of Odessa, where the shops are neither buildings nor stalls; rather, they are shipping containers stacked two high, in long and overcrowded alleys, where 1,600 traders and 1,200 janitors and security staff welcome daily over 150,000 shoppers from as far as 300 miles away.[28] From the containers' steel gates "spills a consumer abundance of inexpensive clothes, shoes and toys, kitchenware, hardware and software, cosmetics, sporting goods and various sundries...Jeans for $9. Turkish suits, marginally stylish, for $60. Dior, Chanel and Armani are all a steal, if one harbors no complexes about authenticity. Speaking of complexes, there are no dressing rooms in shipping containers. Modesty, though, is in short supply, unlike anything else here, and men and women strip unabashedly in search of a proper fit."[29]

More upscale retailing interiors and atmospherics have a very different aspect. Consumers, in their search of Western opulence, appear to be drawn to audacious retail environments; in the case of cosmetics retailing, stores are often garish, visually chaotic environments, adorned with gold and mirrors and creating a sensory overload reminiscent of the disco era.[30] Many shops and restaurants have blaring music, and partnerships between radio stations, discos, and fast-food establishments are common.

The CEE consumers have shown a strong preference for supermarkets and hypermarkets: 23 million people in the national and regional markets of the Czech Republic, Hungary, Poland, Romania, Serbia and Montenegro, Slovakia, and Russia prefer the supermarket format above all others.[31] Hungarian supermarkets/hypermarkets experienced growth rates primarily at the expense of independent food stores and discounters, whose shares decreased dramatically.[32] Supermarkets/hypermarkets account for just under 50 percent of the retail market.[33] Foreign retail chains with operations in Hungary include Auchan (France), METRO GROUP (Germany), Match/Smatch (Belgium), Penny Market (United Kingdom), Cora (France), and Tesco (United Kingdom).[34] Tesco entered the Hungarian, Polish, Slovak, and Czech markets in 1996 and has performed very well across the board.[35] Most of the hypermarket newcomers in the CEE have initially relied heavily on an expatriate workforce; they are now in the process of reducing the number of expatriates, primarily to reduce costs, but also to forge closer relationships with the host countries and with the local consumers.[36]

Nurturing a close relationship to consumers is imperative as CEE consumers tend to respond swiftly to alternative offerings. For example, Billa, a chain supermarket/hypermarket that is part of the German Rewe Group, has 210 stores in Eastern Europe. In Romania, it opened its first store in Bucharest in 1999, and it has had great success, subsequently opening over 20 stores in the country. However, consumers found that competitors such as Metro Cash and Carry, Selgros, Carrefour, Mega Image, La Fourmi, XXL, Profi, Artima, Universal, Intermarché, Praktiker, and Bricostore were competing for their business with low prices and innovative merchandising, and currently Billa is not achieving the growth it has previously anticipated.

In general, however, the outlook is promising for retailers in Central and Eastern Europe. It is clearly a growth market, as Table 3.3 illustrates, and there are still many opportunities for new entrants, as the Eastern European average retail growth rate has been steadily above 4 percent.[37]

Table 3.3
Yearly Retail Growth (percent forecasted change)

	2004	2005	2006	2007
Bulgaria	4.3	4.4	4.1	3.9
Czech Republic	7.3	5.8	5.3	4.8
Hungary	5.3	4.7	4.4	2.6
Poland	3.5	3.2	3.3	3.1
Romania	2.5	2.6	2.5	2.2
Russia	5.4	5.6	4.7	4.6
Slovakia	3.8	5.8	7.8	8.4
Ukraine	8.4	6.0	4.3	5.5
Eastern European Average	4.9	4.8	4.4	4.1
Western European Average	1.5	1.9	1.6	1.2

Source: Economist Intelligence Unit, Eastern Europe industry: Consumer goods gain from influx of large retailers, EIU ViewsWire, New York: February 12, 2003.

Retailers operating in the CEE have often found that they were forced to react swiftly to competitors' moves because consumers quickly become aware of any differences and flock to better deals. When Tesco first entered Hungary in 1994, there were no "high-street" retailers, no other hypermarkets, and no category killers; however, this is changing. There are now two IKEAs, and Media Markt and Electroworld (both large Western electronics retailers) opened in Hungary near a Tesco hypermarket in 2001. Moreover, since Electroworld opened next door to Tesco, sales of electrical goods in the store have dropped sharply.[38] In other examples, Carrefour, the world's largest hypermarket retailer, has a store directly opposite Tesco's main Bratislava store in Slovakia, open from 8 A.M. to 11 P.M. Tesco is open 24 hours, and this strategy has been successful in the Slovak market; Tesco now has two stores in Bratislava and two outside of the capital city.[39]

Pricing

With energy costs increasing dramatically and the cost of living prohibitive for the average middle-class family, consumers in Central and Eastern Europe find themselves squeezed in today's marketplace. Even prices of locally produced staples stretch the budgets of retirees, who must often rely on relatives to be able to sustain themselves in the current economy. Extended families find that they are forced to live under one roof, and grandparents continue in the traditional role they held during Communism, of primary caregivers for the children, as both parents are employed.

Price considerations coupled with national pride have created a strong preference for local products, especially for products in the staples category. For example, consumers in Poland have high ethnocentric purchasing tendencies and prefer domestic brands; moreover, they consider these brands much more economical, leading to a strong position for Polish brands in the local marketplace.[40] It is well documented that changes in product demand and brand attitudes tend to adapt to the changing level of economic development in transitional economies.[41] It is believed that, at first, new high-quality, high-status brands sold by more efficient foreign competitors are likely to cause job loss and social upheaval; these brands will thus first experience a transference of ethnocentrism to consumers' brand attitudes.[42] However, as the CEE countries continue to develop rapidly, and as consumers' wealth grows, consumers can more readily afford Western products. As they become more familiar with foreign brands, their ethnocentric behavior is also more likely to subside.[43]

In spite of the existing ethnocentric tendencies of consumers in Central and Eastern Europe, and in spite of the fact that these consumers have a very limited disposable income, it is surprising that they continue to spend exorbitant amounts—relative to their income—for visible luxury items, such as designer clothing, automobiles, fragrances, and toiletries. Furthermore, their budgets are additionally stretched as, unlike in the past when most consumers rented their apartments, consumers nowadays are increasingly purchasing their homes as rents are becoming prohibitive.

One reason behind these developments is increased financial facilitation. Much has changed in this regard since the mid-1990s, when one could find automated teller machines (ATMs) only in international hotel chain lobbies located in the capital cities and when withdrawing from the very few ATMs that worked, customers were often met with inquisitive glances from the hotel staff. When opening a bank account, consumers had to spend two days; they often had to wait a month to receive a credit card.[44] Nowadays, numerous Western banks regard Central and Eastern Europe as their primary venue for expansion. The banks come from Germany (Commerzbank, Deutsche Bank, and HypoVeriensbank), from Austria (Raiffeisen Bank, Oberbank, and Bank Austria Creditanstalt), from the United States (Citigroup Inc.), from the Netherlands (ABN AMRO), and others. Foreign banks control, for example, 83 percent of the assets of Bulgaria's banks and 70 percent of Poland's.[45] These banks are aggressively expanding into Central and Eastern Europe, readily offering credit to consumers, and the consumers respond, raking up credit at a breakneck pace.

Credit cards, personal loans, and mortgages are now widely available, and consumer debt is becoming a major concern. For example, in Bulgaria, consumer loans (excluding mortgage) increased by almost 50 percent, and overdue credit accounts rose by 73 percent in 2004 alone.[46] These banks are rapidly attracting customers using Western sales methods and creating a customer-service culture never before encountered in the banking sector in the region.

Promotion

The privatization of broadcast and print media in the mid-1990s in the former Eastern Bloc provided consumers access to advertising. Most multinational companies engaged in heavy advertising, placing signage on the main boulevards of capital cities, wrapping town squares in images of people happily drinking Coke or smoking Marlboros, dangling Ronald McDonald on the main thoroughfare, and adorning kiosks and umbrellas with international brand names. Pepsi ONE offered free sampling in front of main university squares, Danone, the French leading multinational retailer of fresh dairy products, offered different yogurt flavors at busy bus stations, and consumers first learned about free sampling at cosmetics counters, as sales staff included miniature bonus samples in the shopping bags of their preferred customers.

Local television stations engaged in heavy advertising blitzes that consumers did not find especially appealing at first. For one reason, advertising in the early 1990s was promoting a good life that locals could attribute only to a lifestyle in the West; they portrayed providential relationships for the happy consumer (that is, a blonde supermodel, a Porsche, and Gauloises cigarettes). Furthermore, consumers in post-Communist societies reported strong skepticism about advertising, which often had been viewed as government propaganda intent on unloading low-quality, outdated goods on consumers.[47]

With time, however, consumers started to perceive advertising as informative, teaching them about new brands and appropriate product uses. Consumers would see the product often, hear about it, and then go to the retail outlet and request it; in effect, consumers perceived advertising as providing valuable product information later in the 1990s, suggesting a stronger relationship between advertising and product knowledge for this target market.[48] As the CEE countries have become more important target markets for multinationals, more and more informative advertising campaigns were created specifically for them. Companies offering feminine hygiene products, for example, started to broadcast campaigns in the local languages, explaining the use of their different products. However, once they were able to capture a substantial market share, these same companies resorted subsequently to dubbing their pan-European advertisements in the local language.

Among the Western companies omnipresent in these markets is The Coca-Cola Company. One ad series that the company is using to target this market is the teddy bear series. One advertising analyst inquires,

Is there anyone who is not familiar with the Coca-Cola polar bear ad series? If yes, it means you do not have a TV (which is somewhat understandable), or that you are not watching (which is hard to comprehend). In any case, it shows a family of fluffy polar bears, dexterously animated, drinking all the Coke they can...The moon is used as a bottle opener.... It persuades you through the feeling it creates, through the ideal meshing of innocent teddy bears (which you can only love), through fantasy and dream, through innocent humor and reverie...[49]

Much advertising in Central and Eastern Europe uses humor. In some examples, Milka, the Swiss chocolate manufacturer purchased by Kraft almost two decades ago, suggests that the marmot, a giant squirrel, wraps the chocolate in foil; Santa, lured by a child with Jacobs coffee (another Kraft pan-European brand), finds that there are several other Santas in the house, drinking coffee and confusing the child; the Danish Carlsberg Beer ad shows young people producing a tune by blowing into Carlsberg Beer bottles; and Blend-a-Med has a dentist running through the streets and parks in search of cavities and tartar and, invariably, finding them everywhere.[50]

According to ZenithOptimedia, one of the world's leading media services agencies, Poland and Russia are among the top ten contributors to advertising growth, with Russia predicted to be one of the top markets by the end of 2008 as it will more than double the size of its expenditures from 2005.[51] See Table 3.4. According to ZenithOptimedia, Romania is the world's fastest-growing ad market with a

Table 3.4
Top Ten Contributors to Advertising Expenditure Growth 2005–2008 (U.S.$million, current prices)

	Contribution U.S.$Millions	Percent of Market 2005	Percent of Market 2008
United States	23,318	41.9	40.5
China	6,441	2.4	3.5
Russia	5,968	1.3	2.3
Japan	4,444	10.3	9.7
United Kingdom	3,118	5.4	5.2
Indonesia	2,512	0.8	1.2
Brazil	1,661	1.6	1.7
Spain	1,443	2.1	2.1
Mexico	1,382	0.9	1.0
Poland	1,239	0.9	1.0

Source: ZenithOptimedia, Advertising Expenditure Forecasts, www.zenithoptimedia.com, April 2006.

growth of 43.2 percent per year in 2004 alone, and the Economist Intelligence Unit predicts that the numbers will increase as the country joins the European Union in 2007; also in the top 20 countries by ad expenditure growth are Lithuania, Hungary, and Estonia.[52]

A large proportion of the media (80–90 percent) in the CEE is dominated by foreign-owned enterprises. For example, in Poland, the Norwegian Orkla concern, the German Passauer Neue Presse, and Springer-Verlag dominate the market; in Hungary, the German WAZ group and the Swiss Ringier Verlag have a substantial influence; in Serbia and Montenegro, WAZ is steadily strengthening its position.[53] Western European firms dominate the printed press, whereas U.S. firms dominate private radio, films, and television, especially in Poland, Romania, and Slovenia. U.S. advertising firms use these media to sell their products in the CEE, and they are using children's programming to target children.[54]

INSIGHTS AND COMMENTARY

An overview of the CEE general marketing environment suggests that this broad market shares commonalities with other large and small emerging markets.[55] The marketing and the overall infrastructure development are at different levels in each country, and it can readily be assumed that the variance is large. This is an important consideration, as it has direct implications for marketing strategy and for effective approaches to these diverse consumer markets. Decidedly, a regiocentric approach to the CEE consumer will probably not work as well as a polycentric or modular approach.

Generally speaking, the risks in these markets are becoming more manageable—certainly more so than the risks in most other developing economies. Moreover, the income growth in the CEE is higher than even that of highly developed, industrialized countries, as CEE countries are becoming technologically competitive and consumer purchasing power is increasing significantly. Central and Eastern Europe offers many opportunities with its large untapped consumer markets and low-cost, high-quality resources.[56] This progress is particularly attractive today, especially when compared to the 1990s—when this region presented high-risk challenges for foreign businesses, as the countries were emerging from an environment characterized by economic crises, dated technology, infrastructural voids, excessive bureaucratic and administrative controls over business operations, and low consumer purchasing power.[57]

Key questions remain. Are the CEE emerging markets developing knowledgeable consumers? Are local and international companies serving these consumers efficiently? Managers in the CEE countries believe they are. When asked to compare their management style with that of EU managers, they rate themselves higher on certain dimensions—they see themselves as more professional, more dynamic, tougher, and more client oriented[58]—these are all dimensions that spell success in developed market economies. Typically, however, companies in CEE countries seem to be less focused on strategic issues, which means that they are assumed to have less explicitly defined core competencies.[59] The quest for further modernization is therefore important to implement market-oriented—specifically, consumer-oriented—company strategies and operational policies.

Consumers in the CEE answer these questions quite differently, and their responses are likely to differ depending on whether they come from the more advanced transition economies—especially from those countries that recently joined the European Union or are prospective members in the short term. These consumers tend to be more optimistic compared to those in the less advanced economies, who have less reason for optimism. One resonant perspective is offered in the *Chisinau Journal* in the Republic of Moldova:

> [T]he post-Soviet democracy in Moldova preferred to build its market economy edifice by legislating rich social gifts, with agricultural exports or exports from the modest left-over soviet reserves, and with massive imports (state or private) of quasi-waste of production from the East, West, Turkey, Israel, or Burundi—cheap and poorly made or expired merchandise...and dubious credits. We are coming back to the point where we have started—a wild, mangy capitalism, greedily chewing the imaginary bone of communist wellbeing, and cooks... gone directly to the pots and pans of governing, mixing everything into the national economy, creating an inedible porridge.[60]

This chapter offered an overview and analysis of developments affecting and shaping consumers in Central and Eastern Europe and companies targeting these consumers. The future of market development and consumer development remains to be seen, and evaluations of that development will continue to represent an issue of perspective—a domestic, local perspective versus scrutiny from companies with primarily an advanced-markets experience and perspective. Western analysts are often too eager to generalize in their discussions of consumer-related developments in the region and suggest that these consumers will want to wear jeans, buy Coke, and drive BMWs. While not totally off the mark, such analyses will benefit from focusing on the specifics of each market in the CEE, and from understanding a strongly emerging ethnocentrist attitude. It has been suggested that ethnocentric sentiment is becoming one of the strongest motivators in consumer purchase behavior, particularly in economies undergoing major reforms such as those in the CEE.[61]

There seems to be a danger of a fundamental inconsistency in the emerging market strategies of multinational firms. On the one hand, they seek billions of new consumers in the CEE markets, but their marketing programs are scarcely adapted for these markets, targeting the heavily sought-after affluent premium segment while forgetting the base of the pyramid. Moreover, many multinational firms have resisted targeting local consumers, opting to use offerings and related marketing programs developed for their traditional markets. As a result, the outcome for many multinational enterprises was low market penetration, disappointing market share, and poor profitability; consequently, these firms were forced to rethink their marketing programs from the ground up.[62] This large consumer market in Central and Eastern Europe will respond well if marketing strategies are adapted for a better local fit, especially if prices are established relative to local purchasing power. In effect, in the short term, pricing must dominate marketing programs and drive product, packaging, distribution, and communication for companies to be able to successfully establish themselves in Central and Eastern Europe.

NOTES

1. Singer, Jason, Carrick Mollenkamp, and Alessandra Galloni, "Plastic Curtain: In Eastern Europe, Western Banks Fuel Growth, Fears"; "As Giants Rush In, Bulgaria Tries to Slow Flow of Credit"; "Big Gamble for UniCredito"; and "Maria Ilieva's Dream House," *Wall Street Journal,* October 5, 2005, A1.

2. Singer, Jason, A. Manrai, and D. Lascu, "Eastern Europe's Transition to Market Economy: An Analysis of Economic and Political Risks," *Journal of Euromarketing* Vol. 5, No. 1, 1996, pp. 7–35; Bilgin, F. Zeynep, Ven Sriram, and Gerhard A. Wührer, "World Trade Trends," in *Drivers of Global Business Success: Lessons from Emerging Markets,* ed. F. Zeynep Bilgin, Ven Sriram, and Gerhard A. Wührer (London: Palgrave Macmillan, 2004), p. 11.

3. "Consumer Demand Growing in Eastern Europe," *Journal of Commerce,* May 10, 2006, p. 1.

4. IMF, *International Financial Statistics,* www.europaworld.com/comparative-statistics, 2006.

5. Manrai, L.A., D. Lascu, A.K. Manrai, and H.W. Babb, "A Cross-Cultural Comparison of Style in Eastern European Emerging Markets," *International Marketing Review,* Vol. 18, No. 3, 2001, pp. 270–285.

6. "Brand Papers: Hungarian Cool," *Brand Strategy,* March 4, 2005, p. 37.

7. Manrai et al., 2001.

8. *Brand Strategy,* 2005.

9. Karenova, Marta, "The Rise of Private Labels: Hungary a Booming Market for Retailers," *Budapest Week* 2006, www.budapestweek.com.

10. Karenova, 2006.

11. Grubow, Liz, "Branding Eastern European Shoppers," *Global Cosmetic Industry* Vol. 173, No. 2, February 2005, pp. 30–32.

12. Grubow, 2005.

13. Grubow, 2005.

14. Grubow, 2005.

15. Reardon, James, Chip Miller, Irena Vida, and Irina Kim, "The Effects of Ethnocentrism and Economic Development on the Formation of Brand and Ad Attitudes in Transitional Economies," *European Journal of Marketing,* Vol. 39, Nos. 7/8, 2005,

pp. 737–54; Irena Vida and Ann Fairhurst, "Factors Underlying the Phenomenon of Consumer Ethnocentricity: Evidence from Four Central European Countries," *International Review of Retail, Distribution and Consumer Research,* Vol. 9, No. 4, 1999, pp. 321–37.

16. Shimp, T.A., and S. Sharma, "Consumer Ethnocentrism: Construction and Validation of the CETSCALE," *Journal of Marketing Research,* Vol. 24, 1986, p. 284.

17. *Brand Strategy,* 2005.

18. *Brand Strategy,* 2005.

19. İrem Eren-Erdoğmuş, Hale Taşdemir-Çaloğlu, and Muzaffer Bodur, "International Market Entry and Expansion Strategies of Anadolu Efes A.Ş.," in *Drivers of Global Business Success: Lessons from Emerging Markets,* ed. F. Zeynep Bilgin, Ven Sriram, and Gerhard A. Wührer, London: Palgrave Macmillan, 2004, pp. 168–181.

20. Rowe, Mark, "Eastern Europe's Attractiveness for the Food Giants—Management Briefing: Local Production and Sales," *Just Food,* May 2005, pp. 3–5.

21. Rowe, 2005.

22. Rowe, 2005.

23. Manrai et al., 2001.

24. Manrai et al., 2001.

25. Grubow, 2005.

26. Coulter, Robin A., Linda L. Price, Lawrence Feick, and Camelia Micu, "The Evolution of Consumer Knowledge and Sources of Information: Hungary in Transition," *Journal of the Academy of Marketing Science,* Vol. 33, No. 4, 2005, pp. 604–619.

27. Coulter, Price, Feick, and Micu, 2005.

28. Myers, Steven L., "From Soviet-Era Flea Market to a Giant Makeshift Mall," *New York Times,* May 19, 2006, Late Edition, Section A, p. 4.

29. Myers, 2006, p. 4.

30. Grubow, 2005.

31. Rowe, 2005.

32. Karenova, 2006.

33. Rogers, Helen, Pervez N. Ghauri, and Katharine L. George, "The Impact of Market Orientation on the Internationalization of Retailing Firms: Tesco in Eastern Europe," *International Review of Retail, Distribution and Consumer Research,* Vol. 15, No. 1, January 2005, p. 53.

34. Karenova, 2006.

35. Rogers, Ghauri, and George, 2005.

36. Rogers, Ghauri, and George, 2005.

37. Economist Intelligence Unit, "Eastern Europe Industry: Consumer Goods Gain from Influx of Large Retailers," EIU ViewsWire, New York, February 12, 2003.

38. Rogers, Ghauri, and George, 2005.

39. Rogers, Ghauri, and George, 2005.

40. Grubow, 2005.

41. Cui, G., and Q. Liu, "Executive Insights: Emerging Market Segments in a Transitional Economy: A Study of Urban Consumers in China," *Journal of International Marketing,* Vol. 9, No. 1, 2001, 84–106; Chandy, R., G. Tellis, D. MacInnis, and P. Thaivanich, "What to Say When: Advertising Appeals in Evolving Markets," *Journal of*

Marketing Research, Vol. 38, No. 4, 2001, pp. 399–415; Reardon, Miller, Vida, and Kim, 2005; Supphellen, M., and K. Gronhaug, "Building Foreign Brand Personalities in Russia: The Moderating Effect of Consumer Ethnocentrism," *International Journal of Advertising,* Vol. 22, No. 2, 2003, pp. 203–226.

42. Reardon, Miller, Vida, and Kim, 2005.

43. Reardon, Miller, Vida, and Kim, 2005; Vida and Fairhurst, 1999,

44. Singer et al., 2005.

45. Singer et al., 2005.

46. Singer et al., 2005.

47. Feick, Lawrence, and Herbert Gierl, "Skepticism about Advertising: A Comparison of East and West German Consumers," *International Journal of Research in Marketing,* Vol. 13, No. 3, 1996, pp. 227–35; Vegh, Csilla, *Hungary-Cosmetics Industry-ISA,* Washington, DC: U.S. & Foreign Commercial Service and U.S. Department of State, 1997.

48. Coulter, Price, Feick and Micu, 2005.

49. IQADS, "Coca-Cola and the Bears," November 2, 2004. http://www.iqads.ro/Analize_Reclame_read_45/coca_cola_ursuletii.html.

50. IQADS, 2004.

51. ZenithOptimedia, Advertising Expenditure Forecasts, www.zenithoptimedia.com, April 2006.

52. "Eastern Europe," *Campaign,* March 11, 2005, p. 15.

53. Schroeder, Renate, "Foreign Concerns Are a Threat to Media Pluralism in Central and Eastern Europe," Council of Europe, October 22, 2003, www.coe.int/t/e/com/files/interviews/20031022_interv_Schroeder.asp.

54. Schroeder, 2003.

55. Bilgin, Sriram, and Wührer, 2004.

56. Cavusgil, S. Tamer, Perven N. Ghauri, and M.R. Agarwal, *Doing Business in Emerging Markets: Entry and Negotiation Strategies,* Thousand Oaks, CA: Sage, 2002.

57. Bilgin, Sriram, and Wührer, 2004.

58. Reichl, Manfred, Gerhard A. Wührer, and Ven Sriram, "Leadership in Central and Eastern European Countries," in *Drivers of Global Business Success: Lessons from Emerging Markets,* ed. F. Zeynep Bilgin, Ven Sriram, and Gerhard A. Wührer, London: Palgrave Macmillan, 2004, pp. 54–60.

59. Reichl, Wührer, and Sriram, 2004.

60. Turcanu, Andrei, "The Wilderness and the Garden," *Jurnalul de Chisinau,* Vol. 198, September 12, 2003, http://www.jurnal.md/articol.php?id=614&editie=198, 1–2; Dawar, Niraj, and Amitava Chattopadhyay, "Rethinking Marketing Programs for Emerging Markets," *Long Range Planning,* Vol. 35, No. 5, 2002, pp. 457–474.

61. Vida and Fairhurst, 1999.

62. Dawar and Chattopadhyay, 2002.

CHAPTER 4

Manufacturing and Selling in China

George O. White III, Yeqing Bao, and Lance Eliot Brouthers

[I]n China everything is possible, but nothing is easy.

(Anonymous)[1]

The People's Republic of China (China) is a country of immense opportunities and is considered by many foreign enterprises to be the next great commercial frontier. China has the largest population in the world, estimated at 1.3 billion people, and its gross domestic product (GDP) has expanded at an average growth rate of 9 percent a year. Once a poor country, China is now the sixth largest economy in the world with a GDP of $1.4 trillion.

Most Chinese, over 64 percent of the population, live in rural areas. However, Chinese who live in urban areas average nearly three times the amount of annual GDP per capita (roughly 7,000 RMB—renminbi, the currency of China) of those living in rural areas (roughly 2,300 RMB). Thus, while China's overall GDP per capita is only around $911—up from $840 a year earlier, yet still ranking China below Namibia, the Republic of Guatemala, and the Kingdom of Morocco—purchasing power parity (PPP) per capita is estimated to be as high as $3,940.

According to the World Development Report, this ranks China 68th in the world on a PPP basis. Economic development in China has produced higher income levels and a burgeoning middle class. This newfound wealth has generated an annual consumer spending growth rate of 8–10 percent per year. Annual earnings and disposable income levels are projected to steadily increase.

Along with the rise in income, several distinct consumer classes have emerged. Based on annual household income they include the following: (1) the rich (earning over 40,000 RMB), (2) the professionals (earning 20,001–40,000 RMB), (3) the salaried class (earning 10,001–20,000 RMB), and (4) the working class (earning less than 10,000 RMB). These classes are not uniform in size; the lower classes are much larger than the upper classes. For example, in urban areas the working class is by far the largest class (55 percent of the population), followed by the salaried class (25 percent of the population), the professionals (15 percent of the population), and then the rich (less than 5 percent of the population). The Chinese government recognizes these groupings, announcing an emergence of divergent social classes in China, including a middle class (known as *Xiao Kang* families). These classes form a "Chinese consumer pyramid."

The Chinese business environment is both complex and unique. It is a mixed economy—a hybrid blend of both market- and Communist-driven economies —which is often referred to as a socialist-market economy. One consequence of this complexity is that multinational enterprise (MNE) success in penetrating the vast Chinese consumer market has been relatively uneven. Thus far, most MNEs have been successful in penetrating only the top income class. This is unfortunate because many Chinese consumers now wish to purchase more expensive foreign-made products.

How can MNEs entering China create better strategies to successfully penetrate the Chinese consumer market and capture a greater market share? Why have global firms not been very successful thus far at selling products to the other economic classes in China? Are there strategies the MNEs can employ to reach more Chinese consumers? In this chapter we explain how the classes differ from each other in ways other than income and discuss strategies foreign MNEs can use to penetrate deeper into the Chinese consumer pyramid. See Figure 4.1.

BACKGROUND

For most of the 20th century China was a poor agrarian society with a closed economy. Prior to the 1980s, less than one urban household in 100 owned a refrigerator and less than 6 percent of the population owned a washing machine. However, since 1979, under Deng Xiaoping's open-door policy, the Chinese economy has opened up and developed rapidly. One aspect of the open-door policy is that foreign products are now able to flow freely into China.

Currently China has a vibrant domestic consumer market, one that interests foreign MNEs. Several factors contribute to this burgeoning marketplace: (1) Chinese household income is steadily rising; (2) the one-child policy has created a large, unique, youthful consumer group within Chinese society; (3) modernization has resulted in women developing more Western buying habits; and (4) the increasing complexity of this rapidly growing economy is reflected in a Chinese consumer pyramid, which includes a burgeoning middle class.

Numerous MNEs such as Anheuser-Busch, The Coca-Cola Company, General Motors Corporation (GM), Motorola, Ericsson, Nestlé, Procter & Gamble, Wal-Mart, Unilever, and McDonald's Corporation are active in the Chinese market. Unfortunately for them, sales of consumer goods have been predominantly

Figure 4.1
The Chinese Consumer Pyramid

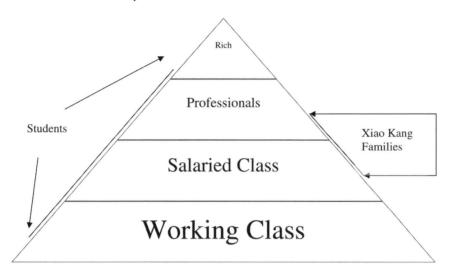

confined to the rich and, to a minor extent, to the professionals. This represents 30 to 70 million people. In comparison to a total population of 1.3 billion Chinese, this is a very small segment.

THE CHINESE CONSUMER PYRAMID

As previously mentioned, the Chinese consumer pyramid is made up of four distinct consumer segments. The rich are the consumer segment at the top of the pyramid. They are by far the smallest consumer segment. Nevertheless, this segment is growing in size and diversity; it currently consists of roughly 2 million people, who predominantly live in prosperous urban areas such as Dalian, Beijing, Tianjin, Hangzhou, Shanghai, Shenzhen, Ningbo, and Guangzhou. They represent the most affluent segment of consumers, coming from a wide range of professions including celebrities, sports stars, entrepreneurs, businesspeople, and government officials and generally earning over $5,000 a year.

These individuals range in age from 30 to 65 years old, typically on the older side of this demographic. Most have little knowledge of the English language or of international matters. Consumers in the rich class are very confident individuals with active lifestyles. They are both brand conscious and increasingly value conscious. Most in this segment are very eager to purchase foreign products that are perceived in China's Confucian materialistic society as status symbols, such as luxury cars, fancy cell phones, large color TVs, new computers, name-brand clothing, alcohol, and cigarettes.

The professionals are the next segment of the Chinese consumer pyramid. This segment consists of roughly 60 million people, which predominantly live, like the rich, in the prosperous urban areas. They, combined with the lower ranks of the rich and the upper ranks of the salary class, make up what we deem to be the new emerging middle class in China, the *Xiao Kang* families. They are better off than most ordinary Chinese, are well educated (typically having a university education or at least some form of college training), have knowledge of and often fluency in the English language, and have a high level of knowledge of international matters. Many are Western educated, now returning to their home country to take advantage of the new economic opportunities opening up in China, and have separated themselves from the traditional notions of their elders.

These individuals tend to work in new start-up enterprises, foreign firms, or international joint ventures operating in China. Many are also small to medium-sized business owners. They earn anywhere from $1,800 to $5,000 a year. These individuals are younger than the rich, ranging in age from 25 to 45 years of age, often have more than one child, and are an upwardly mobile segment that are more open to new ideas and products. "They are socially active and brand conscious[;] however, they feel insecure and concerned about the future."[2] Most in this consumer segment desire many of the same products that the rich wish to acquire.

A third segment of the Chinese consumer pyramid is known as the salaried class. This segment consists of roughly 330 million people, scattered throughout Chinese society. These individuals have a more moderate level of education, ranging from high school to having some college education, generally have relatively little knowledge of the English language, and relatively little knowledge of international matters. Historically, they have worked for state-owned enterprises or government and township enterprises. Their annual household income ranges from $1,100 to $1,799 a year. This segment is conservative in nature, thereby representing the average Chinese consumer who, on occasion, may wish to purchase a foreign product. But they will purchase foreign products only by using long-term savings; therefore, their purchases are carefully premeditated even though they aspire to have the same spending potential as the professionals.

Last, at the bottom of the Chinese consumer pyramid is the working class. This vast segment comprises the majority of individuals in the Chinese consumer pyramid. It is estimated that there are over 800 million individuals in working-class families in China. This segment includes the overwhelming majority of Chinese peasants and retirees with limited incomes. They typically have low education levels, no knowledge of the English language, and no knowledge of international matters. The working class has benefited the least from economic reforms; therefore, they are largely indigent, without steady work, unable to move at will, and the least satisfied with the current state of China's rapidly booming economy.

Table 4.1
Characteristics of the Chinese Consumer Pyramid

Consumer Characteristics	Rich	Professionals	Salary Class	Working Class
Location	Prosperous Urban Areas	Prosperous Urban Areas	Nationwide	Poor Rural and Urban Areas
Population	2,000,000	60,000,000	330,000,000	800,000,000
Age	30–65	25–45	All ages	All ages
Education	All Levels	University or College	College or High School	Some High School or Less
Annual Income (RMB)	40,000+	40,000– 20,001	20,000– 10,001	10,000–
Knowledge of English	Low	Very High	Moderate	Very Low
Knowledge of Intl. Matters	Low	Very High	Moderate	Very Low
Foreign-Brand Consciousness	Very High	High	Moderate	Very Low

This segment is price sensitive and does not care about purchasing foreign products. See Table 4.1.

It must also be noted that university and college students are an underexplored segment of the Chinese population. These individuals come from a wide array of family backgrounds ranging from the rich to the working-class segments. Members of this group, although being full-time students, do have a disposable income that is largely determined by their parents. They have a favorable opinion of foreign brands predominantly because of their access to the Internet, high educational level, and high understanding of the English language. Chinese students consider Western products more fashionable and superior in quality to domestic products. Therefore, they are willing to pay a higher price when purchasing a foreign product.

STRATEGIES FOR PENETRATING THE CHINESE CONSUMER PYRAMID

Previous research has suggested a number of market penetration strategies in China. Combinations of expanding market coverage, focusing on dramatically lowering costs, streamlining distribution channels, localizing research and development, and driving industry consolidation have been suggested to create opportunities for success in conquering the China market. Some scholars have posited that MNEs have divergent strategic options depending on the market segment they wish to enter. Others mention that in order for MNEs to successfully reach consumers in China, they should adopt a *guo qing* (meaning special Chinese characteristics) approach to delivering products "with the value, quality, and convenience that will appeal to Chinese consumers."[3]

We suggest that MNEs should adjust their strategies according to how deeply they wish to penetrate the Chinese consumer pyramid. Strategies include promoting and packaging products according to *guo qing:* implementing brand loyalty discount programs, establishing successful servicing mechanisms, creating diversified branding options, pricing products according to domestic market demands, unbundling products for greater market penetration, and using a product cluster diffusion strategy. Most MNEs have already been successful at penetrating the richest class. Thus, these strategies are aimed at MNEs in achieving greater success in penetrating beyond the rich, moving deeper into the Chinese consumer pyramid. The chosen strategies are based on an understanding of China's unique Confucian materialistic society where brand name and prestige, if used properly, can improve and/or enhance an individual's place in contemporary Chinese society.

Product Packaging

While MNEs have been relatively successful at effectively manufacturing and packaging products for sale to the rich and professional classes, they have yet to be very successful at manufacturing and packaging products that appeal to the salaried-class segment of the Chinese consumer pyramid. One product strategy MNEs can use to further penetrate this consumer segment is to focus on manufacturing and packaging products in smaller units for easy use, convenience, and cost-effectiveness. Consumers in the salaried class do wish to purchase foreign products. This is especially true with regard to durable goods. For example, Whirlpool Corporation was not very successful at introducing large, impressive-looking washing machines in China. Yet when Haier Group, the leading Chinese white-goods firm, introduced a small machine called the "Little Prince," it was successful in selling millions of units. Haier achieved this by understanding that there is little room in China and that the average Chinese home is much smaller than a home in the United States. It also recognized that the Chinese salaried class and *Xiao Kang* families prefer to wash clothes daily during the hot summer months. Thus, Haier made the Little Prince washing machines for easy use, convenience, and cost efficiency. Also, Haier understood that the name "Little Prince" tapped into the sentiment regarding China's one-child policy. Furthermore, Haier understood manufacturing and packaging that appealed to the middle class, unlike Whirlpool. This led to immediate success in penetrating deeper into the Chinese consumer pyramid.

A second strategy MNEs may be able to use in public settings, particularly those in the food-service industries, is to focus on manufacturing and packaging products in larger units for convenience and cost effectiveness. For example, Budweiser quickly became the number one premium beer in China when it entered the market in 1997.

Before entering China, Anheuser-Busch (the parent company of Budweiser), carefully analyzed the market and learned that it was much different than the market in the United States. Anheuser-Busch came to the realization that the majority of premium beer is consumed in restaurants and bars. This is because Chinese consumers will typically drink cheap beer when at home or with their family, but will drink expensive premium beer when eating out with their superiors, colleagues, and friends in order to "save face."

In restaurants, beer is often shared out of large bottles for the purpose of enjoying friendship and extending courtesy. Unlike in the United States, large bottles of beer are cheaper than canned beer because aluminum is in short supply in China and the labor to make cans is costly. Thus, Anheuser-Busch, unlike its primary U.S. competitor, Miller Brewing Company, picked up on this *guo qing* by producing a large 22-ounce bottled beer for consumption in Chinese restaurants and pubs.

This strategy has proven very successful for Anheuser-Busch since members of the salaried class (and members of *Xiao Kang* families) spend a considerable amount of time eating at restaurants with their colleagues and superiors in order to develop *guanxi* ("connections" and "relationships") and would otherwise not have the opportunity to drink premium beer. As a result, Anheuser-Busch has been very successful in penetrating the salary class (and *Xiao Kang*) segment(s) of the Chinese consumer pyramid due to adjusting its product packaging strategies to account for *guo qing*.

MNEs have had little to no success at penetrating the working-class segment of the Chinese consumer pyramid. This is because most of these consumers are from rural areas; therefore, they have different tastes, desires, and needs than consumers from other segments.[4] These consumers often do not have access to modern shopping facilities and often lack adequate product knowledge.[5]

One strategy that MNEs can use to better penetrate this consumer segment is to create graphically oriented package designs and product names that will appeal to auspicious and/or powerful images. For example, a Hangzhou equipment manufacturer tried on several occasions to manufacture a successful product line of kitchen utensils, but was unsuccessful primarily because the product name did not bode well with consumers. It tried several product names such as "Red Star," "Treasure," and "Prosperity," but none of these names seemed to work.[6] After a long period of time the firm's sales dramatically rose when it chose the product name "Boss"; the name was considered by consumers to mean good fortune and was more robust sounding than prior names chosen.

Furthermore, once a product name has been properly chosen, a graphically oriented package design should be created in order for the product to stand out and appeal to the working-class consumer segment. For example, Giant Bicycle, a Taiwanese bicycle firm, has been very successful at selling a wide range of products to working-class consumers by properly naming, designing, and subsequently manufacturing its models more stylishly than other local models while adhering to *guo qing*.

Its models are packaged in a way that appeals to the working-class desires of riding for fun, adventure, and exercise, while being given auspicious names such as Forever (meaning longevity) and Phoenix (an auspicious animal in Chinese folklore).[7] Because it properly adapted its manufacturing strategy to *guo qing*, Giant has captured over 5 percent of the Chinese bicycle market, selling roughly 30 million bicycles a year. A large proportion of its sales are to the working-class segment of the Chinese consumer pyramid.

Pricing

International pricing is a very complex process due to there being so many subjective domestic market variables involved in an international strategic pricing decision. Rao and Bass state that "[c]ompetition is modeled by postulating that firms behave non-cooperatively, maximizing their own profits, and each firm correctly anticipates its rivals' strategies and the effects of those strategies on the firm's profits."[8] Thus, firms entering and operating in emerging markets have used many types of pricing strategies such as generic, market-based, and cost-based pricing strategies. This is particularly true for MNEs wishing to enter and continue to successfully operate in China. In addition, they must consider the consequences of using a particular pricing strategy when trying to penetrate and survive in China's turbulent consumer market.

With this in mind, the working-class segment of the Chinese consumer pyramid purchases products based primarily on price sensitivities. This segment's overriding concern is the ability to pay for a product, not the product's brand name or country of origin. Pricing wars in China are frequent and brutal. But, because pricing is a very sensitive topic for the working-class consumer segment (representing over 800 million consumers), MNEs wishing to establish sustainable competitive advantages, leading to a higher market share in China, should predominantly use a market-based pricing strategy when selling their products.

Some MNEs have figured this strategy out. For example, Procter & Gamble cut the prices of many of its leading products by as much as 40 percent in order to compete with local Chinese companies. Nestlé and Unilever drastically reduced prices on their ice cream products in order to be competitive with local ice cream manufacturers. Also, McDonald's reduced prices in order to stay competitive with local fast-food chains. This strategy allowed McDonald's to successfully penetrate the working-class segment. Because of this strategy, more traditional and less affluent Chinese consumers can afford to purchase MNE products, thereby allowing MNEs implementing this strategy (especially for consumer products) to penetrate deeper into the working-class consumer segment of the Chinese consumer pyramid.

Also, in conjunction with pricing products based on market competition (for example, direct-cost pricing strategies), MNEs should also unbundle their products when trying to penetrate the predominantly rural working-class consumer segment. When coupled with low pricing, this strategy allows for MNEs to sell smaller, lower priced products that appeal to a large indigent segment that is more mobile and less materialistic than the upper segments of the pyramid. For example, Procter & Gamble increased its market share in China by introducing unbundled products normally sold bundled together to wealthy consumers to rural working poor consumers in remote provinces. While many other MNEs such as Nestlé and Coca-Cola implemented strategies similar to Procter & Gamble, most MNEs operating in China have yet to follow suit in forming creative unbundling strategies targeted at penetrating the often neglected working-class consumer segment of the Chinese consumer pyramid.

Promotion

MNEs have had some success at penetrating the rich segment of the Chinese consumer pyramid. However, MNEs can use promotion and advertising strategies centered on *guo qing* to increase their market share of this small but rapidly growing segment. Since this segment is not price sensitive and is commercialized, MNEs should further penetrate this segment by promoting their products through flashy, trendsetting advertising campaigns. Flashy, trendsetting advertising strategies that are most popular and effective in China are ones concerning a son or daughter graduating from college, foreign travel, and/or luxurious living. This strategy is a very effective tool for penetrating the rich-class segment of the Chinese pyramid because it appeals to this segment's ever-present desire to achieve the aforementioned objectives, while also appeasing the desire to be seen wearing or using a foreign-made product. If properly implemented, this strategy will reduce consumer incentives to try other brands, thereby enhancing brand loyalty.

For example, when Ericsson was an upstart in the Chinese market, it captured a large segment of Motorola's market share by launching a flashy, state-of-the-art advertising campaign promoting cellular phones as fashion accessories. Ericsson was successful in doing this by hiring a series of popular actresses, such as Gong Li and Maggie Cheung, to introduce color cellular phones targeted at trendy women. This strategy focused on a growing demand from wealthy women for greater style and practicality in products such as cellular phones. Within three years of implementing this promotion strategy centered on *guo qing* Ericsson had captured 40 percent of the cellular phone market in China, making the company a household name among the rich.

MNEs wishing to capture a greater portion of the rich-consumer segment should also focus on promotional programs (such as advertising campaigns) that emphasize prestige and status. Many consumers in this segment have prestige sensitivity to products; they have a positive view of high prices based on the mind-set that higher prices signal status and prominence to other Chinese consumers. Prestige sensitivity plays a large role in China's Confucian materialistic society where consumer behavior is spurred by brand name and prestige, which, if used properly, will improve an individual's place in society.

Certain companies have capitalized on this cultural trait. For example, several MNE car manufacturers such as Toyota Motor Corporation, Honda Motor Co., Ford Motor Company, Volkswagen, BMW, Mercedes-Benz, and Cadillac have recognized the rich-consumer segment's potential for purchasing products based on prestige sensitivity. Therefore, they have all launched promotional advertising campaigns targeted at this segment by emphasizing luxury and prestige. Sales of luxury cars manufactured for the Chinese market are estimated to be only around 2–3 percent (roughly 120,000 cars) of car sales in China. But, with sales rising, other high-end luxury car manufacturers, such as Ferrari, are now also targeting this Chinese consumer segment. Other MNEs wishing to capture a greater portion of this consumer segment should follow the luxury car manufacturer's strategy of promoting products by emphasizing prestige and status, which appeals to this consumer segment's prestige sensitivities.

MNEs have had less success at penetrating the professional-class consumer segment of the Chinese consumer pyramid. One strategy that can be used to improve market share in this consumer segment is by using *guo qing* to promote products emphasizing Chinese needs and styles, not foreign needs and styles. For example, Yue Sai Kan Cosmetics, which was founded by a famous television personality, has helped influence Chinese women to purchase cosmetics for personal use. Instead of using blonde-haired and blue-eyed foreign models, the firm used Chinese models in its advertising and promotional activities. In doing this, the firm convinced Chinese women, predominantly from the top segments of the Chinese consumer pyramid, to quit imitating foreign styles and start imitating Chinese beauty through its products. To reinforce this effect, the firm trained its sales associates on how to give advice and demonstrate the proper use of its products at the point of sale. This strategy of empowering Chinese women to feel confident and satisfied with the way they looked proved so successful that Yue Sai Kan Cosmetics has become a national leader in the Chinese cosmetics industry. Recently, L'Oréal acquired the firm hoping to continue with its success by using *guo qing* in promotional campaigns to further penetrate the professional-class (and *Xiao Kang*) segments of the Chinese consumer pyramid.

We also suggest that MNEs wishing to penetrate deeper into the professional-class segment of the Chinese consumer pyramid develop product discount promotion strategies in order to create greater brand loyalty. Chinese consumers crave brand loyalty programs. This mentality is largely historical and can be traced to Confucianism. Adherence to the Confucian precept of *guanxi* signifies how important loyalty is in Chinese society. *Guanxi* pertains to the cultivation of long-term relationships to an individual, group, or institution consisting of unpaid reciprocal obligations. In Chinese society, these relationships can often result in the success or failure of an undertaking. For example, Xerox Corporation has used *guanxi* in creating the best dealer network in China. Because of this Xerox is number one in China with a market share of around 43 percent.[9]

Brand loyalty discount programs use *guanxi* to promote products. It takes a considerable amount of time and money for businesses to establish relationships with customers. However, it is essential for MNEs to establish *guanxi* in order to foster trust and a sense of commitment from the professional class. Brand loyalty programs can do this by using high-technology databases that can track and analyze professional class loyalty and product procurement. MNEs can then establish *guanxi* with professional class consumers by offering incentives such as discount rewards programs for repeat purchases. Besides being able to track their customer base, this strategy will also allow MNEs to set goals and objectives for retaining the growing professional-class consumer segment that is loyal to their brand.

MNEs should construct campaigns focusing on coupon rebates as a way to promote products and cultivate greater brand loyalty in the salaried- and working-class consumer segments. This is because the salaried and working class will typically purchase a foreign-made product out of long-term savings. Because of this, MNEs wishing to capture a greater portion of salaried- and working-class markets will have to slowly introduce their products over a long period of time often through specialized promotions. However, coupon rebates and related promotional activities last only for a short period of time. Because of the time incentive, this strategy will speed the purchasing process up by making it cheaper for salaried- and working-class consumers to purchase a foreign-made product that would otherwise be at arm's length.

Chinese consumers have historically doubted the legitimacy of promotions such as coupon programs because of widespread scams and the misuse of these techniques during the Cultural Revolution, but now they are less inclined to doubt a foreign MNE product promotion. This poses a sustainable competitive advantage for foreign MNEs. Furthermore, MNEs wishing to further penetrate the salaried and working classes should construct promotions centered on rebate strategies that will generate greater brand loyalty within these consumer segments.

MNEs should also craft service mechanisms (an indirect way of promoting products) that target the salaried and working classes because these consumer segments have a limited amount of knowledge regarding foreign-made products, yet they do aspire to occasionally purchase foreign-made products after careful premeditation. These consumers are quickly becoming more sophisticated and crave service programs that cater to customer satisfaction. Thus, MNEs such as in the durable goods industries should find ways to offer better services as a marketable incentive in promoting products for consumers in these segments to purchase their products.

Two Chinese MNEs—Haier and Legend Group Ltd.—have penetrated the salaried and working classes by recognizing the utility of the servicing promotion strategy. Haier is considered one of the pioneers of service quality in China. Haier has a nationwide network of call and service centers. In fact, its motto is "all you do is call, and Haier does the rest."[10] Repair technicians from in-house service centers or a nationwide contractor's network can be dispatched at a moment's notice. Haier's technicians are renowned for taking care of its customers; this includes wearing protective shoe covers, placing protective coverings over furniture prior to servicing a product, and vacuuming once repairs are finished. This service promotion strategy has led Haier to be well known throughout China as a durable goods service leader.

Also, Legend quickly took the reigns away from IBM and Compaq Computer Corporation as the number one computer company in China by establishing a nationwide network of sales outlets that offer services that are unique to the Chinese consumer. These services included free "language installation, utility, and tutorial programs" to first-time consumers.[11] This promotion service strategy proved successful for Legend because it offered much needed services not available from other MNEs. In both of the aforementioned cases, Chinese MNEs filled a void by providing services not originally offered by other MNEs. This allowed these companies to capture a dominant market share through promoting high-quality customer service. Other MNEs should follow their lead in introducing service promotion mechanism strategies in order to penetrate the salaried- and working-class segments of the Chinese consumer pyramid.

Product Distribution

MNEs wishing to distribute products only to the rich segment of the Chinese consumer pyramid should start by focusing on selling their products in a single flagship city—predominantly large coastal cities such as Beijing, Guangzhou, Hangzhou, Shanghai, Shenzhen, and Tianjin. Most rich consumers live in these cities due to the high levels of economic growth and prosperity. For example, MNEs such as Prada and Louis Vuitton have chosen this strategy in Shanghai because they are currently testing the Chinese market and are interested in attracting high-end clients wanting to purchase luxury products. This segment of the Chinese consumer pyramid is wealthy and buys a considerable amount of MNE goods, but is only a small portion of the Chinese populace. If successful, MNEs such as Prada and Louis Vuitton would then want to possibly jump to other flagship cities with similar demographic characteristics.

MNEs wishing to penetrate deeper into the professional-class segment of the Chinese consumer pyramid should use a product cluster diffusion strategy in flagship and secondary cities, initially introducing a narrow range of products into the marketplace. First, MNEs that are interested in targeting this consumer segment should develop a dominant market presence in a flagship city where a large percentage of the professional class lives. Flagship cities can act as a test market for initial product entry before expanding market coverage by way of product diffusion into other areas of the region. This is because professional-class consumers are the innovators and opinion leaders of Chinese society. Therefore they will be more receptive to purchase new and interesting foreign-made products.

Once this objective has been achieved, MNEs can then extend their market dominance by diffusing products into adjacent secondary satellite cities clustered around the flagship city. Secondary satellite cities will consist of a relatively large number of consumers from the professional-class segment of the pyramid because many of these consumers own small to medium-sized businesses or work for MNEs operating in these cities. Also, a large number of students from this consumer segment attend universities and colleges in secondary satellite cities.

This strategy allows MNEs to prioritize resources in markets likely to pay the biggest rewards. A good example of implementing this strategy can be seen when China's travel industry exploded in the 1980s; a small Taiwanese company by the name of Tingyi developed and manufactured products targeted at managers and students traveling on business to and from flagship and secondary satellite cities in certain regions. Initially, the market leader in this niche industry was another Taiwanese MNE named President Enterprises. However, President Enterprises did not have a proper product diffusion strategy. However, Tingyi's product cluster diffusion strategy proved very successful, ultimately allowing the company eventually to take away market leadership from President Enterprises through growth and targeted regional expansion. Thus, by initially targeting products at a single closely linked region consisting of a flagship city and a cluster of surrounding secondary satellite cities, MNEs may be better able to penetrate the professional-class consumer segment.

MNEs that wish to further penetrate the salaried-class segment of the Chinese consumer pyramid should extend their product cluster diffusion strategy to include towns within close proximity of the secondary satellite cities of a targeted region. This is because many surrounding towns are home to large numbers of mid-to-low level government and provincial officials and employees of state-owned enterprises and township enterprises. As previously mentioned, these individuals represent a relatively large segment of the Chinese consumer pyramid that has income; they are occasionally willing to spend on foreign-made products.

Procter & Gamble and Unilever have been successful at capturing a large percentage of this market by using the product cluster diffusion strategy to penetrate deeper into this consumer segment. They achieved this by introducing personal care products such as soaps and shampoos to stores in small townships outside of flagship and secondary satellite cities. This strategy allowed these MNEs to leverage influential information emanating from the flagship and secondary satellite cities and to take advantage of similar consumer preferences and efficiencies associated with proximate transportation linkages. Other MNEs could follow Procter and Gamble and Unilever's product cluster diffusion strategies in order to penetrate deeper into the salary-class segment of the Chinese consumer pyramid.

MNEs wishing to penetrate the vast working-class segment need to extend their product cluster diffusion strategy to include surrounding provinces within the region(s) they are operating in. While some of the working class are employed in city factories, an overwhelming majority live on farming communities outside the proximity of cities or towns. Selling foreign products in provincial areas is a difficult task. MNEs wanting to further penetrate the working-class consumer segment need to aggressively distribute their products in the province(s) since this segment is immobile and lacks interest in purchasing foreign-made products. There are several examples of MNEs using the product diffusion cluster strategy to do this. For example, Eastman Kodak Company launched a campaign named "Marching West" in which it extended its product penetration from the coastal cities into the working-class segments of western provinces. While this strategy proved to be time-consuming and costly, it allowed Kodak to penetrate a distant portion of the working-class consumer segment in rural provinces.

Another example of how the product diffusion cluster strategy can be applied to penetrate the working-class consumer segment is Avon Products, Inc.'s recruitment of over 40,000 women in the southern and eastern regions of China to sell beauty products in provincial areas by bicycling, sometimes for several miles, in order to obtain purchase orders from their predominantly working-class clients. If Avon had not implemented this strategy, it may have never reached the isolated areas where rural working-class consumers live and may have lost prospective foreign product purchasers. But, by extending the cluster strategy to include the provinces where the majority of the working class live, Avon has been successful in capturing a greater market share, thereby penetrating deeper into the Chinese consumer pyramid. See Table 4.2.

Table 4.2
Strategies for Penetrating the Chinese Consumer Pyramid

Marketing Strategies		Rich	Professionals	Salary Class	Working Class
Product Packaging	Use *guo qing* to penetrate the bottom segments of the pyramid	• Western standards	• Western standards	• Durable goods: Smaller units • Perishable goods: Larger units	• Graphically oriented designs and names • Auspicious and/or powerful images
Pricing	**Diversified strategies**	• Premium	• Premium	• Market based	• Discount and unbundled
Promotion	**Brand loyalty strategies**	• Flashy, trendsetting advertising campaigns • Focus on prestige and status	• Emphasize Chinese needs and styles • Product discount promotions	• Coupon rebate schemes • Servicing promotion mechanisms	• Coupon rebate schemes • Servicing promotion mechanisms
Product Distribution	**Product cluster diffusion strategy**	• Flagship cities (modern shopping facilities)	• + secondary cities (shopping facilities)	• ++ townships (local stores)	• +++ surrounding provinces (door-to-door sales)

CONCLUSION

China is still a relatively underexplored commercial market. Once a poor country, it is now rapidly developing into one of the world's premier economic powerhouses. The advent of a socialist-market economy has dramatically increased China's development and produced newfound wealth. These events have spurred high levels of consumer spending by China's unique materialistic Confucian society. In turn, a consumer pyramid with various consumer segments has emerged. The different segments of the Chinese consumer pyramid have different buying behaviors and product needs. MNEs have yet to fully realize this. For these reasons, we have offered a series of strategies that MNEs can use in order to achieve greater success at penetrating different segments in the Chinese consumer pyramid. Furthermore, it is our hope that these strategies will assist MNEs in being more efficient and effective in their China strategies, thereby capturing a greater share of the Chinese marketplace.

NOTES

1. Williamson, P., and Zeng, M. (2004) "Strategies for Competing in a Changed China," *MIT Sloan Management Review,* 45(4), 85–91.

2. Cui, G., and Lui, Q. (2001) "Emerging Market Segments in a Transitional Economy: A Study of Urban Consumers in China," *Journal of International Marketing,* 9(1), 84–106.

3. Yan, R. "To Reach China's Consumers, Adopt to Guo Qing," *Harvard Business Review,* 72(5), 66–74.

4. Cui, G. (1997) "The Different Faces of the Chinese Consumer," *China Business Review* 24(4), 34–38.

5. Sun, T., and Wu, G. (2004) "Consumption Patterns of Chinese Urban and Rural Consumers," *Journal of Consumer Marketing,* 21(4), 245–253.

6. Yan, 1994: 70.

7. Williams, C.A.S. (1993) *Chinese Symbolism and Art Motifs,* Tokyo: Charles E. Tuttle Company, Inc.

8. Rao, R.C., and Bass, F.M. Bass (1985) "Competition, Strategy, and Price Dynamics: A Theoretical and Empirical investigation," *Journal of Marketing Research,* 22 (August), 283–296

9 Standifird, S.S., and Marshall, R.S. (2000) "The Transaction Cost Advantage of *guanxi* Based Business Practices," *Journal of World Business,* 35(1), 21–43.

10. Crocker, G., and Tay, Y. (2004) "What It Takes to Create a Successful Brand," *China Business Review,* 31(4), 10–16.

11. Cui and Liu, 2001: 104; Williamson and Zeng, 2004.

CHAPTER 5

COMPLEXITIES OF THE INDIAN CONSUMER MARKET

Rajshekhar (Raj) G. Javalgi and Ashutosh Dixit

India is one of the fastest-growing emerging economies in the world. With a population of over 1 billion people and linguistic and cultural diversity, India represents an economic opportunity on a gargantuan scale, both as a domestic market and a global platform. While mired for many decades in economic isolation, its reform process is now giving hope for a better future for its 1 billion people. With a rich reservoir of natural and human resources and with labor wages significantly lower than the global average, India's economy is a mixture of traditional village farming, modern agriculture, handcrafts, and a multitude of small, independent, owner-managed jobs. Since its economic reform in 1991, the country has made major strides toward liberalization in a variety of sectors. India's Prime Minister Manmohan Singh stated, "If I have any message, it is that it is our ambition to integrate our country into evolving global economy. We accept the logic of globalization."[1]

With over 1 billion people, India's consumer market is largely untapped, although it is changing—changing quickly. With advancements in communication and information technologies and rising affluence, and an increasing pool of skilled workers, Indian consumers are becoming increasingly sophisticated and knowledgeable about foreign products. Consumers are witnessing more choices, getting richer, and becoming more and more brand conscious. The result is that foreign companies are increasingly interested in better understanding the complexities of the Indian consumer market.

The goal of this chapter is to discuss the complexities of India's consumer market. The chapter is organized as follows: The first section of the chapter provides a brief outlook on India's economy. The second section focuses on the characteristics of the Indian consumer market. The third section looks at the purchasing behavior of Indian consumers. The fourth section of the chapter deals with international marketing challenges, followed by our conclusions.

THE ECONOMIC OUTLOOK

India's economic reform has witnessed unprecedented changes, including rising international trade and foreign direct investment, faster infrastructure developments, rising consumer income, and growing consumer demand for foreign products. There have been fundamental changes in economic activities, the emergence of new industries, and a new mind-set on the part of Indian consumers. Simply put, India has undergone a noticeable paradigm shift. In the first quarter of 2006–2007 the Indian economy grew at 8.6 percent, making it the second fastest-growing economy in the world. According to the World Bank forecasts, India could become the fourth largest economy by 2010.[2] The growing affluence of a large, skilled, younger population and the construction of infrastructure ranging from airports to teleports are setting the stage for economic success.

India's economy can be characterized by three types of sectors: the "modern sectors," with a production process resembling those in modern economies, provide 24 percent of employment and 47 percent of output. The second sector can be characterized as the "transitional sectors," which provide 16 percent of employment and close to 30 percent of output. The third and the largest sector is agriculture, which provides 60 percent of employment and 26 percent of output.[3] The transitional sectors include those responsible for the informal goods and services consumed by a growing urban population (for example, street vending, small grocery shops, small scale food processing, and so forth). Here, workers use labor-intensive, low-tech materials and technologies, or business processes. Since jobs in the transitional sectors require little capital and only elementary skills, workers are easily able to move out of agricultural into these low-skilled jobs.[4] The result is new consumers in rural areas with a growing appetite for foreign goods.

The current positive trends are noticeable in most sectors of the economy such as manufacturing (automobiles, textiles, foods, building materials, foods, and cosmetics), the service sector [information-technology (IT) software, banking, insurance, consulting, and retailing], and research and development intensive sectors such as pharmaceuticals.[5] In addition, India is the world's largest producer of milk and the second largest producer of food, including fruits and vegetables.[6] The software sector is one of the fastest-growing, dynamic industries in the Indian economy, thus building its competitive edge in the IT sector. India has the second largest group of software developers after the United States. Since 1991, this sector has witnessed an average annual growth rate of over 50 percent to total sales of $8.3 billion in the year 2000.[7]

Significant reforms have been made in the telecommunications, financial, insurance, and shipping sectors. The United States is the main trading partner of India; nearly 20 percent of India's exports go to the United States. The other significant trading partners to India include the United Kingdom, Japan, and Germany. Table 5.1 provides a brief overview of the Indian economy on a variety of indicators including gross domestic product (GDP), total trade, size of the middle class, and the power of the youth segment.

Table 5.1
Key Economic Indicators of India

Economic Indicators	Value	Explanation (Country/Market Potential)
GDP	$659 billion	
Economic Growth	7-percent growth in 2004–2005; expected to be 7–8 percent or higher in 2005–2006	India is the tenth largest economy in the world and one of the fastest growing; it is the fourth largest in purchasing power parity.
Per Capita Income	$640 in 2004–2005	Income is growing rapidly among urban consumers.
Purchasing Power	In 2005, approximately 170–300 million people had purchasing power.	New policies fueled by the new economy are creating a growing middle-class population.
Youth Power	Over 58 percent of the Indian population is under the age of 20.	This represents over 564 million of the total Indian population, nearly twice the total population of the United States.
U.S. and India Bilateral Trade	In 2005, it was $26.77 billion.	In 2005, U.S. exports to India totaled $7.96 billion, a 30.3-percent increase from the previous year. In 2005, imports from India totaled $18.81 billion, a 20.8-percent increase from the previous year.
Population	Over 1 billion	Urban population is approximately 28.4 percent.
Growing Middle Class	Approximately 300 million people.	Middle-class population is estimated to grow at 5 percent annually.
Retail Market Size	$286 billion (only 3.9 percent is organized retail)	Retail trade is booming due to the rising disposable incomes of middle- and upper-middle-class populations.

Source: www.buyusa.gov (accessed September 13, 2006).

CHARACTERISTICS OF THE INDIAN CONSUMER MARKET

Rural versus Urban Markets

India is primarily rural, but is becoming increasingly urban. It is estimated that by the year 2010, one in three Indians will be living in towns and cities.[8] In fact, there will be more inhabitants in urban India than in almost any country in the world except China. It is noted that 60 million people are living in India's eight largest cities (Mumbai, Calcutta, Delhi, Madras, Hyderabad, Bangalore, Ahmedabad, and Pune). The urbanization pattern in India is different from the other Asian countries. By 2001, 28 percent of Indians were living in towns, compared to 39 percent of Chinese and 83 percent of South Koreans.[9]

Urban and rural consumers differ vastly in terms of spending power, consumption behavior, and willingness to try new products and services. The rural population, consisting of three-quarters of the Indian population, lives in around 627,000 villages.[10] The rural consumer market is becoming an important target market for fast-moving consumer goods (FMCG) as well as consumer durables. The market size for the FMCG sector is projected to more than double from the current U.S.$11.16 billion to $23.25 billion by 2010.[11] This presents a huge opportunity that multinational enterprises cannot afford to ignore.

The Indian middle class, which is the urban embodiment of the best aspirations of globalization, appears to have great potential market. The consumption behavior of this group is defined by the purchase of products such as color televisions, washing machines, and cell phones. This middle class represents a particular segment of the professional middle classes, particularly those related to the new economy jobs such as the information technology sector.[12]

India's middle class is growing; the size is estimated to be 300 million people, which is the size of the U.S. population. Moreover, the middle class is expanding by about 20 million per year and is expected to grow 445 million within a decade. The size of the middle class depends on the variables used to define it. For instance, income-based definitions include both rural and urban consumers, with the majority being urbanites. "In the face of such diversity, the identity of the new Indian middle class provides a kind of normative standard, which this larger group can aspire to. Thus, the boundaries of the middle class are fluid precisely because they hold the prominence of access.[13] The middle-class consumer segment represents cultural symbols of a nation that has opened its borders to consumer goods and services that were unavailable a few decades ago.

Income distribution is unequal compared to other emerging economies. Income is concentrated in urban areas and is visible among affluent classes that can afford consumer durables (for example, color televisions, air conditioners, and so forth). The products are out of range for most rural consumers. However, many are aspiring to the level of income that would allow them to enjoy the lifestyles of urbanites. There about 8 million people earning over $20,000 per annum, with a high desire to purchase foreign products. Over 20 million house-holds earn over $1,500 per year, and 65 million people are in the income category of $10,000–$20,000, with a medium to high level of willingness to buy foreign products. About 130 million people fall in the category of $5,000–$10,000 and have some appetite to buy foreign products.[14] Increasingly, India's rural market, with very rich farmers and countryside business people, is becoming important.

India's Demographic Advantage

India is comprised of 29 states that differ vastly in resources, culture, language, and religion. While the majority of the populous is Hindu (83.2 percent), there are different groups, including Muslims (11 percent), Christians (2 percent), Jains and Buddhists (less than 1 percent), and Sikhs (2 percent).[15] India's large English-speaking population certainly makes it an attractive business destination for trade and foreign direct investment, but also represents a potential consumer market for foreign products and services. India is one of the world's largest civilizations, and rather than dispense with traditional values, it has wrapped modernity around its traditional core values and beliefs. Consumerism is becoming a way of life. "[A]lmost half of India's urban population had adopted a 'work hard and get rich' ethos by 1996; another 9% had done so by 2006."[16]

Consumerism is taking off in India. More and more Indians are motivated by material success, and materialism is becoming a sign of prosperity, especially among the younger generation, which has the drive, energy, and willingness to try new things. Indians constitute one-fifth of the world's population below age 20, suggesting a youthful generation geared toward consumerism, which is becoming a new way of life.[17] While most of the emerging economies are experiencing a decline in their working-age population, India is witnessing growth among this vibrant segment, giving it a demographic advantage.

With a large proportion of people in the 18–35 years of age group, and with rising salaries, this segment presents tremendous potential as consumers of luxurious goods and services. According to the National Council of Applied Economic Research, the changing demographics in India, the young working population's driving innovation and personal consumption, will be an important factor to the expansion of consumer markets.

INDIAN CONSUMERS' PURCHASING BEHAVIORS

India's consumers are family oriented. This value is more important than the values of individualism and achievement. However, changing demographics indicate that the younger population is slowly embracing the culture of ambition and materialism.

Global consumer spending will expand at an annual rate of 5.6 percent to $62 trillion by 2020, compared to $27 trillion today. The United States will continue to be the most attractive and the largest consumer market, followed by China and India. India's share in world consumer spending will increase from 1.9 percent in 2005 to 3.1 percent in 2020.[18]

Household spending in India has grown by 5.3 percent a year for the past ten years.[19] More and more multinational corporations are taking advantage of the changing demographic characteristics of the Indian consumer market. Table 5.2 shows the percentage of annual earnings spent on different product categories. It is clear from Table 5.2 that the Indian consumers' spending habits are changing in a variety of ways. Over 40 percent of income is spent on food; however, the portion of income spent on food is steadily declining as the spending is increasing in other areas as personal care, books/music, movies and entertainment, and vacation/eating out. Also, the percentage of earnings used on savings and investments is declining.

Table 5.3 further shows the relationship between age and spending pattern. Those who are between 15 and 19 years of age are spending the maximum share of their annual income on books, music, and footwear; those who are between 20 and 24 years of age tend to spend on home appliances and movies; those who are between 25 and 44 years of age tend to spend in such areas as eating out, clothes, furnishings, and personal-care products; and those who are between 45 and 58 years of age emphasize vacations and entertainment.

Changing demographics and spending patterns are pushing India into new consumer markets that emphasize excitement and novelty. Many households that previously spent most of their money on basic necessities, such as food and shelter, are now spending a portion of their income on consumption of discretionary

Table 5.2
Percentage of Annual Earnings Spent by Indian Consumers

Product Categories	1992	2002
Groceries	46.2	42.1
Personal Care	6.2	8.8
Appliances/Durables	8.6	5.0
Book/Music	5	6.7
Movies/Entertainment	2.9	5.8
Vacation/Eating out	10.8	15.6
Savings and Investments	12.1	5.2

Source: Basu Indrajit, "India's Growing Urge to Splurge," 2003, www.atimes.com/atimes/South_Asia/ (accessed April 26, 2006).

Table 5.3
The Maximum Share of Annual Earnings Spent on a Particular Product Category (by age groups)

Age Categories	Product Category
15–19	Books, music, and footwear
20–24	Home appliances and movies
25–34	Eating out
35–44	Clothes, furnishings, and personal-care products
45–58	Vacations/eating out

Source: Basu Indrajit, "India's Growing Urge to Splurge," 2003, www.atimes.com/atimes/South_Asia/ (accessed April 26, 2006).

goods and services—everything from air conditioners and motor scooters to movie tickets, eating out, and vacations. An increasing number of people are vacationing outside their home countries for shorter periods of time. The ability of Indian consumers to spend on travel and luxury goods is rising as they are earning more income. Among durable goods, high-tech luxury goods are in demand. For instance, to examine the changes in attitudes of Indian consumers in the decade from 1996 to 2006, the Gallup Organization conducted a survey of over 2,000 respondents. Its report indicated the following consumption behavior patterns[20]: The percentage of Indians who use or own consumer products is up 100 percent for laptops and computers, 83 percent for refrigerators, and a mind-boggling 1,600 percent for mobile phones. Indians are becoming more materialistic, especially urban consumers.

While consumption can be funded by a variety of means (for example, current income, savings, and borrowing), the majority of Indians seem to spend their current income and rely less on borrowing and loans; however, in India the credit boom is fueling spending to a large extent. Even though consumer credit is still in the fledgling stage, the indications are that Indian consumers are quickly gaining access to credit cards.

INTERNATIONAL MARKETING CHALLENGES

Changing consumption patterns and growth in discretionary spending is of strategic significance to the foreign companies that are vying to take a share of the market and penetrate the Indian markets. The new Indian consumer is eager and willing to try new, foreign-made products and services. The rules of the game for businesses operating in the Indian market are changing rapidly, presenting both challenges and opportunities. With a large and complex market like India, looking at economic indicators like per capita income may be misleading because it masks the real purchasing power of dynamic consumer segments in both urban and rural markets. Over the past few decades, as a result of the increasing literacy in the rural areas, exposure to Western culture, and foreign magazines and newspapers, there is a significant increase in consumer sophistication and openness to foreign culture.

From the international marketing perspective there is no simple strategic formula for targeting Indian consumers, comprising different segments of consumers based on status, income, and class. The next section presents strategic challenges that cannot be overlooked.

Product Considerations

In the United States, the volume-price discounting concept works well; that is, consumers are used to buying large quantities of products based on volume-price discounting. In emerging markets this concept does not go well. In the Indian fast-moving consumer goods industry, large multinationals, such as Hindustan Lever Limited (HLL), Procter & Gamble (P&G), Colgate-Palmolive, and so forth found that a strategy exclusively focused on price reductions was not the way to allure consumers to their products. Since over 70 percent of the Indian population lives in rural areas, the demand for smaller quantity packaged products is increasing. Companies are realizing that there is a demand for such products as cosmetics (for example, lipsticks, nail polishes, perfumes, and deodorants), ice creams, shampoos, detergents, ready-to-eat food products, tea, coffee, toothpaste, soaps, and so forth. Foreign multinationals must develop product strategies that focus on smaller quantity packaged goods at lower costs. Small size packaged products increase trial purchase and give the consumer the satisfaction of using a brand-name product at an affordable price. In addition to making the products affordable for the lower-income segments and rural consumers, it also attracts semiurban consumers.

Although there are benefits of offering products in small packs, there are also disadvantages to this approach. Packaging the low per unit price of the product in a sachet, especially products such as shampoos and detergent, may lead to a shift of customers from large packs to small packs.[21] When providing premium brands at a lower price in small packs, the customers who buy cheaper brands switch to the premium, which erodes the market share of the cheaper brands of the same company. India's consumer market is large enough that any scale and scope economies are still achievable with product adaptation and careful product market considerations.

Pricing Considerations

Price is the most significant factor for most Indian consumers in their purchase decisions. Indians tend to be price conscious for various reasons, including low income, a frugal mentality, buying only on needs-based consumption, and saving for tomorrow.[22] Although low-priced products constitute the majority of sales volume, and lower-income and lower-middle-income consumers account for over 60 percent of sales, foreign multinationals must not think that they can penetrate the Indian market with low-quality products and gain a foothold. Indian consumers searching for quality choose expensive brands because they feel that price is an indicator of quality.[23] In the absence of well-known brands, however, consumers are more likely to rely on cues from well-established retail outlets and/or family and friends.

Indian consumers prefer high-value consumer products, but often settle for what is considered to be affordable. These decisions often affect their purchasing habits when searching for products that communicate feelings and emotions. Simply put, for Indian consumers price is a significant factor in purchasing decisions given the large size of the low-income population. A simple conversion of Western currency to Indian currency (rupees) does not work.[24] As discussed above, lowering prices by reducing package sizes and simplifying designs may be necessary to get a foothold, but these practices may not be necessarily the best long-term strategy. J. K. Johansson[25] points out that since price is a salient factor for Indian consumers, the best way to lower prices may be by shifting some assembly into the country or by establishing a joint venture with local business partners who can bring local cultural market knowledge and help succeed in the market. Multinationals that understand the Indian consumers' expectations and price sensitivities can tap into a promising market.

Companies such as LG Electronics (LGE), Hindustan Lever Limited (HLL), Nestlé, The Coca-Cola Company, and P&G, to name a few, have succeeded in the Indian market. HLL and Nestlé, for instance, have embraced the fact that price is the key determinant of purchase decision for the Indian consumer and are enjoying the benefits of launching low-price small unit packs. Coca-Cola purchased Thums Up, thereby acquiring the country's largest bottling and distribution network; Coca-Cola has addressed the affordability issue by introducing the returnable 200-milliliter glass bottle priced Rs 5.[26] By doing so Coca-Cola has tapped into the rural market.

Distribution Consideration

Unlike developed economies, India does not have an efficient distribution infrastructure, though significant improvements have been made in building all kinds of public works, including roads, railroads, transportation systems, airports, and communication systems. The vast majority of the Indian population lives in small villages and cities, so reaching the fragmented and dispersed markets increases the complexity of the distribution structure for companies. Beginning in 1988, Amway India Enterprise engaged in direct selling of personal-care and home-care products. It consists of a network of over 800,000 independent distributors spread across 500 cities, achieving a business of over U.S.$104 million.[27]

Most companies selling in India use a tree-tier distribution system that has evolved over many decades: distributor, wholesaler, and retailer. Foreign firms that do not possess the necessary skills to distribute and sell effectively to Indian consumers should consider outsourcing the distribution of products to Indian firms that are well established and well regarded.[28] However, the main disadvantage with this approach is loss of control.

While department stores and supermarkets are emerging and becoming more popular in bigger cities, family-run stores comprise the majority of selling outlets. Here, buying and selling is often a process of bargaining and negotiation, an activity that is common for Indian consumers. In sum, the Indian distribution system continues to improve, but still remains a challenge for foreign firms.

Promotion

Due to technological advancements and changing perceptions and attitudes of Indian consumers, the reach of media is still fairly limited due to the diverse population and hundreds of regional groups living in cities and towns with their own languages, tastes, and preferences. Therefore, the advertising task becomes complex. Foreign companies have to select the right media for the right market. For instance, compared to urban areas, where there is over 90 percent penetration of at least one medium, in rural areas it is only 66 percent.[29] Media penetration has grown significantly in urban areas, where the television reach is over 77 percent; in the villages radio has the highest reach (over 40 percent), and the press has the lowest reach (about 20 percent).[30] If foreign multinationals want to target rural consumers, advertisements must be grounded in rural consumer values and traditions. Advertising media must focus on local language, color, and modes of communication to make it relevant to the rural market.

Any media vehicle or advertisement in rural India will be successful if it is built around the following three strategies: influencer strategies, participatory strategy, and show-and-tell strategy.[31] In the influencer strategy, the advertisements actually depend on the influence of celebrities or influential people/event in the villages. An example of this kind of advertisement may be brand endorsement by any influential person in the village. In the participatory strategy, events like festivals, games, and sports competitions are used as promotion venues for the product. In the show-and-tell strategy, the focus is to educate rural consumers about brands and their usage to rural consumers. Kellogg Company, the American cereal company, used this approach to educate Indian consumers, especially rural consumers, who were not accustomed to eating cereal for breakfast. On top of the cereal box, information was given about how to mix the milk and cold cereal. The key to this advertising and promotional campaign was to convince

Indian consumers to change their breakfast-eating habits.[32] Colgate-Palmolive, the U.S. consumer products multinational, has devised a highly effective, creative advertising campaign for rural India: video vans. The vans show the villagers an infomercial that attempts to educate the benefits of toothpaste and the proper method of brushing one's teeth.[33] Hence, the video van is one of the effective ways of reaching out to the rural consumers and educating them.

CONCLUSIONS

India is one of the most exciting and complex emerging economies in the world, with a young and skilled population, a rising middle class, and a great appetite for foreign goods and services. In the service sector, which is its major source of economic growth, India is gaining a competitive advantage globally. No foreign multinational denies that India and Indians have undergone a paradigm shift in the past few decades. The fundamental and irreversible changes in the economy, new governmental policies, and rising consumerism have made India globally competitive and of great interest to international marketers.

When compared to the urban markets, rural consumers are primarily driven by their basic needs and are therefore price sensitive. Although rural consumers are motivated by their traditions, customs, and values, their mind-set is changing. Indian consumers have developed lifestyles that have emerged from openness to foreign culture, especially Western culture, and the need for self-gratification. Indian consumers are also traveling abroad a lot more. They get exposed to new products, new designs, and new technologies. Simply put, Indian consumers are getting the attention of multinationals. Those foreign companies that better understand the dynamics of the Indian consumer market and develop innovative strategies to meet unmet needs of consumers and satisfy these needs in a unique way will survive and succeed.

NOTES

1. V. T. Bharadwaj, Ireena Vittal, and Gautam M. Swaroop (2005), "Winning the Indian Consumer," *The McKinsey Quarterly,* September, pp. 20–32.

2. Budhwar Pawan (2001), "Doing Business in India," *Thunderbird International Business Review,* Vol. 43(4), pp. 549–568.

3. Di Lodovico, Amadeo, William W. Lewis, Vincent Palmade, and Shirish Sankhe (2001), "India—Form Emerging to Surging," *McKinsey Quarterly,* Vol. 4, pp. 28–50.

4. Ibid.

5. Som, Ashok (2006), "Bracing for MNC Competition through Innovative HRM Practices: The Way Ahead for Indian Firms," *Thunderbird International Business Review,* Vol. 48(2), pp. 207–237.

6. See www.buyusa.gov.

7. Chandra, Aruna (2003), "Interview: Marketing IT in India, Perspectives of Mr. Murali Raman, Country Manager, IBM India," *Thunderbird International Business Review,* Vol. 45(4), pp. 399–407.

8. Bullis, Douglas (1997), *Selling to India,* Westport, CT: Quorum Books.

9. "Consumer Markets in India—The Next Best Thing?" KPMG 2005, accessed at www.kpmg.com.

10. Goel, A., and Narvankar, S. (2004), "Rural Markets: The Next Frontiers of FMGC Companies," www.indiainfoline.com/bisc/rura.html.

11. Chennai, Matrade (2005), "Product Market Study: Consumer Behavior in India," www.edms.matrade.gov.

12. Fernandes, Leela (2004), "The Politics of Forgetting: Class Politics, State Power and the Restructuring of Urban Space in India, *Urban Studies,* Vol. 41(12), pp. 2415–2430.

13. Ibid., p. 2418.

14. Ramachandran, Raja (2000), "Understanding the Market Environment of India," *Business Environment,* January–February, pp. 44–52.

15. Budhwar Pawan, op. cit.

16. Gopal, Ashok, and Rajesh Srinivasan, "The New Indian Consumer," *Harvard Business Review,* October, p. 22.

17. Ibid.

18. Cisco Systems (2006), "India to Contribute 12.2 Percent to Global Economic Growth by 2020," www.domain-b.com/companies/companies_c/cisco_system/20060626_contrubute.html.

19. Asia Now (2005), "Cycles of Consumption," www.micm-asianow.com/cycles.htm/ (accessed April 26, 2006).

20. See Gopal and Srinivasan, op. cit.

21. Dubey, Jayashree, and Rajni P. Patel (2003), "Small Wonders of the Indian Market," *Journal of Consumer Behavior,* Vol. 4(2), pp. 145–151.

22. Ramachandran, op. cit.

23. KPMG, op. cit.

24. Johansson, Johny K. (2006), *Global Marketing: Foreign Entry, Local Marketing, and Global Management,* New York: McGraw-Hill, p. 127.

25. Ibid.

26. Datta, S. (2003), "Modeling the Effects of Corporate Images and Brand Images," in Proceedings of the 2003 Academy of Marketing Science Conference.

27. Dasgupta, Subhasish (Ed.), (2005), *Encyclopedia of Virtual Communities and Technologies,* London: Idea Group Publishing.

28. Ramachandran, op. cit.

29. Bullis, op. cit.

30. Ibid.

31. Kanjilal, Abir, Indranil Das, and Rohitash Srivastava (2004), "Media Effect and Its Measurement in Rural India," www. Exchange4media.com/e4m/media_matter_110804/ (accessed September 3, 2006).

32. Johansson, op. cit.

33. Ramachandran, op. cit.

CHAPTER 6

WHAT IS IN A NAME? TRANSFERRING BRANDS TO CHINA

Julie Mo, Jason McNicol, and Lance Eliot Brouthers

Global corporations typically have a vast array of brand logos and brand names. Brands aid the firm in obtaining and retaining customers that can potentially lead to greater profits for the multinational enterprise (MNE). However, when entering a new country, particularly in Asia, potential customers may not recognize company logos, may be unable to read brand names, and/or may not associate meanings with sounds when pronouncing the brand name.

In international business, this scenario is becoming more common as businesses expand, particularly in Asia. Between Western and Asian countries, there is a vast difference in written and verbal communication. For example, writing the word "Coca-Cola" means nothing to rural Chinese or Indians; moreover, the sounds associated with the word Coca-Cola are also meaningless.

When a MNE decides to expand into Asia, the firm expects to invest resources and money to promote its brands. But what is the proper way to do this given written and verbal communication differences? More specifically, when firms begin expanding current brands into China, what new and different strategies should be developed in order to ensure the successful transfer of a brand name?

Based on past research it appears that successful transfer of brand names contains three key components: language, sound, and meaning. When these three components are used properly in China, a brand name can evoke cultural and personal desired meanings that help promote the brand more effectively than just creating a brand name that sounds similar to the original. The current chapter compares linguistic features of U.S. brand names with the Cantonese and Mandarin brand names chosen by selected U.S. companies.

Understanding communication differences between the United States and China can help lead to creating a valuable brand name, which in turn is critical to a firm's success. The impact of language differences must be understood if a brand name is to be successfully transferred since key elements of the marketing communication mix used to sell products, like brand names or advertising campaigns, are language based.

In this chapter we propose that when entering the Chinese market, three decision rules should be followed in order to successfully transfer a brand name to China: First, the brand name should accurately reflect the "unique selling proposition" or the "basis of sustainable competitive advantage" of the product/brand. Second, a successfully transferred brand name has a "symbolic" as well as a literal meaning: one that induces positive associations between the transferred brand and the preferred cultural practices or personal goals. Third, a successfully transferred brand name should be memorable; it should enter the evoked set with top of the mind recall. Each of these rules is based on differences between Western and Asian languages and cultures.

THE MEANING OF LANGUAGE

Culture within a country is reflected and transmitted via that county's language. Language includes a country's history and culture revealing a peoples' view of life and manner of thinking. A common known fact about language is that fundamental language differences hamper communication.

For example, most Western languages use alphabetic phonetic systems (letters used to create words with meaning) when the common trait among many Asian countries, like China, is ideographs (the use of symbols or characters for meaning). The difference between alphabetic phonetic systems and ideographs may render brand names meaningless when transferring Western brands to an Asian country. Thus, transferring brand names from West to East may become problematic because it is very difficult to replicate sounds cross-culturally resulting in English phonetic-based names that are difficult to pronounce and/or understand in Chinese.

Transferring brand names from phonetic-based cultures to ideographic cultures requires that three key rules be followed to ensure a successful brand name transfer. First, a country's language should be understood because a lack of understanding in language results in a lack of culture and history understanding resulting in poorly created brand names that will be ineffective. Second, sound helps customers recall the product; a good-sounding product helps customers remember the products. Third, the meanings and visuals associated with a brand name in China are very important because the language is ideographic; the product may sound similar to the original, but poor meanings and visuals hamper the successful transfer of a brand name. Each rule is discussed in more detail.

The rapid growth of international business has caused brand naming to become global and forces MNEs to consider language when transferring a brand. When transferring brand names from one language to another, brand naming should keep its original position; put simply, brand names that are atop their markets should try to maintain their dominance in other markets. Understanding the Chinese language allows MNEs to create a brand name that appeals to the culture and history of the Chinese people in a positive manner, which leads to greater sales; otherwise, the new brand name will be unsuccessful and cause loss of company profits in a very attractive market.

Understanding the language is the first step in successfully transferring a brand name, but sound is also very important in this process. One example of a brand name that sounds similar to the original and was able to maintain success is Coca-Cola's Chinese brand name, ko-kou-ko-le in Mandarin and ho-hau-ho-lohk in Cantonese. These names closely sound like the English brand name while having a positive related meaning, "tasty and happy" (Schmitt and Pan, 1994).

Johnson & Johnson has had success in China by transferring its brand name to "Qiang-sheng." The Chinese brand name sounds similar to the original name and means "strengthen the life," which also relates to most products sold by Johnson & Johnson (Zhang and Schmitt, 2001).

Colgate also translated its brand name to a successful Chinese brand name that means "highly clear and clean." Such successes are difficult to obtain because of the linguistic barriers that exist when translating an English brand name into a Chinese brand name.

Expanding a brand name into international Asian markets must be done carefully so the brand name translated does not have a negative connotation. Such mistranslations can have very negative consequences (such as loss of sales or damaged credibility).

Creating a new brand name may also create difficulty. The new brand name may not convey a desirable connotation or meaning and may be difficult to pronounce (Francis, Lam, and Walls, 2002).

Several companies have successfully transferred a brand name that conveys a positive meaning and is easy to pronounce. For instance, "7-Up" was translated into "qixi" in Chinese, which means "seven happiness." This translation comes from an original meaning that translated the "up" into "happiness" instead of its original meaning.

7-Up's competitor Sprite pursued a similar strategy. Sprite's Chinese brand name is "Xue-bi" meaning "snow and green," which corresponds to the drink: cool, clear, and in a green bottle. "Pepsi" was translated into "baishi kele." It means "being happy for everything"; "baishi" sounds close to "Pepsi," which is a good translation on both meaning and pronunciation "Fu-te" is Ford's brand name in China, which means "happy and special." All of these are good names for products being sold in China. The decision rule all the above examples are

based on is this: in China when translating a brand name to something easily pronounceable, it is important to be sure that the new translation also bears a positive
meaning.

BRAND NAMES

A brand name contains thoughts and characteristics within a symbol, but the
meaning of the brand comes from associations built over time by the perceptions
of customers (Francis, Lam, and Walls, 2002; Gardner and Levy 1955). The
product's image perceived by customers is based on the brand name; hence, a
brand name should be chosen carefully so it may potentially add direct value to
the brand (Kohli and LaBahn, 1997). If done properly, a good brand name can
potentially have characteristics that increase the value of the brand name. Such
characteristics include product relevance, positive association, and a competitive
image over competitors (Francis, Lam, and Walls, 2002).

To illustrate, a French brandy company has had much success with its brand
name. Bisquit, the French brandy company, is translated into Chinese as "baishiqi," which means being fortunate in everything. Many Chinese are superstitious
when it comes to numbers; the numbers three and eight both have good meanings. Three represents growing and money growing, while eight means getting
rich. Eight pronounced in Chinese is "ba," which is very close to the first letter
of the Chinese translation "baishiqi." Therefore, it becomes a very popular brand
name that people like buying as gifts for friends or family.

Another good example is BMW whose Chinese name is "Bao-ma." In China,
horses are considered sacred creatures that have a very high value. "Bao-ma" translated means "precious horse"; the value associated with the car becomes very high
because of the relevance of the horse in Chinese cultures, providing a competitive
advantage over competitors.

The uniqueness and identifiability of a brand name lies within the linguistic
component of the brand name (Charmasson, 1988; Huang and Chan, 1997).
The linguistic components, the pleasure obtained from the brand, and any other
associations may heavily influence the success of a brand; brand names are not just
read, but thought and spoken when the mind converts words into sound (Trout,
1997). The brand name chosen then becomes a strategic choice because the brand
name helps position the brand.

Hewlett-Packard (HP) is a good example of using a brand name to position a
product. "Hui-pu" is the translated Chinese brand name and appeals to everyone
(Dong and Helms, 2001). "Hui-pu" means "practical and popular," which
implies that HP products are for everyone and not reserved for people of stature.
The chosen brand name in Chinese helps position HP products for all Chinese
and not just select groups.

Procter & Gamble is another company that has successfully positioned its product in the market via its brand name Oil of Olay. Translated in Chinese as "Yu-lan-you" (oil of orchard flower), the product's name suggests that it may be produced from natural elements, like orchids. In addition, the orchid in Chinese culture is a representation of beauty, gentleness, tenderness, and pureness, characteristics often considered in Chinese culture to be associated with a young female. The Chinese brand name chosen for Oil of Olay is a great illustration how the proper brand name can strategically position the product with characteristics of the target group.

Last, brand names may contain characteristics that identify the product's country of origin. Even when the brand name is transferred to a Chinese name, the name itself may give Chinese consumers the impression that the product is "Western."

Typically, when companies pursue a Western brand name strategy, the product will sound similar to the original, but in ideographic cultures, the words used do not have any specific meaning. Hence, the branding strategy chosen influences the impression that the brand name gives. As part of their branding strategy firms need to decide if they want their brand to have a Western or Eastern type of connotation.

Motorola is an example of a company pursuing a Western-type strategy. In Chinese "Mo-tuo-luo-la" means nothing and was originally targeted toward higher educated individuals who may have had previous experience with Motorola in other countries. The initial strategy worked well. However, Motorola underestimated the growing demand for pagers and phones in rural areas of China where entrepreneurs are aiding the increased economic growth of China; the name did nothing to help in these areas. Therefore by pursuing this strategy, Motorola's brand name helped initially but hurt it later on (Dong and Helms, 2001). This illustrates the hazard of following a Western-type strategy.

Head & Shoulders represents a counter example. Head & Shoulders chose to follow an "Eastern" brand name characteristic in China. In China, silky smooth hair is often associated with black silk. Understanding this cultural trait, Head & Shoulders created a Chinese brand name that means "sea with flying silk." Unlike Motorola, Head & Shoulders chose to create an Eastern brand name that was a reflection of the local culture, and, as a result, it faired much better in the overall Chinese market.

DIFFICULTIES IN TRANSLATION

Successfully transferring a brand name is quite difficult. As mentioned earlier, the language must be considered prior to any translation. Moreover, the MNE wishes that the brand name transmits a proper meaning and positive connotation. The difficulties typically associated with transferring a brand name are tone, meaning, word expression, and rhetoric. Each is discussed in more detail below.

Difference in Tone

Word pronunciation can create differences in how people hear the brand name; different sounds create different reactions physiologically. Advertising uses language, onomatopoeic motivation, sound symbolism, and echoism to create a sense of uniformity among the words heard. However, when pronunciation differences exist between Chinese and English, onomatopoeic motivation and rhythm are not easily transferable, creating differences in how people hear words; the tone from one message to the next is not easily transferable, creating discrepancies in meaning between cultures.

Maxwell House Coffee had this problem. China is not known for growing coffee so when Maxwell created a Chinese brand called "Maishi" (meaning the mai family brand), Chinese customers were confused and were not aware of the quality associated with that brand (Dong and Helms, 2001). This illustrates why it is important for the brand meaning to be transferred effectively; otherwise customers will be confused and uninterested in purchasing the brand.

Words mean different things in different cultures. For instance, there exist some interesting examples with car brand names that have been translated into Chinese. Honda "Civic" was translated into "siyu" in Hong Kong, which means "miss a place." This translation was not successful because it is too philosophical and also could mean getting lost. "Civic" was then translated into "ximei" in Taiwan, which means "happiness and beauty"—a much better translation; when Taiwanese people think of "ximei," they think of newlyweds, happy and beautiful, which seems appropriate when thinking about the Civic, an entry-level family car.

Difference in Meaning

A country's language is a means to reflect a country's culture and convey that culture to others. Language contains many country characteristics such as history, cultural background, and people's view of life and way of thinking. When trying to translate the brand to a new country, not only does the direct meaning need to be understood, but the cultural and historical meanings of that country should be understood. Language can then be influential when used in advertising because advertising can then reflect the culture.

Some companies have been successful in transferring brand names. McDonald's Corporation is one such success story; when translated into Chinese, McDonald's is "maidanglao," which sounds very close to its original pronunciation. "Maidanglao" means "danglao"; translated into English this means hardworking, which fits the image of McDonalds's as a fast-food chain. Cadillac has also been successful in transferring its meaning into Chinese. Cadillac was translated into "jiateli," meaning "it's good, special, and pretty"; the translation is a good representation of both meaning and pronunciation.

Difference in Words

Word choice is an important component when transferring a brand name because word preferences differ among countries; words mean different things in different countries. Chinese people prefer words that illustrate long life, good luck, happiness, and other words pertaining to such things. However, according to the American writer Irving Wallace, Americans prefer words like chime, golden, lullaby, melody, and so on. Americans prefer these kinds of words because they look good and sound good. In ideographic countries, such as China, more emphasis is placed on the visual emphasis of the ideographs; how words look is more important than how they sound. Hence, choosing proper words in Chinese to transfer a brand name is important because the meaning of the word in Chinese can be seen just by looking at the word; words that are attractive draw attention and inspire Chinese customers.

Nike, Inc. is one company that chose its word choice carefully. Nike in old Greece means "Victoria," the goddess of victory. If this were translated on pronunciation alone, it would not have any specific meaning, which does not transfer to Chinese customers well because it does not make sense to them. However, Nike was translated into "naike," which sounds similar to the original brand name, but is actually quite different. The two words used to make up the word "naike" mean long lasting, wear resisting, and can always defeat enemies. The transferred Chinese brand name creates inspiration for Chinese to win or be victorious.

Not all companies enjoy success when they first enter the Chinese market. When Procter & Gamble (P&G) first entered the Chinese market, Chinese consumers did not perceive the initials P&G as being Western; P&G was seen as "precious cleanness," where the "p" was considered rude because it stood for intestinal gas. This example illustrates the need for Western firms to be careful with Chinese word choice so potential consumers are not offended and proper meanings are transferred.

Difference in Rhetoric

Rhetoric is used in advertisement and brand naming to make a product more vivid, more specific, and easy for people to remember. However, translation difficulties result because there are differences between Chinese and English traditional rhetoric. In English rhetoric tends to be geared toward the individual and the achievement of personal goals. In China, rhetoric tends to be more philosophical emphasizing harmony and a good life.

Moreover, Chinese are more dependent on information gathered from previous experiences than from seeing a catchy brand name (Li and Shooshtari, 2003). Thus, many Western slogans do not translate well to Chinese culture because the Chinese do not have similar aspirations.

PepsiCo represents an example of one such company that tried to translate its slogan into Chinese but failed in the attempt. At the time, Pepsi's slogan was "come alive with the Pepsi generation." However, when this slogan was translated into Chinese, the meaning was quite different; "come alive with the Pepsi generation" was translated into "Pepsi brings your ancestors back from the grave." This obviously poorly translated slogan had a not surprisingly negative impact on Pepsi's sales.

TRANSLATION SKILLS

Brand names are symbols that reflect quality, product image, and property right of knowledge. Naming a product in a foreign market is very important, and caution should be used when translating a brand name; a well-translated brand name positively impacts a product's global image, whereas a poor translation leads to loss of sales in the local market and a damaged global image.

Translations should not focus only on literal translations, but how words look. From the view of aesthetics, people enjoy rhythm and expect something more when this technique is used. Rhythm in poems, parallelism in articles, and overlapping objects in photographs provide a sense of beauty and are all examples of how to satisfy expectations. Translating a brand name should follow a philosophy that translates the beauty of the brand. Thus, translated words should maintain the brand's aesthetics and meaning. Several methods are discussed below on how this can be accomplished.

Save Syllables

When doing translations, two or three syllables are typically used; two- or three-syllable words are commonly used, but two-syllable words fit Chinese customers' sense of aesthetics. Three-syllable words often come from traditional old China's naming, but two-syllable words create better transferability of brand names. For example, "Pentax" was translated to "binde," "McDonald's" was translated to "maidanglao," "Sprite" was translated to "Xue-bi," and "Aquafresh" was translated to "jishu," all of which represent excellent translated names.

Adding Syllables

Saving syllables may not always fit the global strategies of firms. After initial translation of the main syllables, additional syllables may need to be added to fit the products' characteristics and special meaning; syllables can be added to show product specialty and attract consumers. One such example is "rock," which translated means "gunshi." Other examples include "power" soap, translated to "jie er fu," and "Colgate" translated to "gao lu jie." When additional syllables are added, meanings and tones should remain the same between translated brand names and the original.

Additional Words

Adjusting the number of syllables works best when it matches the strategies of the firm. However, in order to maintain a brand name, different words should be chosen; some instances require the use of words that fit the tone of the brand better. "Ricon" was translated into Chinese as "li guang" and is one such example of a translated brand name where additional words were added to fit the original brand name. Other successful translations with additional words include "Cannon" translated to "jia neng," "Seiko" translated to "jing gong," "Comfort" translated to "jin fang," and "Reebok" translated to "rui bu."

TRANSFERRING BRANDS TO CHINA

Prior marketing studies suggest that differences between the Chinese and English languages may influence a brand name's success. How a brand name sounds (phonemic qualities) influences Americans and Europeans, while for the Chinese how the ideographs look and their meanings are very important and appear to affect the manner in which brand names are recalled or stored in the memory (Schmitt, Pan, and Tavassoli, 1994; Tavassoli, 1999).

A good example of the differences between Western and Chinese cultures is found in the name "Coca-Cola" used to initially enter China. Prior to entering the Chinese market in 1978, The Coca-Cola Company created a brand name based on a phonemic-naming strategy. The product was called "Ke Kou Ke *La*," which was unfortunately associated with the ideographs that meant "bite the wax tadpole."

However, in this instance the firm realized its mistake prior to entering the market. Coca-Cola responded by engaging in examining over 40,000 Chinese characteristics before developing and releasing the new brand name in China. It discovered a phonetic equivalent to the original brand name, "ke kou ke *le*," which means "it tastes good and makes you happy." Coca-Cola marketed this brand name in China and continues to do very well—the number two soft drink in all of China (Wahaha, a Chinese brand, is number one).

DISCUSSION

Based on the above discussions and prior research we conclude that it appears that following three basic principles may result in successful brand transfers in China. Each of the rules is briefly discussed below.

First, the brand name should accurately reflect the "unique selling proposition" or the "basis of sustainable competitive advantage" of the product/brand. For example, the male clothing brand Gold Lion contains a unique selling proposition. "Gold Lion" was first translated according its direct meaning.

However, the brand name needed to be enhanced with rich and powerful boldness to satisfy people who pursue luxury items. The translated brand name went from "Gold Lion" to "LiLai," which means "gold" and "good luck comes." Translating the brand name in that manner allowed the firm to maintain the brand's competitive advantage while providing a unique selling position to its customers. Such a brand name transfer provides greater benefits to a company; the company earns greater profits while providing a brand name in Chinese that sounds more promising and appeals to consumers that prefer goods that represent stature.

Mercedes-Benz also has had success in transferring its stature image to China. In China, "Mercedes" is translated into "Ben Chi," or "dashing speed," and is really a reflection of masculinity. This brand name has done very well by appealing to men of high economic stature.

Not all companies try to appeal to stature; some try to use the translated brand name itself as a sustainable competitive advantage. The name brand Tide was able to provide a unique selling position by creating a Chinese brand name, "Tai-tzi," that means "washing off stains." Tide is effectively demonstrating one of its competitive advantages in its Chinese name: Tai-tzi has the ability to remove stains from laundry. Competitors now must find other ways to try and appeal to customers because the strength of the Tai-tzi name has given the company a competitive advantage in the marketplace.

Second, a successfully transferred brand name has a symbolic as well as a literal meaning: one that induces positive associations between the transferred brand and preferred cultural practices or personal goals. In China it appears that the meaning of the brand name is more important than sounding similar to the American/European sound of the brand name.

However, it is even better to find a combination of sounds that are similar to the Western name that also create a positive meaning for the Chinese customer. One such example of this is the life insurance company Prudential. "Pu Tian Shou," or "long life for everybody under the sky," was selected as its Chinese brand name. The name sounds similar, and the meaning is quite pleasing.

Finally, a successfully transferred brand name should be memorable; it should enter the evoked set with top of the mind recall. One good example is the translation of "Yahoo!," or "beautiful tiger," in Chinese. Appealing to traditional folklore, the tiger allows the brand to become associated with a key element of the culture making it memorable; when the product becomes memorable, consumers are likely to purchase the product more frequently.

CONCLUSION

As firms seek to expand internationally, it has been argued that only the best-managed and strongest brand names will survive (Ourusoff, Ozanian, Brown, and Starr, 1992). A strong brand name enables a company to earn above-average return by creating a loyal consumer following that protects the firm from competitive encroachments on its franchise.

First, a brand name is the foundation of the product, an asset to the company, and an important consumer cue that is critical to the success of a new product (Kohli and LaBahn, 1997; Lubliner, 1993). As firms expand abroad, a key decision that must be made is the degree to which the brand name will be standardized or localized to adapt to the local market conditions.

Linguistic and cultural diversity make it difficult for firms to standardize brand names globally. Firms moving into linguistically different countries should expect to localize their brand names. In such a situation, they are unlikely to be able to transfer the names as they are because the names may not be pronounceable or may have unfortunate or unrelated meanings attached to them, even if they can be pronounced. This is particularly true when transferring brands from Western nations to Asian countries. Language differences are quite fundamental.

Based on the above discussion we suggest that a more proactive strategy should be used when entering foreign markets. When initially developing global brand names, firms should investigate how pronounceable a brand name is in major language groups and whether it carries an appropriate meaning (Trout, 1997).

It may prove beneficial to actually make up a name that has no known meaning but has pleasing connotations. For instance, this is what Toyota did when coming up with its brand name "Lexus." The word has no meaning in any major language, but evokes the Latin root "Lex," which means king or regal. It is an excellent choice for a luxury brand name.

Second, a brand name is more likely to build equity if it accurately reflects the unique selling proposition or the basis of sustainable competitive advantage of the product/brand. Recall our "Gold Lion" example. The brand name Gold Lion contains a unique selling proposition by enhancing its original brand name with a rich and powerful boldness that appealed to people in pursuit of luxury items. The translated brand name "LiLai" (gold and good luck comes) provides a competitive advantage and enhances the benefits (profits) to the company by appealing to customers who prefer goods that represent stature.

Third, particularly when selling in China the brand name is more likely to be effective if it contains a symbolic as well as a literal meaning. The symbolic meaning should evoke positive associations between the product and positive cultural attributes.

Finally, firms will benefit by creating a brand name that can be recalled easily; the transferred brand name will perform better if it is memorable.

Thus, we have provided three strategic brand-naming strategies. First, the brand should contain a unique selling proposition or a basis of sustainable competitive advantage. Second, the brand should carry a symbolic as well as a literal meaning and be recalled easily. Third, a successfully transferred brand name should be memorable; it should enter the evoked set with top of the mind recall. Each of these brand-naming strategies is based on differences between Western and Chinese languages, cultures, and thought processes.

If all three of strategies are followed simultaneously, we suggest that it will result in a very effective transfer of a Western brand to China. In this chapter we have given numerous examples of firms that followed this advice with success or ignored it and suffered poor market outcomes.

We suspect that the three strategies of (1) unique selling proposition, (2) symbolic and literal meanings, and (3) top of the mind, easily recalled names will also work in other ideographic-based societies, like India. However, this notion needs to be rigorously tested. If future research supports our proposed approach to brand transfer, we will have successfully developed a method that will allow West to meet East on the field of international commerce.

REFERENCES

Agrawal, Madhu (1995), "Review of a 40-Year Debate in International Advertising: Practitioner and Academician Perspectives to the Standardization/Adaptation Issue," International Marketing Review, 12 (1), 26–48.

Agres, Stuart J., and Tony M. Dubitsky (1996), "Changing Needs for Brands," Journal of Advertising Research, 36 (1), 21–30.

Alden, Dana L., Jan-Benedict E.M. Steenkamp, and Rajeev Batra (1999), Brand Positioning Through Advertising in Asia, North America, and Europe: The Role of Global Consumer Culture," Journal of Marketing, 63 (1), 75–87.

Caller, L. (1990), "Effective Management in Brand and Advertising Development," Marketing and Research Today, 18 (June), 106–115.

Chan, Allan K.K. (1990), "Localization in International Branding: A Preliminary Investigation on Chinese Names of Foreign Brands in Hong Kong," International Journal of Advertising, 9 (1), 81–91.

Chan, Allan K.K. (1997), "Localization in International Branding: A Longitudinal Comparison of the Chinese Names of Foreign Brands in Hong Kong Between 1987–1988 and 1994–1995," Journal of Marketing Communications, 3 (2), 127–137.

Charmasson, H. (1988), The Name Is the Game—How to Name a Company or Product. Homewood, IL: Dow Jones-Irwin.

Cobb-Walgren, Cathy J., Cynthia A. Ruble, and Naveen Donthu (1995), "Brand Equity, Brand Preference, and Purchase Intent," Journal of Advertising, 24 (3), 25–40.

Collins, L. (1977), "A Name to Conjure With," European Journal of Marketing, 11 (5), 339–363.

de Chernatony, Leslie (1993), "The Seven Building Blocks of Brands," Management Today, (March), 66–68.

Domzal, Teresa J., and Lynette S. Unger (1987), "Emerging Positioning Strategies in Global Marketing," Journal of Consumer Marketing, 4 (4), 23–40.

Dong, Lily C., and Marilyn Helms (2001), "Brand Name Translation Model: A Case Analysis of US Brands in China," Brand Management, 9 (2), 99–115.

Douglas, Susan P., and Yoram Wind (1987), "The Myth of Globalization," Columbia Journal of World Business, 22 (4), 19–29.

Francis, June N.P., Janet P.Y. Lam, and Jan Walls (2002), "Executive Insights: The Impact of Linguistic Differences on International Brand Name Standardization: A Comparison of English and Chinese Brand Names of Fortune-500 Companies," Journal of International Marketing, 10 (1), 98–116.

Gardner, Burleigh B., and Sidney J. Levy (1955), "The Product and the Brand," Harvard Business Review, 33 (2), 33–39.

Halliburton, Chris, and Ratna Bernath (1995), "International Branding: Demand- or Supply-Driven Opportunity?" International Marketing Review, 12 (2), 9–21.

Harvey, Michael G. (1993), "A Model to Determine Standardization of the Advertising Process in International Markets," Journal of Advertising Research, 33 (4), 57–64.

Huang, Yue Yang, and Allan K.K. Chan (1997), "Chinese Brand Naming: From General Principles to Specific Rules," International Journal of Advertising, 16 (4), 320–335.

Jones, John Philip (1986), What's in a Name? Advertising and the Concept of Brands. Lexington, MA: D.C. Heath and Company.

Kanungo, N. (1968), "Effects of Fittingness, Meaningfulness and Product Utility," Journal of Applied Psychology, 52 (2), 290–295.

Kohli, Chiranjeev, and Douglas W. LaBahn (1997), "Creating Effective Brand Names: A Study of the Naming Process," Journal of Advertising Research, 37 (1), 67–75.

Lannon, Judie (1991), "Developing Brand Strategies Across Borders," Marketing and Research Today, 19 (3), 160–168.

Lee, Paul (1995), "Hong Kong to Lose Its Tax Advantages?" International Tax Review, 6 (4), 15–20.

Levitt, Theodore (1983), "The Globalization of Markets," Harvard Business Review, 61 (3), 92–102.

Li, Fengru, and Nader H. Shooshtari (2003), "Brand Naming in China: Sociolinguistic Implications," The Multinational Business Review, 11 (3), 3–21.

Lubliner, Murray J. (1993), "Brand Name Selection Is Critical Challenge for Global Marketers," Marketing News, 27 (16), 7, 11; McDonald, Gael M., and C.J. Roberts (1990), "The Brand-Naming Enigma in the Asia Pacific Context," European Journal of Marketing, 24 (8), 6–19.

Ourusoff, Alexandra, Michael Ozanian, Paul B. Brown, and Jason Starr (1992), "What's in a Name? What the World's Top Brands Are Worth," Financial World, 161 (17), 32–49.

Schmitt, Bernd H., and Yigang Pan (1994), "Managing Corporate and Brand Identities in the Asia-Pacific Region," California Management Review, 36 (4), 32–48.

Schmitt, Bernd H., Yigang Pan, and Nader Tavassoli (1994), "Language and Consumer Memory: The Impact of Linguistic Differences Between Chinese and English," Journal of Consumer Research, 21 (3), 419–431.

Tavassoli, Nader T. (1999), "Temporal and Associative Memory in Chinese and English," Journal of Consumer Research, 26 (2), 170–181.

Trout, Jack (1997), "Minds Work by Ear," in *The New Positioning: The Latest on the World's #1 Business Strategy,* Jack Trout and Steve Rivkin, eds. New York: McGraw-Hill, 101–109.

Zhang, Shi, and Bernd H. Schmitt (2001), "Creating Local Brands in Multilingual International Markets," Journal of Marketing Research, 38, 313–325.

Part III

MANAGING WORLD MARKETS

CHAPTER 7

CULTURE AND INTERNATIONAL MARKETING

Vern Terpstra

What is culture? The simplest definition is that culture is the distinctive way of life of a group or nation of people. A dictionary[1] puts it in more detail. It is "the totality of socially transmitted behavior patterns, arts, beliefs, institutions, and all other products of human work and thought characteristic of a community or population." Culture is also learned behavior. It depends on the environment, not heredity; it is not biologically transmitted.

In other words, culture is a very complex phenomenon and a challenge to firms that wish to market internationally (interculturally). How does the firm's product or service fit in with the foreign market's culture? How must it be adapted to fit? Every firm must make its own adjustment and adaptation to satisfy foreign customers. We look at various dimensions of culture and their significance for international marketing. A very simple illustration of cultural differences was used by Hong Kong Shanghai Bank in advertising on an international airport poster. It showed an image of a grasshopper and the following message:

USA—Pest

China—Pet

Northern Thailand—Appetizer

LANGUAGE

Language is the most obvious difference between cultures. Inextricably linked with all other aspects of a culture, language reflects the nature and values of that culture. For example, the English language has a rich vocabulary for commercial and industrial activities, reflecting the progressive nature of the English and U.S. societies. Many less industrialized societies have only limited vocabularies for those activities, but richer vocabularies for matters important to their cultures.

For example, Eskimo has many words to describe snow, whereas English has one general term. This is reasonable because the differences in forms of snow play a vital role in the lives of Eskimos. The kinds of activities they can engage in depend on the specific snow conditions. Of course, in the United States, the subculture of skiers has a richer vocabulary for snow than that of nonskiers.

Because language is such an obvious cultural difference, everyone recognizes that it must be dealt with. It is said that anyone planning a career in international business should learn a foreign language. Certainly, if a person's career involves dealing with a particular country, he or she will find learning the country's language to be very useful. Because it is usually impossible to predict to which countries a career will lead, it is best to study a language spoken by many people (for example, Mandarin Chinese) or a language that is commonly used as a first or second language in many nations (for example, English, French, or Spanish). Whether or not it is a primary language of the parties involved, English is frequently used in negotiations, legal documents, and business transactions.

This does not mean, however, that American firms can bask in their knowledge and use of English. Language still provides a challenge to international marketing. Frequently, translation will be needed, and translation can be expensive. The World Trade Organization spends over one-fifth of its budget translating its documents. The European Union (EU) spends over $1 billion for translators and interpreters, and that is just for EU members, not the rest of the world.

It is said that a language defines a cultural group, that nothing distinguishes one culture from another more than language. What does it mean, though, when the same language is used in different countries? French, for example, is the mother tongue not only for the French, but also for many Belgians and Swiss. Spanish plays a similar role in Latin America. The anthropologist, however, stresses the spoken language as the cultural distinction. The spoken language changes more quickly than the written language and reflects the culture more directly. Although England, the United States, and Ireland use the same written English, they speak somewhat different dialects. These three cultures are separate yet related, as are the Spanish-speaking cultures of Latin America.

Even where a common language is spoken, different words signifying the same meaning are occasionally used, as are different pronunciations. In England, people say "lorry," "petrol," and "biscuits"; in the United States, people say "truck," "gasoline," and "cookies." Incidentally, even within one country—for example, the United States, where almost everyone speaks "American" English—there are different cultural groups, or subcultures, among which the spoken language varies.

Language as a Problem

Activities such as advertising, branding, packaging, personal selling, and marketing research are highly dependent upon communication. If management is not speaking the same language as its various audiences, it is not going to enjoy much success. In each of its foreign markets, a company must communicate with several audiences: its workers, its managers, its customers, its suppliers, and the government. Each of these audiences may have a distinctive communication style within the common language.

A Japanese company provides an example of dealing with the language problem. If an employee wants to be promoted at Matsushita Corporation (the makers of Panasonic and other global brands), he or she must pass a proficiency test in English. Toyota Motor Corporation, Komatsu Ltd. (earth-moving equipment), and NCE (computers) have also tied promotions to English-speaking abilities. The reason for this is explained by the director of human resources for Matsushita: "Japanese are insulated by their language and do not have a global mentality because of this language barrier."

Language diversity in world markets could be an insurmountable problem if managers had to master the languages of all their markets. Fortunately, that is not the case. To be effective, any person assigned to a foreign operation for a period of a year or more should learn the local language. However, cultural bridges are available in many markets. For example, in countries where a firm is operating through a distributor, the distributor may act as the bridge between the firm and its local market. In advertising, a firm may be able to rely on a local advertising agency. Agency personnel, like the distributor, probably speak the advertising manager's language—especially if the firm communicates principally in English. For example, the Dutch firm Royal Philips Electronics uses English as the official company language even though it is domiciled in the Netherlands. Because of its widespread operations, the company finds English to be the most useful language for its markets. Furthermore, in the Chrysler/Daimler-Benz merger, American English was made the corporate language.

SOCIAL ORGANIZATION

The social organization of a group of people helps define their roles and the expectations they place upon themselves and others in the group. Concepts such as family vary from group to group, which becomes evident when talking about these concepts to people from other cultures. The nature of people's friendships with others—how quickly the relationships develop, how the friendships are nurtured, and how long they last—also reflect on the social organization within the culture or group. Social organization is formally defined in the government and the laws that proscribe certain behavior among people. The nature of social organization and the impact on business is discussed next.

Kinship

Kinship includes the social organization or structure of a group: the way people relate to other people. This differs somewhat from society to society. The primary kind of social organization is based on kinship. In the United States, the key unit is the family, which traditionally included only the father, the mother, and the unmarried children in the household. Of course, the definition is changing, as is reflected in each census. The family unit elsewhere is often larger, including more relatives. A large, extended family is common in many less-developed nations. Those who call themselves brothers in Congo, for example, include cousins and uncles.

In developing countries, the extended family fulfills several social and economic roles. The family unit is not prescribed or defined by a specific religious restriction, as does the *baradari* of Hinduism. The extended family provides mutual protection, psychological support, and economic insurance or social security for its members. In a world of tribal warfare and primitive agriculture, this support was invaluable. The extended family, still significant in many parts of the world, means that consumption decision making takes place in a larger unit and in different ways. Pooled resources, for instance, may allow larger purchases; for this reason, per capita income may be a misleading guide of market potential. The researcher may find it difficult to determine the relevant consuming unit for some goods. Is it a household or a family? How many members are there?

The size of households varies greatly around the world. The United States and other first-world countries generally have three or fewer occupants per household on average, whereas many poorer countries, such as India and Pakistan, have six or more.

Common Territory

In the United States, common territory can be a neighborhood, a suburb, or a city. In many countries of Asia and Africa, common territory is the tribal grouping. In many countries, the tribe is often the largest effective unit because the various tribes do not voluntarily recognize the central government. Unfortunately, nationalism has not generally replaced tribalism. Tribalism and religious or ethnic divisions often lead to bloody conflict, as in Congo, Ireland, Israel and Palestine, Pakistan, the Philippines, Rwanda, and Sudan. Even in Europe, the Scots and the Welsh are not happy about being under British rule. For businesses, in many countries, groupings based on common territory may be a clue to market segmentation.

Special Interest Group

A third kind of social grouping, the special interest group or association, may be religious, occupational, recreational, or political. Special interest groups can also be useful in identifying different market segments. For example, in the United States, the American Association of Retired Persons, the Sierra Club, and the National Rifle Association represent market segments for some firms.

Teens—The New Global Consumers?

The finding of many cross-cultural studies are that young people, because of their exposure to new ideas and to one another through television and the Internet, as well as their willingness to take risks and try new things, are similar in those respects that are not confined to a particular geographic area or culture. That is, certain characteristics, beliefs, attitudes, and behaviors are common to teenagers around the world; and because of that fact, firms can get teenagers' attention in similar ways.

Look in teens' bedrooms in cities around the world: Des Moines, Los Angeles, Jakarta, Mexico City, Paris, Santiago, Singapore, and Tokyo. You will find an amazing similarity of items: Nikes and Reeboks, Levis, MP3 players, PCs, and NBA jackets. Teens everywhere watch MTV and the World Cup, and most of them shop in malls that look amazingly alike.

These are promising developments for international firms making consumer goods. Caution is necessary, however, before firms implement a one-size-fits-all strategy. Many seasoned observers note that cultural differences persist. For example, one survey found that American teenagers prefer to eat on the run, while teens elsewhere prefer meals they can savor. The same survey showed that American teenagers use fewer features on their cell phones than their European and Japanese counterparts. So despite similarities among teenagers around the world, firms are unable to use identical practices to reach teenagers in all markets.

Other Kinds of Social Organization

Some kinds of social organization cut across the categories just discussed. One is the caste system or class groupings. These may be detailed and rigid, as in the Hindu caste system; or they may be loose and flexible, as in U.S. social classes. The United States has a relatively open society, but there is still concern about social standing and status symbols. While social class is more (or less) important and rigid in comparing countries, each country has its own social and ethnic groupings that are important for its society and the economy. These groupings usually mean that some groups are discriminated against and others are favored. Different groups may require different marketing strategies.

Other groupings based on age occur especially in affluent industrialized nations. For example, senior citizens usually live as a separate economic unit with their own needs and motivations. Age groupings are a major market segment in industrialized countries. As noted in the discussion of the extended family, much less separation between age groups exists in less-developed areas. Generally, strong family integration occurs at all age levels, as well as a preponderant influence of age and seniority, which is in contrast to the youth motif prevalent in the United States. Of course, Generation X and Baby Boomers are important age groupings in the United States.

A final aspect of social organization concerns the role of women in the economy. Women seldom enjoy parity with men as participants in the economy, and their participation is related to the economic development of nations—the poorer the nation, the fewer women are seen in jobs outside the home. The extent to which women participate in the money economy affects their role as consumers and consumption influencers. Even developed countries exhibit differences in attitudes toward female employment.

For example, significant differences in female employment exist among the United States, several European countries, and Japan. These differences are reflected both in household income levels and in consumption patterns. In spite of the constraints noted, the economic role of women is undergoing notable change in many countries. Many believe this change is occurring too slowly, however.

TECHNOLOGY AND MATERIAL CULTURE

Material culture includes the tools and artifacts—the material or physical things—in a society, excluding those physical things found in nature unless they undergo some technological transformation. For example, a tree as such is not part of a culture, but the Christmas tree is. Technology refers to the techniques or methods of making and using that which surrounds us. Technology and material culture are related to the way a society organizes its economic activities. The term "technology gap" refers to differences in the ability of two societies to create, design, and use that which exists in nature or to use that which has been transformed in some way.

When referring to industrialized nations, developing nations, the nuclear age, or the space age, one is referring to different technologies and material cultures. One can also speak of societies being in the age of the automobile, the bicycle, or foot transportation—or in the age of the computer, the abacus, or pencil-and-paper calculation. The relationships between technology, material culture, and the other aspects of life are profound, but not easily recognized because people are the products of their own culture. It is primarily as people travel abroad that they perceive such relationships.

When discussing this topic, Karl Marx went so far as to say that the economic organization of a society shapes and determines its political, legal, and social organization. His view was termed "economic determinism," his materialist interpretation of history. Few people today would take such a strong position, but they may recognize many examples of the impact of tools, techniques, and economic organization on the nature of life in society. For example, people's behavior as workers and consumers is greatly influenced by the technology and material culture.

The way people work and how effectively they work is determined in large part by their technology and material culture. Henry Ford's assembly line revolutionized U.S. productivity and, ultimately, the standard of living. The U.S. farmers' use of equipment and technology has made them the world's most productive agriculturalists. Ironically, agriculture is one of the most capital- and technology-intensive industries in the United States. The farmer does not do the research and development, however, but land-grant universities, equipment manufacturers, and chemical companies do. The computer, as one of the newer artifacts, affects the way people work, the kind of work they can do, and even where they work. If you consider the nature of the factory and agricultural methods and the role of the computer in an African nation, you can see technology and material culture as a constraint on work and productivity in a culture.

One of the most striking examples of the potential impact of technology is India. In the 20th century, India was almost a third-world country. In the 21st century, India is a world leader in computer and information technology and sells its services to the United States and other first-world countries. Most of the world's poorest countries are not able to imitate India's success, but technology can help them also.

In 2005, the United Nations launched a "Digital Solidarity Fund" to finance projects that address "the uneven distribution and use of new information and communication technologies" and that will "enable excluded people and countries to enter the new era of the information society."

One of the simpler new technologies, the mobile phone, is having the greatest impact on economic development. The world's poorest are rushing to embrace mobile phones because of their benefits. They can be used by illiterates and do not depend on a permanent electricity supply. They are shared and rented out by the call. Farmers and small businesses can shop around for the best place for supplies and equipment, as well as the market with the best price for their products, reducing the need for travel.[2]

How people consume and what people consume are also heavily influenced by the technology and material culture. For example, the car has helped to create the conditions that made suburban living possible, with the accompanying lifestyle and consumption patterns. Television has a wide-ranging impact on consumer and voter behavior. The microwave oven influences not only the preparation of food, but also the nature of the food consumed. Considering artifacts such as the digital camera and the cellular telephone, one can imagine further ramifications of each new project on the life of the consumer. Knowing the impact of these products in the U.S. culture, one can conjecture how consumer behavior might be different in countries with much lighter penetration of such products.

Material Culture as a Constraint

Managers need to develop insight into how material culture in foreign markets affects their operations abroad. In manufacturing, foreign production by a firm may represent an attempt to introduce a new material culture into the host economy. This is usually the case when a firm builds a plant in a less-developed country. The firm generally checks carefully on the necessary economic prerequisites for such a plant: for example, raw-material supply, power, transportation, and financing. Frequently overlooked, however, are the other cultural preconditions for the plant.

Before making foreign production decisions, a firm must evaluate the material culture in the host country. One aspect is the economic infrastructure—that is, transportation, power, and communications. Other questions are these: Do production processes need to be adapted to fit the local economy? Will the plant be more labor-intensive than plants at home? The manager discovers that production of the same goods may require a different production function in different countries.

In large diversified markets such as the United States, almost any industrialized product can find a market. In developing nations, however, firms that make industrial goods find increasingly limited markets in which they can sell only part, or perhaps none, of their product line. The better the picture of the material culture in world markets, the more able a firm is to identify the best prospects. The prospects in countries where the principal agricultural implement is the machete differ from those in countries where farmers use tractors.

Firms that manufacture consumer goods are also concerned with the material culture in foreign markets. Simple considerations such as electrical voltages and use of the metric system must be taken into account. Product adaptations may also be necessitated by the material culture of the family unit. Does the family have a car to transport purchases? Does the family have a stove to prepare foods or a refrigerator in which to store foods? If electrical power is not available, electrical appliances will not be marketable unless they are battery powered. To those people who wash clothes by a stream or lake, detergents and packaged soaps are not useful; the market is for bar soaps only.

Large multinational companies are learning from entrepreneurs in developing countries that the key to success in markets where income is low is to sell products that come in small sizes, are relatively cheap, and are easy to use. Unilever packages its shampoo in single-use sizes, selling it for a few cents in India. Other examples include 3-inch square packages of margarine in Nigeria that do not need refrigeration and an 8¢ tube of Close-Up with enough toothpaste for about 20 brushings. Unilever expects that developing markets will account for 50 percent of all sales by 2010, up from 32 percent in 2005. Freeplay Energy in London designed and sold 3 million hand-crank radios. Since many people in developing countries have no electricity and cannot afford to purchase batteries, these units are popular for listening to farm and health reports. Philips of the Netherlands has developed its own version, which the firm is now selling in India for around $20. Indian firms located in Madras and Bangalore are developing wireless kiosks that allow users to access the Internet for as little as 3¢ an hour and computers with voice recognition software, which is aimed at users who cannot read.

Marketing strategy is influenced by the material culture. For instance, the promotional program is constrained by the kinds of media available. The advertiser wants to know the availability of television, radio, magazines, and newspapers. How good is the reproduction process in newspapers and magazines? Are there advertising and research agencies to support the advertising program? The size of retail outlets affects the use of point-of-purchase displays. The nature of travel and the highway system affects the use of outdoor advertising.

Modification in distribution may also be necessary. These changes must be made based on the alternatives offered by the country's commercial infrastructure. What wholesale and retail patterns exist? What warehouse or storage facilities are available? Is refrigerated storage possible? What is the nature of the transport system—road, rail, river, or air? What area does it cover? Firms that use direct channels in the United States, with large-scale retailers and chain-store operations, may have to use indirect channels with a multitude of small, independent retailers. These small retailers may be relatively inaccessible if they are widely dispersed and transportation is inadequate.

If local storage facilities are insufficient, a firm may have to supply its own packaging or provide special packaging to offer extra protection. Whereas highways and railroads are most important in moving goods in the United States, river transport is a major means in other countries. And in still other countries, air is the principal means of transport. Thus, in numerous ways, management is concerned with the material culture in foreign markets.

Perhaps the subtlest role of international business is that of the agent of cultural change. When a firm introduces new products into a market, it is, in effect, seeking to change the country's material culture. The change may be modest, such as a new food product, or it may be more dramatic, such as a machine that revolutionizes agriculture or industrial technology in the host country. The product of the international firm is alien in the sense that it did not originate in the host country. The firm must consider carefully the legitimacy of its role as an agent of change. It must be sure that any changes it introduces are in accordance with the interests of the host country. When the product is coming from a developed nation and sold in developing countries without modification, people may resent the firm's product as a form of "neocolonialism," "Westernization," or "imperialism." Along this line, someone coined the term "cocoa colonization" concerning U.S. cocoa business abroad.

EDUCATION

In developed nations, education usually means formal training in school. In this sense, those people without access to schools are not educated; that is, they have never been to school. However, this formal definition is too restrictive. Education includes the process of transmitting skills, ideas, and attitudes, as well as training, in particular disciplines. Even so-called "primitive" peoples have been educated in this broader sense. For example, regardless of formal schooling, the Bushmen of South Africa are well educated in relation to the culture in which they live.

One function of education is to transmit the existing culture and traditions to the new generation. Education plays an important role in cultural change in the United States, as it does elsewhere. For example, in the past, developing nations' educational campaigns were carried out with the specific intent of improving techniques used in farming and in reducing the population explosion. In Britain, business schools were originally established to improve the performance of the economy. Some attribute the rapid economic development of Singapore to formal apprenticeship programs.

International Differences in Education

When looking at education in foreign markets, the observer is limited primarily to information about the formal process, that is, education in schools. This is the only area for which the United Nations Educational, Scientific and Cultural Organization (UNESCO), the World Bank, and others have been able to gather data. Traditionally, literacy rates have been used to describe educational achievement; recently, however, international agencies have been measuring inputs as well as educational system outputs other than literacy. For example, the World Bank still includes adult and youth illiteracy rates in its reports. Now it has begun measuring participation in education, which includes enrollment ratios in primary, secondary, and tertiary levels of education, and educational efficiency, which includes completion rates at different levels of education and average number of years in school. In addition, the World Bank also reports on inputs such as expenditures per student, teachers' compensation, number of faculty with appropriate qualifications, and pupil-teacher ratios. Perhaps most importantly, the goals of the World Bank have changed from activities aimed merely at increasing literacy rates to measures designed to ensure that "all children complete a full course of primary education," a target it hopes is achieved by 2015. (See Table 7.1.)

The education information available on world markets refers primarily to national enrollments in the various levels of education—primary, secondary, and college or university. This information can give an international marketer insight into the sophistication of consumers in different countries. There is also a strong correlation between educational attainment and economic development.

One could argue that qualitative measures such as math and science scores on international achievement tests should also be used as indicators of human capital development and long-term economic prospects. Because U.S. students consistently score lower on these exams than students in other countries, some fear that the United States may lose its technological edge in the future.

Because only quantitative data are available, there is a danger that the qualitative aspects of education might be overlooked. Furthermore, in addition to the limitations inherent in international statistics, the problem exists of interpreting them in terms of business needs. For example, a firm's needs for technicians, marketing personnel, managers, distributors, and sales forces must be met largely from the educated population in the local economy. When hiring people, the firm is concerned not only with the level, but also with the nature of the applicants' education.

Training in law, literature, or political science is probably not the most suitable education for business needs. Yet in many nations, such studies are emphasized almost to the exclusion of others more relevant to commercial and economic growth. Too often, primary education is preparation for secondary, secondary

Table 7.1
World Education

Country by Income Group	Primary School Teacher-Pupil Ratio	Secondary School Enrollment	Adult Literacy Rate (%)	
			Male	Female
Low Income	40	46	72	53
Lower Middle Income	22	75	92	82
Upper Middle Income	21	81	95	92
High Income	17	100	99	99
World Average	28	70	84	71

Sources: World Bank, 2004 World Development Indicators; Table 2.10 Education inputs, pp. 72–75; Table 2.1 Participation in Education, pp. 76–79; Table 2.13 Education Outcomes, pp. 84–87, UNESCO, Institute for Statistics, July 2004.

education is preparation for university, and university education is not designed to meet the needs of the economy. In many nations, university education is largely preparation for the traditional prestige occupations. Although a nation needs lawyers and philosophers, it also needs agricultural experts, engineers, managers, and technicians. The degree to which the educational system provides for these needs is a critical determinant of the nation's ability to develop economically.

Education and International Marketing

The international marketer must also be something of an educator. The products and techniques a firm brings into a market are generally new to that market. The firm must educate consumers about the uses and benefits. Although a firm may not make use of a formal educational system, its success is constrained by that system because its ability to communicate depends in part on the educational level of its market. An international marketer is further concerned about the educational situation because it is a key determinant of the nature of the consumer market and the kinds of marketing personnel available. Some implications for businesses include the following:

- When consumers are largely illiterate, existing advertising programs, package labels, instructions, and warranties need to be adapted to include fewer words and more graphics and pictures.

- When women are largely excluded from formal education, marketing programs may differ from those aimed at female segments in developed nations. When a firm is targeting women audiences with less education, messages need to be simple, perhaps with less text and more graphics.

- Conducting marketing research can be difficult, both in communicating with consumers and in getting qualified researchers. If few people are able to read, written surveys would be an ineffective tool in gathering data. Personal interviews, although more costly, would tend to increase response rates and accuracy.

- Cooperation from the distribution channels depends partly on the educational attainments of members in the channel. When overall levels of education are low, finding local qualified marketing employees for certain service or managerial positions may be difficult and very competitive. Long-term training programs and commitments to employee education may raise local operating costs.

RELIGION

If you are to gain a full understanding of a culture, you must become familiar with the internal behavior that gives rise to the external manifestations. Generally, it is the religion of a culture that provides the best insights into this behavior. Therefore, although an international company is interested primarily in knowing *how* people behave as consumers or workers, management's task will be aided by an understanding of *why* people behave as they do.

Numerous religions exist in the world. This section presents brief overviews of animism, Hinduism, Buddhism, Islam, Shintoism, Confucianism, and Christianity. These religions were selected based on their importance in terms of numbers of adherents and their impact on the economic behavior of their followers. Adherents to these religious beliefs account for over three-fourths of the world's population. The animists alone have a reported number of adherents varying from 100 to 245 million.

Animism or Nonliterate Religion

"Animism" is the term used to describe the religion of indigenous peoples. It is often defined as spirit worship, as distinguished from the worship of God or gods. Animistic beliefs have been found in all parts of the world. With the exception of revealed religion, some form of animism has preceded all historical religions. In many less-developed parts of the world today, animistic ideas affect cognitive behavior.

Magic, a key element of animism, is the attempt to achieve results through the manipulation of the spirit world. It represents an unscientific approach to the physical world. When cause-and-effect relationships are not known, magic is given credit for the results. The same attitude prevails toward many modern-day products and techniques.

For example, during the author's years in Congo, he had an opportunity to see reactions to European products and practices that were often based on a magical interpretation. In one instance, a number of Africans affected the wearing of glasses, believing the glasses would enhance the intelligence of the wearer. Some firms that manufacture consumer goods in Africa have not hesitated to imply that their products have magical qualities. Of course, the same is sometimes true of firms elsewhere.

Other aspects of animism include ancestor worship, taboos, and fatalism. All of them tend to promote a traditionalist, status quo, backward-looking society. Because such societies are more interested in protecting their traditions than in accepting change, companies face problems when introducing new products, ideas, or methods. A firm's success in bringing change depends on how well it understands and relates to the culture and its animistic foundation.

Hinduism

There are over 900 million Hindus in the world, most of them in India. In a broad sense, about 80 percent of India's population is Hindu; but in the sense of strict adherence to the tenets of Hinduism, the number of followers is smaller.

A common dictum is that Hinduism is not a religion, but a way of life. Its origins go back approximately 3,500 years. It is an ethnic, noncreedal religion. A Hindu is born, not made, so a person cannot become a Hindu or convert to Hinduism, although he or she may become a Buddhist, for example. Modern Hinduism is a combination of ancient philosophies and customs, animistic beliefs, legends, and, more recently, Western influences, including Christianity. A strength of Hinduism has been its ability to absorb ideas from outside; Hinduism tends to assimilate rather than exclude.

Despite this openness, many in India are unhappy about marriages between Christians or Muslims and Hindus because it is viewed as a threat or dilution of Hindutva (Hindu-ness) of the culture. Much violence has occurred between the Hindu and Muslim populations: in one instance over 500 people were killed in Gujarat in early 2002. Because Hinduism is an ethnic religion, many of its doctrines apply only to the Indian situation. However, they are crucial in understanding India and its people.

Sikhism is a religion also practiced in India that represents a combined form of Hinduism and Islam, featuring a much-debated aspect, the caste system. While the Indian government officially abolished it over a half century ago and instituted quotas and job-preferment policies, there are still examples of separate *gurdwarars* (houses of worship) for Sikhs and the *Dalit,* or scheduled caste (formerly called "untouchables"), some of whom are converting to Buddhism, Christianity, and Islam to escape the caste system.

Another element and strength of Hinduism is *baradari,* or the "joint family." After marriage, the bride goes to the groom's home. After several marriages in the family, there is a large joint family for which the father or grandfather is chief authority. In turn, the older women have power over the younger. The elders give advice and consent in family council. The Indian grows up thinking and acting in terms of the joint family. If a member goes abroad to a university, the joint family may raise the funds. In turn, that member is expected to remember the family if he or she is successful. *Baradari* is aimed at preserving the family.

Nirvana is another important concept, one that Hinduism shares with Buddhism. This topic is discussed in the following section.

Buddhism

Buddhism springs from Hinduism, originating about 2,600 years ago. Buddhism has approximately 360 million followers, mostly in South and East Asia from India to Japan. There are, however, small Buddhist societies in Europe and America. Buddhism is, to some extent, a reformation of Hinduism. It did not abolish caste, but declared that Buddhists were released from caste restrictions. This openness to all classes and both sexes was one reason for Buddhism's growth. While accepting the philosophical insights of Hinduism,

Buddhism tried to avoid its dogma and ceremony, stressing tolerance and spiritual equality.

At the heart of Buddhism are the Four Noble Truths:

1. The Noble Truth of Suffering states that suffering is omnipresent and part of the very nature of life.

2. The Noble Truth of the Cause of Suffering cites the cause of suffering to be desire, that is, the desire for possessions and selfish enjoyment of any kind.

3. The Noble Truth of the Cessation of Suffering states that suffering ceases when desire ceases.

4. The Noble Truth of the Eightfold Path that leads to the Cessation of Suffering offers the means to achieve cessation of desire. This is also known as the Middle Way because it avoids the two extremes of self-indulgence and self-mortification. The eightfold path includes (1) the right views, (2) the right desires, (3) the right speech, (4) the right conduct, (5) the right occupation, (6) the right effort, (7) the right aware-ness, and (8) the right contemplation. This path, though simple to state, is a demand-ing ethical system. Nirvana is the reward for those who are able to stay on the path throughout their lifetime or, more probably, lifetimes.

Nirvana is the ultimate goal of the Hindu and the Buddhist. It represents the extinction of all cravings and the final release from suffering. To the extent that such an ideal reflects the thinking of the mass of the people, the society's values would be considered antithetical to such goals as acquisition, achievement, and affluence. This is an obvious constraint on business.

Islam

Islam dates from the 7th century A.D. It has over 900 million adherents, mostly in Africa, Asia, and the Middle East. Most of the world of Islam is found across the northern half of Africa, the Middle East, and throughout parts of Asia to the Philippines. Islam is usually associated with Arabs and the Middle East, but non-Arab Muslims outnumber Arab Muslims by almost three to one. The nations with the largest Muslim populations are all outside the Middle East. Indonesia, Pakistan, Bangladesh, and India all have over 100 million Muslims. Although there are two major groups in Islam (Sunni, 85 percent; Shi'ite, 15 percent), they are similar enough on economic issues to permit identification of the following elements of interest to firms.

Muslim theology, *Tawhid,* defines all that one should believe; whereas the law, *Shari'a,* prescribes everything one should do. The *Koran (Qur'an)* is accepted as the ultimate guide. Anything not mentioned in the *Koran* is likely to be rejected by the faithful. Introducing new products and techniques can be difficult in such an environment (see Table 7.2). An important element of the Muslim belief is that everything that happens, good or evil, proceeds directly from the Divine Will

Table 7.2
Islam and Marketing

Islamic Element	Marketing Implication
1. Daily prayers	Work schedules; hours of peak/off-peak customer traffic; timing of sales calls
2. Prohibition on usury and consumption of pork and alcohol	Prohibition of or difficulty in selling certain products (insurance, banking, and financial services); processes used in manufacturing of food and other products for human consumption or use; inappropriateness of layaway and other credit tools
3. Zakat (mandatory alms)	Spending patterns; attitudes toward charity; social consciousness; excessive profits used for charitable purposes
4. Religious holidays (for example, Ramadan) and other religious or sacred periods	Sales and special promotions; lavish gift periods' food distribution and restaurant hours; Muslim "weekend" is Thursday and Friday
5. Public separation of sexes	Access to female customers; direct marketing to women's mixed-gender focus groups

and is already irrevocably recorded on the Preserved Tablet. This belief tends to restrict attempts to bring about change in Muslim countries; to attempt change may be a rejection of what Allah has ordained. The name *Islam* is the infinitive of the Arabic verb to *submit*. *Muslim* is the present participle of the same verb; that is, a Muslim is one submitting to the will of Allah.

The Five Pillars of Islam

The Five Pillars of Islam, or the duties of a Muslim, include (1) the recital of the creed, (2) prayer, (3) fasting, (4) almsgiving, and (5) the pilgrimage. The creed is brief: There is no God but Allah, and Mohammed is his Prophet. The Muslim must pray five times daily at stated hours. During the month of Ramadan, Muslims are required to fast from dawn to sunset—no food, no drinking, and no smoking. Because the Muslim year is lunar, Ramadan sometimes falls in midsummer, when the long days and intense heat make abstinence a severe test. The fast is meant to develop self-control and sympathy for the poor. During Ramadan, work output falls off markedly, which is attributable as much to the Muslim's loss of sleep (from the many late-night feasts and celebrations—as to the rigors of fasting. The average family actually spends more money on the food consumed at night during Ramadan than on the food consumed by day in the other months. Other spending rises also. Spending during Ramadan has been said to equal six months of normal spending, corresponding to the Christmas season elsewhere. Sales increases of 20 to 40 percent of furniture, cars, jewelry, and other large or expensive items are common. One firm stated that between 35 and 40 percent of all auto sales take place during Ramadan.

By almsgiving, the Muslim shares with the poor. It is an individual responsibility, and there are both required alms (*zakat*) and freewill gifts. The pilgrimage to Mecca is a well-known aspect of Islam. The thousands who gather in Mecca each year return home with a greater sense of the international solidarity of Islam. Spending for the pilgrimage is a special form of consumption directly associated with religious behavior.

There is a relationship between culture and law. Behavior deemed acceptable or not acceptable is often reflected in the laws of a nation or group of people. The tie between religion and law is perhaps most clear in Islam. With respect to business, Muslims are not allowed to consume pork or alcohol. Furthermore, people are not allowed to invest in firms whose primary business involves alcohol, defense, entertainment, gambling, or the manufacture of or processes using pork products. Under shari'a law, investors are not allowed to hold any stake in conventional banks or insurance companies because these institutions are believed to engage in usurious practices that are illegal. Even the ability to own stock or shares in companies with large amounts of debt or that make annual interest payments is being called into question. While there is some tolerance for investing in these companies, devout Muslims point out that this is a breach of shari'a rules against usury.

Japan: Shinto, Buddhism, and Confucianism

Japan is a homogeneous culture with a composite religious tradition. The original national religion is Shinto, "the way of the gods." In the 7th century, however, Japan came under the influence of China and imported an eclectic Buddhism mingled with Confucianism. In 604, Prince Shotoku issued a moral code based on the teachings of both Confucius and Gautama Buddha. Its 17 articles still form the basis of Japanese behavior. The adoption of the religions from China was only after the authorities decided they would not conflict with Shinto.

Traditional Shinto contains elements of ancestor and nature worship; state or modern Shinto added political and patriotic elements. Official estimates of 90 million Japanese Buddhists are somewhat misleading. An old refrain is that Japanese are born Shinto, get married as Christians, and die as Buddhists. Figures on followers of Buddhism in Japan vary widely, from 20 to 90 percent of the Japanese population. (The high figures are based on birth records and on Buddhism being the "preferred religion" in a response to research questions posed; the low figures incorporate the response of up to 75 percent of Japanese who claim to be nonreligious.)

Among the more important aspects of modern Shinto are (1) reverence for the divine origin of the Japanese people and (2) reverence for the Japanese nation and the imperial family as head of that nation. The term "modern Shinto" is used because when the imperial powers were restored in 1868, state Shinto became a patriotic cult, whereas sectarian Shinto was purely religious. Of course, sectarian Shinto, through ancestor worship, also affects Japanese attitudes. In many houses, there is a god-shelf (*kamidana*) on which the spirits of the family ancestors are thought to dwell and watch over the affairs of the family. Reverence is paid to them, and the sense of the ancestors' spirits is a bulwark of the family's authority over the individual.

The impact of modern Shinto on Japanese life is reflected in an aggressive patriotism. The mobilization of the Japanese in World War II and their behavior during the war are examples. One longtime observer said, "Nationalism is the Japanese religion." More recently, the economic performance of Japan is due, at least in part, to the patriotic attitude of those working in the economic enterprise. The family spirit is carried over to the firm, which has meant greater cooperation and productivity. Some Eastern religions seek virtue through passivity. Shinto, by contrast, stresses the search for progress through creative activity. Japan's economic performance clearly seems to follow the Shinto path. The aggressive Japanese attitude is reflected in the company song of Kyocera, a Japanese firm.

As the sun rises brilliantly in the sky, revealing the size of the mountains, The market, oh, this is our goal.

With the highest degree of mission in our heart, we serve our industry,

Meeting the strictest degree of customer requirement.

We are the leader in this industry, and our true path

Is ever so bright and satisfying.

Christianity

Christianity is a major religion worldwide, and little time will be spent describing its general teachings. The emphasis here is the impact of the different Christian religious groups (Roman Catholic and Protestant) on economic attitudes and behavior. Two studies have dealt with this subject: Max Weber's *The Protestant Ethic and the Spirit of Capitalism* and R.H. Tawney's *Religion and the Rise of Capitalism*. The Eastern Orthodox churches are not discussed, but their impact on economic attitudes is similar to that of Catholicism.

Roman Catholic Christianity traditionally has emphasized the Church and the sacraments as the principal elements of religion and the way to God. The Church and its priests are intermediaries between God and human beings; apart from the Church, there is no salvation. Another element is the distinction between the members of religious orders and the laity, with different standards of conduct applied to each. An implicit difference exists between the secular and the religious life.

The Protestant Reformation, especially Calvinism, made some critical changes in emphasis, but retained agreement with Catholicism on most traditional Christian doctrine. The Protestants, however, stressed that the Church, its sacraments, and its clergy were not essential to salvation: "Salvation is by faith alone." The result of this was a downgrading of the role of the Church and a consequent upgrading of the role of the individual. Salvation became more of an individual matter.

Another change by the reformers was the elimination of the distinction between secular and religious life. Luther said that all of life was a *Beruf,* a "calling," and even the performance of tasks considered secular was a religious obligation. Calvin carried this further by emphasizing the need to glorify God through one's calling. Whereas works were necessary to salvation in Catholicism, works were evidence of salvation in Calvinism.

Hard work was enjoined to glorify God, achievement was the evidence of hard work, and thrift was necessary because the produced wealth was not to be used selfishly. Accumulation of wealth, capital formation, and the desire for greater production became Christian duty. The Protestant Reformation thus led to greater emphasis on individualism and action (hard work), as contrasted with the more ritualistic and contemplative approach of Catholicism.

Although it is useful to recognize the separate thrust of Roman Catholic and Protestant Christianity, it is also important to note the various roles Christianity generally plays in different nations. Some nations reflect varying mixtures of Catholic and Protestant, and the resulting ethic may become a combination of both doctrines. Of course, within Christianity (as with Buddhism, Hinduism, and Islam), wide variations exist in the degree to which adherents follow the teachings. In all groups, segments range from fundamentalist to conservative to casual.

Religion and the Economy

In discussing various religions, some economic implications were suggested that will be elaborated on here. Religion has a major impact on attitudes toward economic matters. The following section, "Attitudes and Values," discusses the different attitudes religion may inspire. Besides attitudes, however, religion may affect the economy more directly, as in the following examples:

- Religious holidays vary greatly among countries—not only from Christian to Muslim, but also from one Christian country to another. In general, Sundays are a religious holiday where Christianity is an important religion. In the Muslim world, however, the entire month of Ramadan is a religious holiday for practical purposes.

A firm must see that local work schedules and other programs take into account local holidays, just as American firms plan for a big season at Christmas.

- Consumption patterns may be affected by religious requirements or taboos. Fish on Friday for Catholics used to be a classic example. Taboos against beef for Hindus or pork for Muslims and Jews are other examples. The Muslim prohibition against alcohol has been a boon to companies such as The Coca-Cola Company. Heineken and other brewers sell a nonalcoholic beer in Saudi Arabia. On the other hand, dairy products find favor among Hindus, many of whom are vegetarians.

- The economic role of women varies from culture to culture, and religious beliefs are an important cause. Women may be restricted in their capacity as consumers, as workers, or as respondents in a marketing study. These differences may require major adjustments in the approach of a management conditioned in the U.S. market.

  Procter & Gamble's products are used mainly by women. When the company wanted to conduct a focus group in Saudi Arabia, however, it could not induce women to participate. Instead, it used the husbands and brothers of women for the focus group.

- The caste system restricts participation in the economy. A company may feel the effects not only in its staffing practices (especially its sales force), but also in its distribution and promotional programs because it must deal with the market segments set up by the caste system.

- The Hindu joint family has economic effects. Nepotism is characteristic of the family business. Staffing is based more on considerations of family rank than on any other criteria. Furthermore, consumer decision making and consumption in the joint family may differ from those in the U.S. family, requiring an adapted strategy. Pooled income in the joint family may lead to different purchase patterns.

- Religious institutions themselves may play a role in economic matters. The Church, or any organized religious group, may block the introduction of new products or techniques if it sees the innovation as a threat. On the other hand, the same product or technique can be more effectively introduced if the religious organization sees it as a benefit. The United States has seen the growing role of religious groups. This is true in other countries, too, as one can see following the daily news and business press.

- Religious divisions in a country can pose problems for management. A firm may find that it is dealing with different markets. In Northern Ireland, there is strong Catholic-Protestant hostility. In India, Muslim-Hindu clashes led to the formation of the separate nation of Pakistan; but the animosity continues. In the Netherlands, major Catholic and Protestant groups have their own political parties and newspapers. Such religious divisions can cause difficulty in staffing an operation or in distributing and promoting a product. Religious differences may indicate buyer segments that require separate strategies.

Clearly, an international firm must be sensitive to religious differences in its foreign markets and be willing to make adaptations. To cite one example, a firm that is building a plant abroad might plan the date and method of opening and dedicating the building to reflect the local religious situation. In particular, a firm's advertising, packaging, and selling practices need to consider local religious sensitivities.

ATTITUDES AND VALUES

People's attitudes and values help determine what they think is right or appropriate, what is important, and what is desirable. The attitudes that relate to business will be presented. It is important to consider attitudes and values because, as Douglas North, the Nobel Prize–winning economist said, "People act on the basis of ideologies and religious views."[3] People have attitudes and values about work, money, time, family, age, men, women, and a host of other topics that have an impact on business. The list is long; only those topics most important for business will be highlighted here.

Business Activities

Ever since Aristotle, selling activities have failed to gain high social approval. The degree of disapproval, however, varies from country to country. In countries where business is looked upon unfavorably, as a wicked or immoral profession, business activities are likely to be neglected and underdeveloped. Capable, talented people are not drawn into business. Often these activities are left to a special class or to expatriates. One is reminded of the medieval banking role filled by Jews or the merchant role of the Chinese in Southeast Asia. In any case, depending on a country's attitude toward business, an international firm may have problems with personnel, distribution channels, and other aspects of its marketing program.

Wealth, Material Gain, and Acquisition

The United States has been called the "affluent society," the "achieving society," and the "acquisitive society." Those somewhat synonymous expressions reflect motivating values in society. In the United States, wealth and acquisition are often considered signs of success and achievement and are given social approval. In a Buddhist or Hindu society, where nirvana or "wantlessness" is an ideal, people may not be so motivated to produce and consume. Businesses obviously prefer to operate in an acquisitive society. However, as a result of rising expectations around the world, national differences in attitudes toward acquisition seem to be lessening. For example, Buddhist Thailand is proving to be a profitable market for many consumer goods firms.

Work may be an end unto itself for some people, and one's position with a particular organization may be an important measure of the person's social status. For others, family, leisure time, and friends take precedence over money and position.

German and French workers have gone on strike and even rioted over plans to extend their workweek beyond 35 hours, to cut paid vacation time, or to raise the age that one becomes qualified for retirement benefits.

Change

When a company enters a foreign market, it brings change by introducing new ways of doing things and new products. In general, North Americans accept change easily. The word "new" has a favorable connotation and facilitates change when used to describe techniques and products. Many societies are more tradition oriented, however, revering their ancestors and traditional ways of consuming.

Business as an agent of change has a different task in traditional societies. Rather than emphasizing what is new and different about a product, the business might relate the product to traditional values, perhaps noting that it is a better way of solving a consumer problem. In seeking acceptance of its new product, a firm might try to get at least a negative clearance—that is, no objection—from local religious leaders or other opinion leaders. Any product must first meet a market need. Beyond that, however, to be accepted, the product must also fit in with the overall value system.

The Campbell Soup Company met this kind of obstacle when it introduced its canned soups into Italy. In conducting research, it received an overwhelmingly negative response to the question, "Would you marry a user of prepared soups?" Campbell had to adjust its questionnaire accordingly.

Risk Taking

Consumers take risks when they try a new product. Will the product do what they expect it to do? Will purchasing or using the product prejudice their standing or image with their peers? Intermediaries handling the untried product may also face risks beyond those associated with their regular line. In a conservative society, there is a greater reluctance to take such risks. Therefore, a firm must seek to reduce the risk perceived by customers or distributors in trying a new product. In part, this can be accomplished through education; guarantees, consignment selling, and other techniques can also be used.

Risk avoidance is a major factor in the low number of online shoppers. While the number of users is growing exponentially, a recent survey found that one-third of Internet users did not shop online because they did not want to risk providing credit card information over the Internet. One-quarter of those surveyed believed it was safer to purchase at a retail shop. The number of Internet users who are also online shoppers is highest, between 15 and 25 percent, among developed nations and lowest, below 5 percent, among developing nations. Recent research indicates that this differs from one culture to another, but this may also be a reflection of different use patterns; that is, some people use the Internet for entertainment or research, while others use it for shopping.

Consumer Behavior

The attitudes just discussed are relevant to understanding consumer behavior in the markets of the world. International managers must have such an understanding to develop effective programs. Because of the impossibility of gaining an intimate knowledge of a great number of markets, they must rely not only on company research, but also on help from others. Those who can assist managers in understanding local attitudes and behavior include personnel in the firm's subsidiary, the distributor, and the advertising agency. Although a firm is interested in changing attitudes, most often it has to adapt to them. As Confucius said, "It is easier to move mountains than to change the minds of men."

AESTHETICS

Aesthetics refers to the prevalent ideas in a culture concerning beauty and good tastes, as expressed in the arts—music, art, drama, and dance—and the appreciation of color and form. International differences abound in aesthetics, but they tend to be regional rather than national. For example, Kabuki theater is exclusively Japanese, but Western theater includes at least all of Western Europe in addition to the United States and Canada in its audience.

Musical tastes, too, tend to be regional rather than national. In the West, many countries enjoy the same classical and popular music. In fact, due to modern communications, popular music has become truly international. Nevertheless, obvious differences exist between Western music and music of the Middle East, Africa, or India. Likewise, the dance styles of African tribal groups or the Balinese are quite removed from Western dance styles. The beauty of India's Taj Mahal is different from that of Notre Dame in Paris or the Chrysler Building in New York City.

Design

The aesthetics of a culture probably do not have a major impact on economic activities. In aesthetics, however, lie some implications for international business. For example, in the design of its plant, product, or package, a firm should be sensitive to local aesthetic preferences. This may run counter to the desire for international uniformity, but the firm must be aware of the positive and negative aspects of its designs. Generally, Asians appreciate complex and decorative styles, particularly when it comes to gift wrapping, for instance.

A historical example of a lack of cultural sensitivity is illustrated by early Christian missionaries from Western nations who were often guilty of architectural "imperialism." The Christian churches built in many non-Western nations usually reflected Western rather than indigenous architectural ideas. This was not done with malicious intent, but because the missionaries were culture-bound in their aesthetics; that is, they had their own ideas about what a church should look like.

The U.S. government faces a similar problem in designing its embassies. The U.S. Embassy in India received praise both for its beauty as a building and for the way it blended with Indian architecture. The U.S. Embassy in London, however, has received more than its share of criticism, including comments about the size of the sculpted American eagle on top of the building. Some Britons also took exception to the architecture of the London Hilton. For a firm, the best policy is to design and decorate its buildings and commercial vehicles to reflect local aesthetic preferences. In its thousands of outlets abroad, McDonald's Corporation has learned to adapt its facilities to local tastes.

Color

The significance of different colors also varies from culture to culture. In the United States, for instance, people use colors to identify emotional reactions; people "see red," they are "green with envy," and they "feel blue." Black signifies mourning in Western countries, whereas white is often the color of mourning in Eastern nations. Green is popular in Muslim countries, while red and black have a negative connotation in several African countries. Red is an appealing and lucky color in China, blue sometime suggests evil, and yellow is often associated with authority. Certain colors have particular meanings because of religious, patriotic, or aesthetic reasons. Businesspeople need to know the significance of colors in a culture when planning their company's products and the products' packaging. For any market, the choice of colors should be related to the aesthetic sense of the buyer's culture rather than that of the manager's culture. Generally, the colors of the country's flag are safe colors. Japan has a Study Group for Colors in Public Places. It wages war on "color pollution," and its mission is "to seek out better uses for color, to raise the issue of colors."

Music

There are also cultural differences in music. An understanding of these differences is critical in creating advertising messages that use music. The music of nonliterate cultures is generally functional, or has significance in the people's daily lives, whereas the music of literate cultures tends to be separate from people's other concerns. For example, a Western student has to learn to "understand" a Beethoven symphony, but aborigines assimilate musical culture as an integral part of their existence. Ethnomusicologist William Malm stated that understanding the symbolism in different kinds of music requires considerable cultural conditioning. Therefore, homogeneity in music throughout the world cultures is not possible. There are exceptions, of course, but one implication for a firm is that wherever it utilizes music, it should use music of the local culture. Recognizing the importance of music in popular culture, companies such as Coca-Cola, PepsiCo, and Nike, Inc. are frequent sponsors of events such as MTV Video Music Awards, Latin America and WOMAD (Festival of World Music, Arts & Dance).

Paul Anka provides an example of the value of "going native" in music and language. Anka has recorded ten albums that have sold, collectively, 10 million copies, none of which has been heard in the United States. The secret is that the songs in the albums were sung in Japanese, German, French, Spanish, and Italian—songs that Anka composed strictly for those countries in a style indigenous to their musical cultures. Anka is not fluent in those languages. For months, he worked with native musicians on music and lyrics that would appeal to each nation. He sang in the local language phonetically. Mr. Anka succeeded because of his broad appeal, but also because he records his music in so many other languages.

Brand Names

The choice of brand names is also affected by aesthetics. Frequently, the best brand name is one in the local language, pleasing to local taste. This leads to a multiplicity of brand names, which some firms try to avoid by searching out a nonsense word that is pronounceable everywhere, but that has no specific meaning anywhere. Kodak is one example. In other cases, local identification is important enough that firms seek local brand names. For example, Procter & Gamble has 20 different brand names for its detergents in foreign markets.

The aesthetics of a culture influence a firm's strategies abroad, often in ways that businesses are unaware of until they make mistakes. A firm needs local input to avoid ineffective or damaging use of aesthetics. This input may come from local marketing research, local nationals working for the firm, and local advertising agencies or distributors.

NOTES

1. Webster's New Collegiate Dictionary, 11th ed., s.v. "culture."
2. The Economist (March 12, 2005): 11.
3. Douglass North, Understanding the Process of Economic Change (Princeton, NJ: Princeton University Press, 2005), p. 85.

CHAPTER 8

GLOBAL VALUE-ADDED STRATEGIES

John Caslione

In today's competitive marketplace, successful companies develop Value-Added Strategies to build and sustain important customer-supplier relationships, relationships that rise above the traditional confines of both product and price. Both customer and supplier share a common vision: to engage in innovative strategies to enhance their respective long-term profitability in a spirit of mutual self-interest.

Too often, however, suppliers and customers alike have a tendency to become a bit greedy in their approaches to each other, forgetting that the most successful business relationships are founded upon the concept that both parties find value in working together from the very beginning.

After years of feeling as though they have been giving away too much value to customers in the form of value-adding services, many suppliers are now adopting a misguided and short-term strategy in which they attempt to charge the customer for every service provided. This classic "cafeteria"-style pricing approach is nothing more than turning virtually everything that the supplier provides to a customer into a chargeable product or service.

This is not a strategy at all; it is just another desperate attempt by corporate finance departments to wrest every last dollar from their customers under the justification that all things of value provided to customers should result in direct and immediate revenue for the supplier.

A similar situation exists on the customer's side, but with a different directional flow. With the economic slowdown, it seems that customers are trying to take the quick and easy way to meet their company's challenged profit streams. They pressure their suppliers by extracting price reductions first, and then maybe, if the customer is sophisticated enough, by thinking about true cost reductions.

Both supplier and customer must temper their eagerness for quick, short-term gains and look to attack the true enemy for them both: their common operating expenses. Even with today's ultra-short-term focus on profits, both are significantly better off using their respective core competencies to lower each other's operating costs in a spirit of true alliance: a Strategic Supplier Alliance initiated by the supplier.

LUCENT TECHNOLOGIES AND DIGITAL CHINA

Digital China, a spin-off of Legend Group Ltd. in 2000, was listed on the Hong Kong Stock Exchange in 2001. The company embraces innovation to provide first-tier products, solutions, and services for e-commerce infrastructure. Digital China is currently the largest information technology products distributor and systems integrator in China.

Lucent Technologies, with its headquarters in Murray Hill, New Jersey, designs and delivers the systems, services, and software that drive next-generation communications networks. Backed by Bell Labs research and development, Lucent uses its strengths in mobility, optical, software, data and voice networking technologies, as well as services, to create new revenue-generating opportunities for its customers while enabling them to quickly deploy and better manage their networks.

Lucent Technologies and Digital China formed the strategic supplier alliance in 2004. This is a win-win solution. The alliance allows Digital China to become the exclusive general distributor of Lucent's network management software to enterprises in mainland China. Lucent will be able to influence the network of resellers and agents across the United States to provide a broader range of software products and related services to Chinese service providers and enterprises. This will help the Chinese enterprises migrate toward next-generation networking technologies, while minimizing the overall network operations costs for everyone involved.

Digital China has already established a channel network consisting of more than 3,500 integrators, agents, and industrial customers, backed by its strong capabilities in technical support, after-sale maintenance, and customer training. Lucent offers network management software with cutting-edge technologies that best support Digital China's strategy in growing value-added businesses. By forming this strategic alliance, Digital China manages to deliver more products and value-added services to Chinese customers.

Suppliers that engage in real Value-Added Strategy have the freedom to charge a premium for their products and services and refrain from reducing prices. These suppliers often charge a premium because the value they deliver to customers, in the form of increased bottom-line profits, routinely far exceeds the price of the charged premium.

DEVELOPING A GLOBAL CUSTOMER SERVICE STRATEGY

Enlightened customers engaging in such value-adding relationships are typically at the forefront of their industries. While these customers often pay a premium for the products and services their suppliers provide, the overall cost of doing business together may be among the lowest in their respective industries. The customers' selection of suppliers represents the best, most profitable business decisions that these customers can make for their businesses to build market share, increase revenues, and enhance profitability for today and also for the long term.

As both customer and supplier work together, their common vision enables each to rise above the primal desire to operate using traditional competitive product and pricing strategies. Instead, these companies strive to work together in a customer-supplier relationship dedicated to pursuing long-term high profitability for both, in a relationship called a Strategic Supplier Alliance.

For example, a supplier of seals used in automatic transmissions knew that its customers, the major auto manufacturers, were incurring high warranty costs for failed transmissions under warranty. No transmission component supplier in the industry, including the auto manufacturers themselves, knew exactly why the transmissions failed all the time. Some failures were obvious as to the cause, while other failures were not so obvious. In the ambiguous situations, by default, the seal manufacturers were routinely blamed for the failure.

Tired of working in such a contentious environment, one highly motivated U.S.-based seal manufacturer created a customized database to collect data and information from one of its customer's three repositories of failed transmissions, where transmissions were dismantled and tested.

The supplier's goal was to uncover the reasons why faulty transmissions failed and then to provide recommendations to the customer on how to reduce transmission failures and consequently reduce the high warranty costs. Specifically, the seal supplier used this database for its own organization to develop a special knowledge to know how and why transmissions failed all of the time.

With this valuable knowledge and the ability to provide profit improvement recommendations to the customer, the seal manufacturer was able to directly reduce warranty costs by more than $50 million in the first year alone. This seal supplier provided all of this information at no additional charge to one of its carefully selected customers, one of the few customers dedicated to pursuing long-term strategic supplier relationships.

Not surprisingly, this automobile manufacturer promptly gave the seal supplier an exclusive supply contract on its next three transmission platforms for the next five years. Despite paying a slight premium for this supplier's seals, doing business with this particular supplier represented the best, most profitable business decision that the auto manufacturer could make in choosing its seal supplier.

And, unlike most of its competitors in a price-driven industry, this auto manufacturer made its decision based upon lowest total cost and highest overall profitability rather than lowest product price.

WHAT IS "VALUE ADDED?"

True Value-Added Strategy goes above and beyond the product level to create a strategic relationship between the two companies. The product itself does not change, and, in fact, it sometimes becomes almost incidental to the customer-supplier relationship.

Value-Added Strategies are based on the supplier's competencies and other areas of expertise as an organization. They are designed to provide high value to a selected customer's bottom line, versus merely seeking to "add value" to the individual products and services it sells. It is a supplier's organizational value rather than its product or service value that is at the core of Value-Added Strategies.

From the customer's perspective, a Value-Added Strategy enhances profitability. The supplier develops projects and programs that boost the customer's profits in one or more of three ways:

1. Enhancing customer's revenues,

2. Reducing customer's current costs, or

3. Avoiding customer's future costs.

Whether a supplier achieves one, two, or all three of these objectives, the result is that it improves the customer's bottom line. A Value-Added Strategy focuses on achieving these objectives by utilizing core competencies or other areas of special expertise in the supplier's organization to materially benefit the customer's profitability.

VALUE ADDED VERSUS ADDED VALUE

A Value-Added Strategy should not be confused with an Added-Value Sales approach to marketing products and services. While many companies use the terms interchangeably, the difference between the two is significant. It is also essential that companies understand the difference between the two; otherwise a Value-Added Strategy cannot be used effectively to develop marketing differentiation strategy.

With Added Value, a company focuses on the same objective as in a Value-Added Strategy, namely, improving the customer's bottom line, but it does so by increasing the tangible benefits a customer receives from using the actual products and services the supplier sells. In other words, the supplier's product or service is still the source of the value delivered, such as increased customer revenues or reduced or avoided customer costs. See Figure 8.1.

Figure 8.1
Added Value versus Value Added

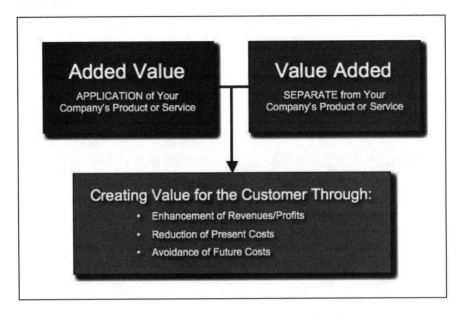

For example, if a supplier's product has lower installation costs and lower life-time maintenance costs, these are Added-Value product benefits, because the source of the value to the customer emanates from the product itself.

This approach does indeed add value, and it makes sense to position products and services sold that way. But customers typically do not perceive one company's product and service offerings to be highly differentiated from another's, especially when they look at the suppliers' product and service portfolios in their entirety.

Today, there increasingly exists product and service parity in customers' eyes. Even if a supplier has great technology or a tremendously valuable product, its biggest and best competitors probably have similar and comparable products. If they do not, it will not be very long before they do, wiping out any competitive advantage that the original supplier had.

Competitive parity of products typically exists between most suppliers' products and services today. Any customer value that may be derived from products is largely the same; the playing field is virtually level. This ultimately leads to more "commoditization" of product and service offerings in the marketplace, which in turn creates increased supplier frustration. They then dismiss the power of Value-Added Strategies, largely because they are mistakenly engaging in Added-Value Sales, which is product-based differentiation in its marketing differentiation strategy and not true Value-Added Strategy.

In today's highly competitive and technology-driven environment, companies must begin to understand and finally accept that product-oriented strategies can no longer provide suppliers with any meaningful or sustainable differentiation from their competition beyond the short to medium term.

A Value-Added Strategy helps overcome the issue of product parity by taking the customer-supplier relationship to a higher level. Value-Added Strategies connect the two companies at the organizational level, not the product level. Value Added is organizationally based value, creating a relationship between supplier and customer through the development of multiple cross-functional department relationships and through the integration of intercompany systems and processes.

If effectively applied in marketing strategy, the competitive advantages gained by a supplier are not easily replicated and can become a sustainable competitive advantage over several years.

In executing Value-Added Strategy, company size does not matter as much as one might think. In the example of the seal manufacturer, its fiercest competitor, a global company with six times more in revenue, is unable to pursue a similar strategy because its management and company culture pursues a product-based differentiation strategy that strives to differentiate by offering a wide product line at discounted prices. At the time of this writing, the gap between the two seal suppliers has closed to less than four times in revenue due to the success of the Value-Added supplier's increased share of the market.

Because so few companies understand the Value-Added approach, let alone have the kind of company culture needed to implement it, significant opportunities to differentiate from the competition await suppliers willing to take the more difficult road by pursuing a Value-Added approach.

TOTAL VALUE PROPOSITION = VALUE ADDED + ADDED VALUE

Countless business books have been written about Value Added and Added Value, and most of these books offer different and conflicting definitions of the two. Still more talk about the "Total Value Proposition" (see Figure 8.2) and usually fail to tie together a clear and concise definition that is both tangible and easy to explain. There should be little mystery or disagreement about what comprises a supplier's total value proposition if one provides clear definitions of Value Added and Added Value. Both enhance the customer's revenues, reduce current operating costs, and avoid future operating costs of the customer. They just approach it from two different and distinct directions.

Simply, a supplier's total value proposition is the sum total of the value its products (Added Value) bring to the customer and the value that the supplier's

Figure 8.2
The Total Value Proposition

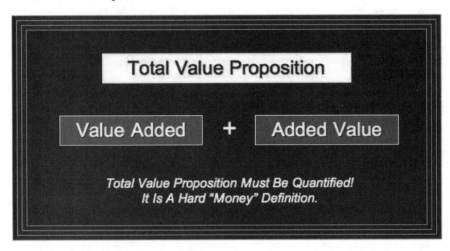

organization brings (Value Added) to this same customer; in other words, product value plus organizational value equals a supplier's total value proposition.

EXAMPLES OF VALUE-ADDED STRATEGIES

United Parcel Service, United States

At United Parcel Service (UPS), a core competency is its understanding and application of information and communications technology. It is unparalleled in the industry and could otherwise match up with even the most successful telecommunications supplier. This expertise came in very handy recently with one of UPS's largest global accounts.

UPS's Global Account Manager (GAM), responsible for the global account of a major European electronics company, had uncovered that this customer was in the early planning stages of building a new, state-of-the-art manufacturing facility for one of its divisions. As part of this effort, this division was preparing to contract with a telecommunications consultancy in Europe to write the technical specifications for a tender (request for proposal). The tender, once developed, would then be let to one of the major telecommunications providers, for example, Nortel, Lucent, and so forth.

Learning of this opportunity, the UPS GAM for the account offered to provide UPS's own telecommunications consultants to write the specifications for the tender at no additional charge to the company. After a bit of initial skepticism with such a generous offer, the customer eventually agreed.

UPS then dedicated four of its telecommunications consultants for a period of almost three months to complete the task, saving this particular customer division over $660,000 in avoided telecommunications consultancy costs.

What did UPS gain for all its effort? It more than doubled its account share within this customer division to more than 80 percent of business in that division that next year. Pursuing similar Value-Added Strategies, it also went on to achieve sizable increases in sales and account share within other divisions of this same global customer.

British Sugar Ltd., Europe

One of the ultimate commodity products in the world is sugar. Companies have tried unsuccessfully for decades to differentiate their sugar from that of their competitors. U.K.-based British Sugar Ltd. succeeded in differentiating sugar by not even trying. It ignored its product and focused upon other sources of value within its organization that it could provide.

British Sugar's Value-Added Strategy was founded upon two key Value-Added Contributions.

Leverage Consulting Expertise

The first strategic Value-Added Contribution involved making use of the environmental consultancy expertise that it had developed over the years for internal use. Many of British Sugar's customers are in the food-processing industry and, like British Sugar, had an ongoing problem of treating environmental waste resulting from the processing of sugar, as well as in the processing of foods.

As part of its strategy, British Sugar offered its environmental consultancy to a selected group of six strategically important customers at no additional charge. All six customers who received the offer accepted. Each was able to significantly reduce and avoid considerable costs in their businesses almost from the first day. Some customers no longer needed to pay outside consultants for these services, and some eventually eliminated the need to maintain an internal environmental consulting department altogether.

Sell Excess Capacity

The second involved selling excess capacity of electricity to this same select group of six customers. One of British Sugar's major cost drivers is electricity (a "20/80 cost"). Years earlier, when the United Kingdom was going through its own deregulation of the electric utility industry, as the United States is currently doing, British Sugar had acquired a power generation company for its own exclusive energy generation and consumption.

Over time, it found that it had more potential power than it could use in its own operations. Instead of selling it outright for a profit, executive management decided to offer its excess capacity at cost to this same group of six strategic customers, and not one pence (cent) more. The price offered to these customers, British Sugar's actual cost, was 70 percent below the lowest wholesale price in the industry. It was also estimated that this excess capacity of electricity would be enough to satisfy anywhere from 25 to 35 percent of the six customers' needs at their U.K.-based facilities.

When offered this opportunity to purchase electricity at a much-reduced price, all six customers were interested, especially after the very positive experience with British Sugar assuming the responsibility for environmental consultancy within their companies.

What was in this for British Sugar? Quite a lot. Not only did all six customers give either all or most of their business to British Sugar, but British Sugar was able to demand a premium price for the sugar it sold to these customers. Moreover, it gained a tremendous amount of control over its business within the customers' businesses.

For example, as a condition under U.K. law, in order for British Sugar to effectively "sell" electricity at its cost, it must have a British Sugar office inside every facility that consumes its electricity. This meant that, as part of the agreement with these customers, there needed to be a British Sugar office inside each of these customers' locations that consumed British Sugar's electricity.

In the world of strategic or global account management, such a cohabitation arrangement is invaluable for the supplier to increase its business in the customer account and to maintain control of its business in that account over the long term.

Some people believe that British Sugar should have made a small profit by charging a slightly higher price for its electricity. Would these same British Sugar customers still be interested in buying electricity if British Sugar offered it at 50 percent below the lowest wholesale price versus 70 percent?

Certainly they would, but two potentially dangerous things would likely happen if it did begin to sell its excess electricity:

First, if British Sugar charged any price above its actual costs, then under U.K. regulatory law it would have to begin to create a number of reports and filings and routinely submit these to the government. This would have created a lot of new internal expenses and a need to staff new departments.

Second, a more insidious problem, such an approach would defocus management from its core business—sugar—onto an entirely new and different industry: electricity. Such a shift into a new complex industry in which it was a novice meant that British Sugar really could not compete successfully long term unless it wanted to refocus its current driving forces from that of a manufacturer and marketer of sugar to a full-time generator and marketer of electricity. Attempting to do both would likely jeopardize the success of both, and British Sugar's executive management was unwilling to take such a dangerous step.

INTERNATIONAL TRADING COMPANIES

The international trading operating system in China is changing dramatically. International trading companies used to specialize in sales and marketing now have started to develop their manufacturing branches in order to provide value-added services to their customers. These trading companies have managed to establish strategic relationships with their customers, obtaining accurate understandings of their needs. This is an effective strategy, because customers tend to pay more attention to the value-added services that the suppliers can bring to them.

Shartex International Trading Co., a Shanghai-based trading company, established its research and development center, engaging in market trend projection, raw material proportion, product design, and product sample development. This enables the company to improve the efficiency of product renovation, hence significantly reducing the time that customers usually spend examining the sample products.

Another international trading company, located in Beijing, specializes in handcrafted products selected from a supplying base of over ten manufacturing factories in Jiangsu and Zhejiang provinces. These ten factories are responsible for manufacturing the products to meet the requirement and demand of the trading company, while the trading company is responsible for the sales of these products to its major customer, a large-scale retailer from South America. By simply contacting the trading company, customers are able to complete their purchasing tasks. The suppliers are able to expand their market share by providing these value-added services to the customers.

WHAT ABOUT VALUE ADDED IN A SERVICES COMPANY?

About a year ago when I was conducting a Value-Added Marketing & Sales management workshop in Europe, a participant asked me how to apply Value-Added Strategy in a services company and not just a product company. My answer was simple. I asked her to truly understand what services her company is currently providing at a specified price and then determine which of these services should become Value-Added Contributions, or services without charge.

This participant provided a great example. She was the senior marketing and sales director for the largest and most prestigious advertising and communications services agency in Germany. She shared with all of us in the workshop group her company's current marketing dilemma.

There were five major companies in Germany that her company was unable to really break into to do a lot of business. The problem was always the same. In this industry, the marketing director was the equivalent of most companies' purchasing directors, and the marketing director routinely prevented access by ad agencies and other suppliers to the company president. Although this ad agency was doing some business with these clients, it was a fraction of the potential that it could be doing.

In the seminar I asked if her company offered speech mentoring and speech writing as a service in her company. She immediately replied that it did and, although it was viewed as the best in Germany in providing this service, it was never a big revenue generator.

After hearing her answer, I offered her a challenge. I told her to send a letter to the presidents of five clients offering private, personalized speech mentoring at no cost to them under a special program with "exclusive clients."

I also instructed her to continue reinforcing this offer every few weeks for at least three months. Finally, I made her promise to notify me at the end of the three months and then after six months with a progress report.

At the end of the second month she contacted me to tell me that three of the five presidents had accepted the offer and had begun their one-on-one, personalized speech mentoring classes. She proceeded to tell me that within a matter of weeks, a great deal of rapport was developed between each client president and his or her personal speech coach.

Not long afterward, the marketing directors from each of these client companies had begun to invite this agency in to bid on more and more business. And even though this agency was usually higher priced than most of its competitors in the bidding process, the agency had begun to quickly increase its business with all three clients.

The agency always had this tool available. At the same time, the agency had never recognized it for what it was, a powerful Value-Added Contribution. Speech mentoring now was a valuable asset that could open doors otherwise inaccessible if kept in the agency's traditional portfolio of services for sale. The same is true for product companies with the services that they sell.

USING VALUE-ADDED STRATEGY IN A TARGETED MARKET SEGMENT

In the telecommunications industry throughout the 1990s, the long-distance providers began to encounter a problem called "churning," in which small business and residential customers would change long-distance carriers, sometimes monthly, to take advantage of promotional discounts and other pricing incentives.

AT&T was one such company that was victimized by the widespread churning in the marketplace, until one day when one of its suppliers presented it with an innovative strategy to help regain customer loyalty and minimize churning.

AT&T SOHO Division

To market to and service small businesses with fewer than 100 employees, AT&T created a dedicated group called the Small Office/Home Office (SOHO) division. This department was charged with the responsibility to build the market share in this fast-growing customer segment that was very vulnerable to being "churned" by competitors. Needless to say, in this very price-conscious segment of the business, churning became almost "sport" for many SOHO small business customers.

A woman whose husband became a victim of a downsizing initiative of his company in the late 1990s relayed a story to me in one of my executive marketing seminars. Her husband had over 25 years of employment with his company and found it difficult to land a new job, so, like so many other middle-aged unemployed business executives, he became a consultant. Having recently seen their last of four children off to college, he converted one of their now vacant bedrooms in their home into his business office. He proceeded to begin his new and exciting career in consulting.

AT&T SOHO Division wants this man's long-distance business, as do all of AT&T's competitors. Over time, it has become increasingly difficult to differentiate long-distance "dial tone" and, not surprisingly, the industry had become commoditized with price discounting running rampant.

As a result, there is little price difference between suppliers in this industry; the spread between the highest priced and the lowest priced competitors is typically less than 5 percent. This creates especially tight operating margins when the average SOHO customer working out of his or her home spends less than $200 each month on his or her long-distance service.

As the story goes, one of AT&T's suppliers of office products proposed an innovative Value-Added Strategy to AT&T in an effort to help it stem the increasing trend of churning. It seemingly caught the attention of the right AT&T executive and led to the development of a full-blown Value-Added Strategy.

The recently unemployed company executive, now-turned-consultant, was offered a full package of inducements if he would sign a one-year service agreement with AT&T. The package included all of the following Value-Added Contributions from AT&T at no additional charge:

- An offer to provide a customized office design to make the most efficient and effective utilization of space within the consultant's "office."

- The ability to purchase everything from computer and office furniture, office supplies, courier and shipping services, and so forth, at AT&T's steep volume price discounts.

- The ability to take advantage of AT&T's discounted group health and life insurance that would save the consultant several hundreds of dollars each month after his former employer's extended insurance coverage ran out.

- A list of accountants and bookkeepers that specialize in working with small businesses in the consultant's local area.

The consultant was provided several hundreds, or even thousands, of dollars each year in savings if he was willing to commit to AT&T for one year. This commitment would require him to pay, at most, a $10.00 price premium each month, calculated at a rate of 5 percent on $200 each month. When he analyzed the total value proposition that AT&T was providing him, it was an easy and quick decision for him. He signed up immediately and has stayed loyal to AT&T for more than three years now.

In this case study, AT&T's service became almost incidental and even unimportant to the relationship as it was tacitly acknowledged by AT&T that the product of long-distance service was a commodity and nearly impossible to differentiate from the competition.

AT&T approached the situation differently than its competitors. It made some minimal investments in developing this new Value-Added Strategy and then, by engaging its own suppliers to help execute the plan, AT&T created such an attractive total value proposition that it began to reduce the problem of churning and once again regain substantial stability in its small business customer base.

WHAT IS "VALUE EXPECTED"?

In my executive management seminars, I am repeatedly asked if there is a logical and inevitable end to Value-Added Contributions, that is, at some point are not all Value-Added Contributions likely to be matched by competitors, thus becoming part of the product offering and eliminating any prior competitive advantage by a competitor? The answer is both yes and no.

Certainly, at the very foundation of free competition, if a competitor has a competitive advantage—especially a significant advantage, competitors in the industry will seek ways to minimize or eliminate that advantage. Sometimes when a Value-Added Contribution becomes something that many competitors have matched, it does become part of the combined standard product offering. This is what is called Value Expected. Technically it is still Value Added, but because it no longer differentiates as it once did, the Value-Added Contribution now becomes an expected Value-Added Contribution, or just Value Expected.

A good example of this is supplier-managed inventory or vendor-managed inventory, wherein a supplier manages the inventory of its products on behalf of the customer. When it was first introduced in the late 1980s and into the early 1990s, it presented a significant competitive advantage for a number of suppliers in many industries. Beginning in the 1990s in many industries, it became a standard service offering and soon it was considered as a basic component of a supplier's product offering. It became Value Expected.

To minimize or delay a Value-Added Contribution from becoming Value Expected, two things can and should be considered.

There is a greater likelihood that a supplier can prolong its competitive advantage if it can proactively recommend Value-Added Contributions before the customer even thinks about it. Too often, most suppliers are reactive in this endeavor and, if they do offer a Value-Added Contribution to a customer, it is done for one of two reasons:

1. The first is that a competitor is already providing it to a customer and has gained a competitive advantage. The market's many reactive suppliers then want to minimize their competitor's advantage, thus creating a motivation to match the competitor's same Value-Added Contribution.

2. The second is when the customer asks or demands that the supplier provide the additional service because it will represent a cost savings to the customer. The trouble with this scenario is that when a customer initiates a cost or revenue improvement initiative, a supplier-provided Value-Added Contribution, the customer typically designs it so there is a high level of substitutability in the service requested; that is, the customer can easily substitute one supplier's Value-Added Contribution for another supplier's Value-Added Contribution.

The key for a supplier is to propose Value-Added Contributions to the marketplace that the customers have not yet even considered. In this way, suppliers can design and engineer their Value-Added Contributions in ways to minimize the degree of substitutability that can exist in the contribution provided. In essence, suppliers can more readily maintain a balanced peer relationship with their customers.

The most effective way to design any Value-Added Contribution to be as nonsubstitutable as possible by a customer is to make the Contribution systemic and as integrated as possible between both the customer's and the supplier's many different functional departments and their business operations.

For example, a manufacturer of flour and other mixing and baking ingredients supplied a leading commercial bakery in North America. The flour supplier was noted for its world-class transportation logistics.

However, when the flour manufacturer's trucks unloaded its raw flour and other mixing ingredients at the customer's commercial baking facilities, some of these trucks "deadheaded" back to the supplier's production locations; they traveled back empty. Not surprisingly, the commercial bakery's trucks also did a lot of deadheading back to their sites after they unloaded the finished baked goods at their customer's locations, the major supermarket chains.

The flour manufacturer proposed that a lot of operating costs between both companies could be driven out if the two companies were to merge their transportation logistics functions, and the bakery agreed. By combining the two transportation-scheduling functions, and by utilizing the supplier's expertise in transportation logistics planning, both companies saved millions of dollars each year in operating costs. Moreover, the supplier was able to maintain a high degree of control of its business within the customer's business because it *systematized* the Value-Added Contribution and made it essential to the operation of both companies.

As compelling as it is, if the supplier were to stop here with only this single Value-Added Contribution as part of its strategy, it would be only a matter of time, even if it were an extended period of time, before a competing flour producer would find a way to replicate and eliminate any competitive advantage in the market.

But what the incumbent supplier does have is access to this customer's people and information in key areas of this customer's business that its competitors do not have. With this proprietary access, the supplier has the ability to pursue additional proactive integrations of customer systems and processes.

In doing so and in pursuing a deliberate, cogent Strategic Supplier Alliance strategy, the supplier can create a multitude of such linkages and entanglements, which can integrate the two companies so much that they create tremendously high barriers of entry to competitors. This prevents, or severely hampers, the competitors' ability to gain a foothold into this customer's business.

Likewise, such a series of entanglements will also be critical in creating the high barriers of exit necessary to make it costly and difficult for the customer to substitute this supplier for another.

VALUE ADDED: KEY TO DEVELOPING ACCESS STRATEGY

Let us examine more closely some of the examples just presented. They underscore the fact that in most companies, the executive management does not know the difference between Value Added and Added Value. Moreover, they often fail to recognize the difference between what are products and services they should be selling and what is customer service that supports the pre-sales and post-sales servicing of the products and services sold.

Even more important, companies are unaware of the Value-Added Contributions they currently or potentially can provide as key components of their total value proposition. These Value-Added Contributions provided by companies facilitate the needed access to people and information within the customer's organization.

When the supplier believes that it has a service that may be of value to a customer, the temptation to put a price tag on it to develop new revenue streams becomes so great that most suppliers end up pricing everything they can. This is almost always a critical mistake.

Imagine three buckets (see Figure 8.3). Also imagine a supplier that understands what should properly go into each of the three buckets. A supplier that understands this is a supplier that can build true strategic market differentiation strategy.

Figure 8.3
Value-Added Strategy

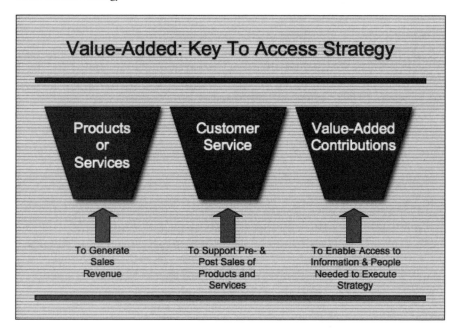

Obviously, the key is to know what rightly goes into each bucket and then how to use each in practical business strategy, particularly Value-Added Contributions.

The fundamental and essential advantage of a Value-Added Contribution is gaining access to people and information in the targeted customer's organization that would otherwise be unattainable by pursuing the traditional sales process. This exclusive access is critical to the successful execution of the supplier's marketing differentiation strategy.

Let us examine the three earlier case study examples.

UPS

In the shipping industry, the customer's traditional buying department typically chooses two suppliers, and then the actual end users of the service in each department of the account are able to use their shipper of choice on a case-by-case basis.

Imagine UPS's telecommunications consultants who have been given free reign to meet with every department manager, every project manager, every secretary, and so forth, within the account. Also imagine that this is being done as an effort to effectively design the voice/data/video specifications for the new telecommunications system, rather than as an effort to sell traditional UPS shipping services.

Over time, UPS telecommunications experts did this. They dug deep into every department within the European Economic Community (EEC) and along the way built a tremendous amount of rapport with virtually everyone in the EEC who could be a potential decision maker in each department.

It is no wonder that UPS became the shipper of choice in eight out of ten times that managers and secretaries had to select their preferred shipper.

British Sugar

Think about all of the customer's different departments and managers that the account team from British Sugar needed to work with to implement the two Value-Added Contributions it offered. With the environmental consultancy at no additional charge, the list of managers in the targeted food manufacturing company includes plant manager, quality control manager, operations manager, CFO, the legal department, and so forth. All of these departments are very influential within these organizations, and British Sugar interacted closely with a large number of them.

These managers have a tremendous amount of influence concerning the decision to use or not use British Sugar as a supplier. Furthermore, this is also the group of managers that will be in the best position to consider British Sugar's Value-Added Contributions and subsequently assess the true total value proposition that British Sugar will bring to their company.

Advertising Agency (Service Company)

As we learned in the example of the German advertising and marketing communications company, the marketing director was the key decision maker, and oftentimes a hindrance in the marketing and sales process. The marketing department routinely withheld access to the client company's president, making it virtually impossible for the ad agency's account managers to develop any real relationship with the client company's president.

Consider that, through this ad agency's Value-Added Contribution, the company president is in a closed room with a speech mentor from the ad agency several times over a month or more. In these sessions, the president allows himself or herself to be exposed to criticisms in a very personal and sensitive area, that of his or her public speaking skills. In addition, the president realizes after a few sessions that there is noticeable improvement in his or her public speaking skills. Imagine the closeness of the relationship and the level of rapport that now exists between the client president and his or her speech mentor.

With such a positive halo effect spilling over to the ad agency overall, it is not surprising that the clients' marketing directors were strongly encouraged to do more business with this particular ad agency, even with its higher fees.

SUMMARY

With a better understanding of the fundamental differences between Value Added and Added Value, a company can utilize Value-Added Concepts in strategy development. Knowing how to do this will assist in avoiding the mistakes commonly made by so many companies, the most common one being the development of product-based marketing differentiation strategies that routinely create higher operating costs and encourage even greater price competition.

In fact, many such purported value-adding programs routinely become nothing more than mere "giveaway programs," or programs that provide ever-increasing benefits to customers, but do very little to actually generate any real reciprocal benefits for the supplier.

The flip side of this approach is to put a price tag on all Value-Added Contributions, turning them into nothing more than Added-Value Services to be sold within the supplier's portfolio of products and services. By doing this over the long term, suppliers inadvertently accelerate the commoditization of their product and service offerings, as well as stimulate even more aggressive price discounting in the marketplace.

One might say that if a "value-adding service" provided by a supplier is so valuable, then a customer should be willing to pay for it. Though this makes sense, it is not always the case. The willingness of a customer to pay is "sometimes yes" and "most often no." The question of whether or not to charge for value-adding services holds dire consequences for suppliers that get the answer wrong.

Most often, by charging for a Value-Added Contribution, suppliers inadvertently enter into new and different industries that provide this Contribution as one of their primary service offerings. When companies mistakenly begin to offer services for a price that are either tangential or complementary to their core business, they end up shifting their companies' driving force and find they are unable to compete in new and different industries: for example, British Sugar and the electric utility industry. The results are usually disastrous, unless the company is willing to make a full commitment to the new industry it is entering, a commitment complete with a long-term plan to compete head-to-head with these new competitors in the new industry.

It is absolutely necessary to understand how to apply Value-Added Contributions in strategy, by utilizing the Strategic Supplier Alliance Continuum to develop long-term, sustainable customer-supplier relationships.

It is only a matter of time before more companies acknowledge that they cannot compete on price- or product-based strategy. They must instead forge true value-adding relationships together. Value-Added Strategies will enable customer and supplier alike to secure a truly beneficial scenario every time.

Part IV

Customers: The Forgotten Participants in World Markets

The Value of Qualitative Research for International Marketers: Cross-Cultural Issues and Recommendations

Rajshekhar (Raj) G. Javalgi, Robert B. Young, and Robert F. Scherer

Increased trade, advancements in information and communication technology, growing wealth and affluence across the globe, and a convergence of consumer tastes and preferences have accentuated the importance of and need for international business research.[1] In fact, it is reported that effective global marketing begins with strong market research.[2] The growth of the international market research business has been accelerating since the mid-1990s. For perspective, the top 25 global market research organizations had aggregate revenues of $5.7 billion in 1995, and 45 percent of their revenues came from outside the companies' home countries. By 2002 combined revenues had grown 84 percent to $10.5 billion, while the out-of-home-country share had grown to 63 percent.[3] It is clear that spending on international market research projects is on the rise in the United States and other countries. Globalization will continue to spread and the world market will reward market research information and competitive advantage without regard to distances and locations.[4] Moreover, the increasing trend toward the globalization of business activities provides a compelling reason for understanding the cultural context of consumer behavior.[5]

Market research is the vital link between the organization and its customers. The objective of sound market research is to interpret consumer behavior and translate the perspective of key customers into actionable marketing strategies. Without this open dialog with customers, companies are unable to keep their pulse on the vital consumer behavior trends and the many other influences on the customers of an organization. In today's consumer environment of overchoice and overcommunication, growth can be realized only by organizations that are very skilled at crafting well-targeted strategies directed at very specific microniches of the larger macro market. Companies that go to market without *first* uncovering specific segment needs and perceptions risk facing the monumental cost of marketing failure. With new consumer product launches typically costing $25 million and often much more, the risk of not incorporating consumer behavior into marketing strategy is considerable. As organizations continue to pursue worldwide markets, an in-depth understanding of both customers and noncustomers is even more critical today.

Thomas V. Bonoma argued for more applications of qualitative market research techniques in marketing science.[6] Ronald J. Cohen suggests the need for generating widespread interest in using psychological expertise in the form of qualitative market research to solve some of the mysteries in marketing.[7] Why do organizations need qualitative marketing research? Organizations committed to growing their markets, either domestically or internationally, need information about target customers, markets, and competitors in order to make effective decisions.

Organizational questions that lend themselves to qualitative marketing research techniques include the following: Why do our customers buy from us? What is the context of our business and competitive environment? How do our customers acquire, use, and discard our products and services? What can be learned by observing our customers interact with our products and services? Do our products and services hold a deeper meaning to our customers and, if so, do we fully understand what it is? Organizations need an increased depth of understanding in order to answer these types of questions. Psychological factors can be added to the list of other "P's" (product, price, place, and promotion) that are important to marketers since psychological variables such as behavior, affect, sensation, imagery, motivation, and cognition are highly relevant to an understanding of the relationships between people and products.[8]

The strategic significance of qualitative research lies in its ability to explore the dynamic, context-rich, and interactive phenomena that are subject to international business research.[9] Qualitative marketing research adds a layer of rich meaning not otherwise provided by its quantitative counterpart. This chapter extends this thought process by arguing that qualitative market research is even more essential in today's global business environment. This chapter underscores the fact that qualitative market research techniques are uniquely positioned to uncover the true motivations of diverse customer segments represented in international cultures. Furthermore, the insight gained from qualitative research is of a sufficient depth that is required by organizations to develop meaningful international marketing strategies.

Marketers are very aware that culture shapes consumer behavior.[10] However, despite this widespread belief, relatively little research concerning consumer behavior and marketing has examined the interaction of consumer behavior and culture. This chapter suggests that conducting and interpreting qualitative market research techniques are more suitable for investigating subtle cultural differences and developing impactful international marketing strategies and tactics.

The primary themes of this chapter are organized into four major sections: The first section provides definitional issues. The second section presents an overview of qualitative marketing research techniques, along with international business applications of the techniques. The third section discusses critical management challenges involved in conducting international qualitative marketing research. Finally, the fourth section suggests proposals for improving international qualitative marketing research studies.

QUALITATIVE MARKETING RESEARCH: DEFINITIONS, DISTINCTIONS, BENEFITS, AND CLASSIFICATIONS

While quantitative marketing research approaches concentrate on large samples, population projection, measurement, and mathematical properties, qualitative marketing research techniques focus on the question of "why" by attempting to understand the depth of meaning and the context of consumer choice behavior.

An important distinction that requires initial clarification is that between qualitative research and qualitative *marketing* research. The broad field of qualitative research, or qualitative inquiry, has application well beyond marketing research. These include qualitative methods and ways of thinking to investigate a wide range of phenomena and spanning a diverse range of disciplines within the social sciences.

Market research is the method by which organizations learn about customer-relevant issues in order to guide organizational strategies and tactics. Consequently, qualitative marketing research is where market research and qualitative methods overlap. Broadly, applications of qualitative marketing research cover issues of diagnosis, prognosis, and the creative generation of ideas or solutions to marketing problems.[11] Mike Imms and Gill Ereaut discuss three broad areas where qualitative methods in general can be used to help solve problems. First are issues related to academic inquiry where research is conducted to extend theories and other constructs. Second is the use of qualitative methods in social or policy research consisting of studies conducted by governments or foundations with the intention of improving social policies or conditions. And third are the commercial marketing research projects conducted to help an organization further its goals and objectives. The focus of this chapter is limited to the applications of commercial qualitative marketing research approaches and their associated management challenges.

Qualitative marketing research offers important advantages to marketers interested in developing meaningful and impactful marketing strategies. Highly structured quantitative techniques are not well suited to yield the rich and potentially insightful findings that are generated using an unstructured approach. The important purposes of qualitative marketing research are discussed by Denise F. Polit and Bernadette P. Hungler and include the following: description, hypothesis generation, and theory development.[12]

- *Description.* When information is incomplete regarding a group of customers, a brand, or a potential strategy, in-depth interviewing and participant observation are good ways to learn more about them. Questioning that elicits more fundamental insight and allows a free flow of communication often provides organizations with the ability to enhance or customize marketing strategies.

- *Hypothesis generation.* A researcher using qualitative techniques often has no explicit *a priori* hypotheses. The collection of in-depth information about some phenomena may indeed lead to the formulation of a set of hypotheses that could be subsequently tested using quantitative techniques.

- *Theory development.* Qualitative researchers often analyze their data with the goal of developing an integrated explanatory scheme. Using field research for data collection, this approach involves generating theory by observing and analyzing information from field interviews rather than investigating preconceived hypotheses about particular phenomena.

Despite potential benefits of qualitative research, the applications of the qualitative methods to the international business research has been a neglected topic.[13] Qualitative marketing research provides the firm with a set of techniques designed to probe meaningful customer-related issues and concerns. A wide variety of qualitative marketing research options are available, which can be broadly classified into the areas shown in Figure 9.1. The following section presents a brief discussion of these techniques along with actual company examples. The remainder of the chapter is devoted to the variety of consumer behavior challenges related to the international environment.

Table 9.1 provides a brief summary of the qualitative techniques discussed in this chapter. A basic working definition as well as a practical company example is provided to help illustrate the use and context of each technique.

INTERNATIONAL CONSUMER BEHAVIOR CHALLENGES

Durairaj Maheswarah and Sharon Shavitt discuss several issues related to conducting cross-cultural market research. Among these were the research orientations of emic (which advocates a within-culture investigation, arguing that

Figure 9.1
Qualitative Research Techniques

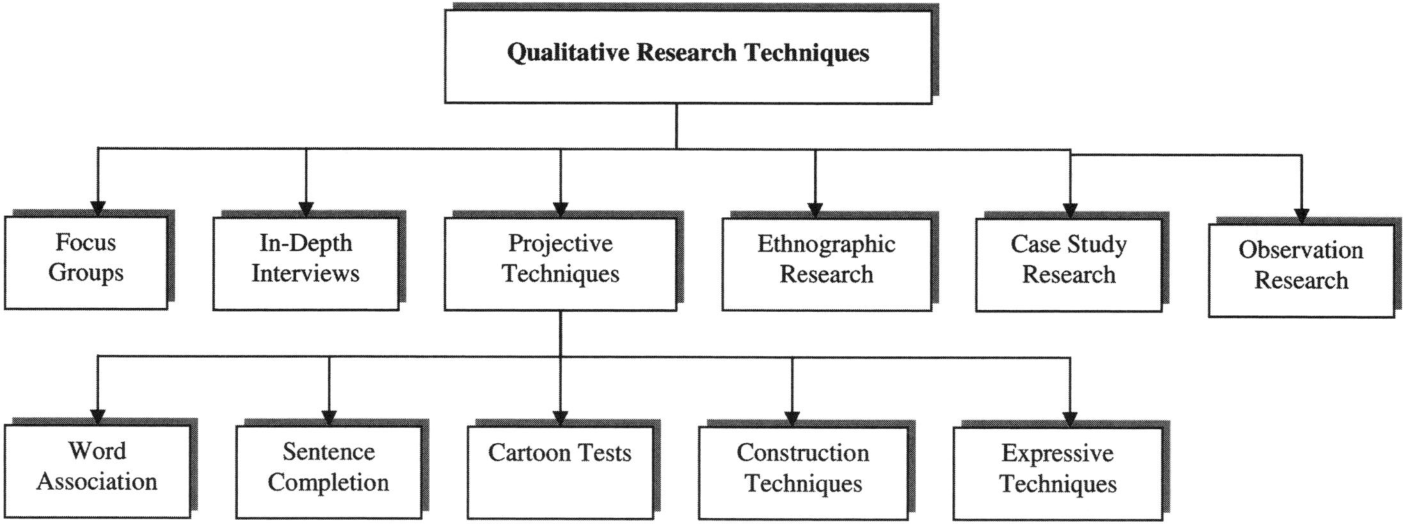

Table 9.1
Definitions and Company Examples

Qualitative Technique	Definition	Company Example
Focus Groups	Focus groups consist of a small group interview among 6–10 respondents that generally follows a semistructured questioning format and is moderated by a trained interviewer. Groups are typically viewed through a one-way mirror by clients and other pertinent stakeholders.	Focus groups were used successfully by a Swedish bus company having difficulty attracting senior citizens to its bus tours.[14] Results indicated that the primary reason, by far, for seniors not taking bus tours was due to the lack of bathroom facilities.
In-Depth Techniques	In-depth techniques involve an unstructured, direct, personal interview in which a single respondent is probed by a highly skilled interviewer to uncover underlying motivation, beliefs, attitudes, and feelings about any given topic.	Chivas Regal conducted an international qualitative project to help its marketing managers evaluate a number of global advertising concepts for Chivas Regal whiskey. This design ensured that the researchers were in tune with the cultural differences between Japan and North America.[15]
Projective Techniques	Projective techniques utilize an unstructured, indirect form of questioning that encourages respondents to project their underlying motivations, beliefs, attitudes, or feelings regarding issues of concern.	Projective techniques including word association, sentence completion, cartoon tests, construction techniques, and expressive techniques have been used by marketers to develop a variety of strategies.
Case Study Research	Case research involves a comprehensive description and analysis of a single situation.	Case research was successfully used by a food company to suggest the attributes that might characterize effective district sales managers.[16] Successful and unsuccessful managers were matched and studied for two weeks, resulting in a profile of effective behaviors.

Qualitative Technique	Definition	Company Example
Observation Techniques	Observational techniques typically do not require the respondent to perform any specific task. Observation is based on watching how respondents behave and, in some cases, videotaping respondents in a specific consumption or purchase environment. These techniques are well suited for the investigation of sensitive topics where social desirability may be a concern.	Observational techniques have been employed in many retail purchase situations as well as home environments. Shopping behavior has been observed both formally within the context of a specific study and informally by interested store personnel.

theorizing is culture specific and should be inductive) versus etic (which argues for generalization and focuses on issues that are universal and common to all cultures), measurement equivalence, and the broad cultural dimensions of individualism and collectivism.[17] These authors also discuss the difficult challenge between theoretical frameworks that can be generalized across cultures versus the need to capture unique cultural insights from cross-cultural studies. This dichotomy of the universal versus the unique makes international qualitative research applications even more useful if used appropriately.

Once the appropriate qualitative research technique has been identified, there are a host of issues that must be dealt with in order to assure that the project meets its stated objectives. Critical project management skills are involved in every market research project, but the international environment adds further complexities all related to project management.

Similar to quantitative research techniques used internationally, the use of focus groups in multicountry research poses a number of other problems. These include comparability of data, multilingual moderator availability, and the interpretation of respondent data. Trained moderators who are familiar with both the appropriate language and also the patterns of social interaction in various countries and cultures are relatively rare. This can pose serious problems in developing countries such as Eastern Europe or Southeast Asia, particularly China, where there is no established research tradition or infrastructure. These problems may require the research organization to train local interviewers to conduct a given project.[18]

The interpretation and analysis of focus group data are subjective in character and require considerable skill and experience. Moderators and analysts are required to understand verbal as well as nonverbal cues such as voice intonation, gestures, and expressions used in other countries and cultures. Incorrect assumptions made at the critical analysis level will result in erroneous findings and lead to off-target strategic recommendations.

The extent to which interpretation and reporting is centralized varies according to the research organization. Some international research organizations centralize transcripts, audiotapes, and videotapes of groups and conduct interpretation and analysis centrally. This typically requires the availability of bilingual research executives at the head office of the research firm. Other firms rely on local interpretation and analysis by moderators and then integrate these findings into a common report. The major consideration in interpretation is to reduce the extent to which findings reflect variations in research technique and traditions rather than true consumer behavior differences that will be meaningful from a strategic marketing and management perspective.

Additional challenges include cultural, language, sampling, interviewer, and cost issues, which are discussed in the following section. The relationship between qualitative techniques, management challenges, and improvement proposals is shown in Figure 9.2.

Figure 9.2
Framework for International Qualitative Consumer Marketing Research

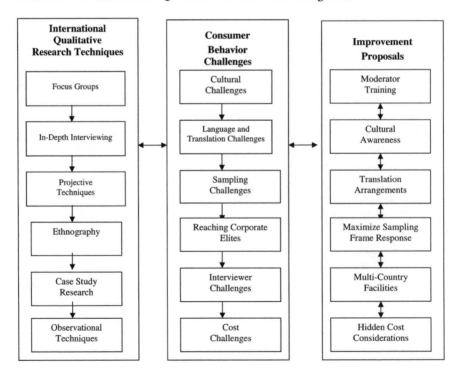

CULTURAL CHALLENGES

Culture is a critically important factor to understand when conducting international marketing research and, as previously discussed, this situation is even more important when conducting cross-cultural qualitative marketing research. Culturally informed researchers should tailor their information-gathering efforts to match the client's cultural expectations.[19] Ignoring subtle cultural differences when conducting global qualitative marketing research results in jeopardizing multimillion dollar marketing strategies that will not impact the organization's targeted customers as intended.

Culture provides people a solid anchoring point, an identity, as well as codes of behavior.[20] Edward T. Hall discussed culture in terms of high- versus low-context cultures. In high-context cultures, such as Japan and Saudi Arabia, the context is as important as the specific words spoken.[21] In low-context cultures, such as in North America and Western Europe, words form the foundation for communication exchanges. Being aware of and managing these differences becomes an integral part of conducting international qualitative marketing research.

The elements of culture are multidimensional and interdependent.[22] Changes in one dimension will necessarily affect other related dimensions as well. Specific components of culture include language, nonverbal communication, religion, values and attitudes, manners and customs, material elements, social institutions, and education among others. Jeffrey S. Nevid and Nelly L. Sta. Maria reviewed the need for international researchers to appreciate cultural differences including ethnicity, gender, values, and trust issues in conducting cross-cultural qualitative marketing research.[23]

Language and nonverbal communication plays a critical role in interpreting qualitative research results. North American cultures with strong oral traditions make a focus group or in-depth interview approach more feasible. But other cultures, notably the Asian culture, are well known for their long traditions of discouraging public disagreement or differences of opinion. Furthermore, Asian societies do not actively encourage the discussion of individual opinions or the discussion of these opinions with people outside the family unit.[24] Similarly, researchers need to be aware and sensitive to the importance of strong religious values and spirituality in African-American communities.

After language the most significant variable in successful foreign market research is culture, which can make the difference between successful product introduction and failure. Furthermore, these differences in culture and cultural norms are usually very subtle rather than blatant and obvious. For example, after learning that ketchup was not marketed in Japan, a U.S. company attempted to sell its product there. Without the benefit of any preliminary research, the large, well-known U.S. company shipped a large quantity of its popular brand-name ketchup to Japan. Unfortunately, the firm did not first determine why ketchup was not already available in Japan. The large, affluent market was so tempting that the company feared any delay would permit its competition to spot the opportunity and capture the market. The market research, had it been conducted prior to the introduction, would have revealed that soy sauce is the preferred condiment in Japan rather than ketchup.[25]

Chase & Sanborn had a similar challenge when it tried to introduce its instant coffee in France. In the French home, the consumption of coffee plays a more significant role than in the English home. Since the preparation of real coffee is a ritual in the life of French consumers, they will generally reject instant coffee because of its impromptu characteristics. Culture has significant effects on many other arenas as well. For example, in many Middle-Eastern countries women would never consent to be interviewed by a man. Furthermore, the idea of discussing grooming behavior and personal-care products with a stranger (that is, moderator) would be highly offensive.[26]

One of the most well-known discussions of culture is Geert Hofstede's four-dimensional structure that includes (1) individualism versus collectivism, (2) large versus small power distance, (3) strong versus weak uncertainty avoidance, and (4) masculinity versus femininity. A brief review of each dimension follows.[27]

According to Hofstede's research, collectivist cultures, such as the Asian culture, place more value on consensus and agreement. In contrast, people in individualistic cultures, such as North America and other Western cultures, place value on the individual and the self. Power distance is the extent to which members of a society accept the unequal distribution of power among individuals. In cultures with large power distance, such as North America, an individual with power has it because he or she deserves it and others simply accept this fact. Strong versus weak uncertainty avoidance refers to the degree to which the members of society feel threatened by ambiguity and are reluctant to take risks. Finally, masculinity versus femininity refers to the degree to which the dominant values in a society emphasize assertiveness, financial acquisitions, and achievement of visible rewards (masculinity) compared to the degree to which the society focuses on relationships, concern for others, and the overall quality of life (femininity).[28] Hofstede's structure provides the basis for a wide array of considerations in conducting qualitative marketing research in the international setting. Given the nature of personal communication in qualitative research techniques, interviewers must be acutely aware of these cultural differences. For example, high-context, collectivist, relationship-oriented cultures like Japan will require interviewers with different sensitivities compared with interviewers operating in low-context, individualistic, achievement-oriented Western cultures. In the Korean culture, it is considered disrespectful to exchange eye contact with strangers, while among Native Americans, it is not unusual for speakers to provide lengthy intervals in order to allow respondents to answer questions.[29] International market researchers clearly need to take these differences into account to assure project success.

Language and Translation Challenges

Now that qualitative market research is being conducted around the globe, researchers must take language and translation factors into account when designing questionnaires and qualitative discussion guides. Language represents the most obvious factor that makes international market research so challenging.

A discussion guide developed in one country may be difficult to translate because equivalent language concepts may not exist or because of differences in idiom, vernacular, and phrasing (that is, syntax). For example, the concepts of uncles and aunts are not the same in the United States as in India. In India the words for aunt and uncle are different for the maternal and paternal sides of the family. Although Spanish is spoken in both Mexico and Venezuela, researchers have found the Spanish translation of the English term "retail outlet" works in Mexico, but not in Venezuela. Venezuelans interpreted the translation to refer to an electrical outlet, an outlet of a river into an ocean, and the passageway into a patio.[30]

International marketing researchers often have questionnaires and interviewer guides *back translated*. Back translation is the process of translating questionnaires from one language to another and then translating them back again by a second, independent translator.[31] The back translator is often a person whose native tongue is the language that will be used for the final questionnaire. This can reveal inconsistency between the English version and the translation, for correction if necessary. For example, in one international advertising research project the advertising slogan "out of sight, out of mind" was back translated as "invisible things are insane."

There are many other examples from around the world of marketers and researchers running into translation problems. Bruce Nash and Allan Zullo provide several examples of translation difficulties.[32] For example, The Coca-Cola Company had to change its name in China in 1986 after it discovered that its phonetic equivalent, "*Ke Kou Ke La*" was translated as "bite the wax tadpole." PepsiCo ran into translation problems in Germany when consumers there interpreted Pepsi's "come alive" advertising campaign to mean "arise from the grave." One of the most well-known translation issues was the General Motors new car campaign in Latin America. The company was having trouble determining why sales of its new economy car, the Nova, was not selling well. Finally, GM learned that in Spanish, "*no va*" means "it doesn't go."

Culture and Sampling Challenges

Consider conducting marketing research in China. China has a population of 1.2 billion of which 350 million are in urban areas: 622 cities and scores of smaller towns. Of the cities, only 32 have populations of at least 1 million, 42 between 500,000 and 1 million, and the remaining 548 less than 500,000.[33] Since almost no small towns or rural areas are included in market research projects, what constitutes a nationally representative sample of the Chinese market? In Germany, for example, telephone penetration did not reach the 80-percent level until the mid-1980s, long after the United States. Less than 10 percent of all households in India have telephones making telephone interviewing difficult to conduct. Furthermore, telephone penetration in Brazil is less than 50 percent in large cities.[34] Considering the low current computer usage in these nations the sample representation problem is even more dramatically exacerbated when using Internet-based samples. Unless and until these nations increase their overall computer and Internet capacity, using the Internet to conduct international market research in less-developed countries is not going to result in sound customer-based business strategies.

Cultural Challenges of Reaching Corporate Elites as Informants

According to Welch et al., corporate elites, defined as senior or middle management executives within an industry who have international experience, a high status and visibility, and possess a broad network of relationships within and outside their organizations, tend to affect the interview situation and the quality of the data.[35] These researchers argue that the challenge of reaching corporate elites as informants in qualitative international business research has received little scholarly attention, although most researchers are likely to interact with elite interviewees at some stage of their research projects. No doubt an understanding of corporate elites as informants in qualitative studies is important when seeking to improve the data-gathering tasks in international business settings. The dialogue between an international business researcher and an elite interviewee has profound implications not only for theory development and testing the reliability and validity of research findings, but also for managerial implications. Such issues are generally not found in most handbooks on qualitative research. Generally speaking, answers to international business issues, concerns, and/or clarifications require answers from a powerful elite person representing, for instance, subsidiary management or headquarters. There is a prevailing view that the higher the status of the company informant being interviewed, the greater the reliability and validity of the data.[36] It is pointed out that "data collection and analysis may be distorted, misleading, and incomplete if researchers find themselves selective and partial access to a company, amending their interview guide, falling captive to the 'hostage syndrome,' encountering negative perceptions of academic or headquarter spies, battling manipulation by elite informants in the interview situation and censorship in the feedback process, and juggling their roles as neutral observer and consultant."[37]

Culture and Interviewer Challenges

To facilitate the already complicated communication process, using native interviewers for international research projects allows multinational clients to exert a form of quality control. It is a matter of courtesy to the local respondents for them to be able to speak with interviewers in their language, and many nationalities, such as the French, are offended by a foreigner calling them to conduct research when it is obvious they are not native themselves. Recruiting native interviewers, although advisable, can also be problematic in countries where the literacy rate is low like rural China and India.

Along with quality control, interviewing consistency is a challenge in domestic research as well as in international market research. One of the many constant market research challenges is interviewer consistency. This concept relates to the difference in findings that are due to the simple fact that the same person cannot possibly conduct all the interviews related to a given project. Rather than uncovering differences due to actual changes in brand awareness, preference, and so forth, interviewer inconsistency introduces the possibility of multicollinearity. So in the case of interviewer (in)consistency, differences in brand performance must be attributed to *real* differences in performance rather than simply differences in the people who interviewed specific respondents. Interviewer consistency is closely related to the measurement equivalence discussion below.

Culture and the Use of Incentives

The cost of international marketing research is affected by a variety of less obvious factors, including the use of incentives, different time zones, and foreign holidays. Each is discussed briefly in the following section.

Incentives

The use of incentives in market research has been debated for as long as research projects have been conducted. The common criticism is that an inherent bias is introduced by paying respondents for their opinions. Using incentives is more complicated in the international setting where in some cultures they are required in order to get respondent cooperation. For example, in Brazil drinking and socializing are expected as part of the research experience. But in other cultures incentives of any kind are regarded as insulting to the respondents.

Culture and Time Zones

Differing time zones make it more problematic to conduct any type of business in foreign markets, and market research is no exception. During fieldwork, market researchers frequently find it necessary to communicate with the facilities that have been hired to conduct the actual interviews. The various time zones in other countries impact project communication and ultimately project timing.

Depending on the specific countries involved in the research project, different time zones are likely to cross over entire work days. Hence additional days are required to field a given research project to allow for communications that may need to occur half way around the world. Even the time of day matters in places like Japan. Business-to-business interviewing in Japan is very difficult to conduct during business hours because the Japanese are so strongly loyal to their employers, and they also believe that they owe absolute commitment to their employees while on the job as well.

Culture and Foreign Holidays

The United States generally celebrates approximately 12 standard holidays per year. In other countries, the number can be much greater and certainly differs from the American calendar. Holidays also add to the total time frame required to complete an international research project. According to Quirk's Marketing Research Review, clients should always check the holiday schedule in the countries prior to starting research as you can be sure that nearly every Monday is a holiday somewhere in the world.

PROPOSALS FOR IMPROVING INTERNATIONAL QUALITATIVE CONSUMER RESEARCH

In order for organizations interested in conducting cross-cultural qualitative market research to improve its effectiveness, Kent D. Hamilton offers several guidelines for managers. They include the following:

1. Have moderators been secured in each country that have the appropriate language and cultural fit to relate effectively to respondents and elicit their feedback?
2. If personnel are attending interviewing sessions that do not speak the local language, have arrangements been made for simultaneous translation?
3. Consider the possibility of matching interviewers to participants along racial or ethnic lines to increase communication flow.
4. Are appropriate procedures in place for simultaneous translation of audio and/or video tapes if necessary?
5. Have additional interviewers been considered who are attuned to the different cultural variations and/or language dialects either within or across countries?
6. Have appropriate arrangements been made for transcripts of qualitative research findings to be translated into English?
7. How will the briefing of interviewers (in-person or via long-distance conference call) for cross-cultural studies be conducted?
8. Are the facilities in different countries suitable for conducting qualitative interviewing? For example, are one-way mirrors or private interviewing rooms available in designated countries?

9. Have adequate sampling procedures been implemented prior to recruiting focus group or in-depth interview participants?

10. Have appropriate steps been taken to maximize the response rates of corporate elites?

11. Have hidden cost implications such as the use of incentives, differing holidays, and varying time zones been addressed?[38]

CONCLUSIONS AND MANAGEMENT GUIDELINES

As the economy continues to go global the need for cross-cultural market research continues to increase. Global market research differs from its domestic counterpart due to its application to a multitude of cross-cultural environments where comparable, relevant data are oftentimes nonexistent. Because of this complexity, conducting international market research requires flexibility and creativity on the part of the researcher. The complexity of the international marketplace, the extreme differences that exist in different countries, and the unfamiliarity of foreign markets demand better information prior to launching costly international marketing strategies. Prior to entering foreign markets, global organizations need accurate information concerning potential market segments, marketing mix options, and potential positioning strategies. Information regarding competitors is also critically needed by global organizations. Qualitative marketing research is uniquely qualified to provide the depth of information required by today's successful international marketers.

This chapter provides a thorough review of qualitative approaches and uses international application examples to illustrate the various techniques. Specifically, the chapter reviews the use of focus groups, in-depth interviews, and a variety of projective techniques, ethnographic approaches, case study research, and observational studies. This review also includes a discussion of the management challenges associated with conducting market research in a global context. These challenges include issues related to culture and language translation, sampling, reaching corporate elites, interviewing consistency, and the increased cost of international market research. Successful international marketers will need to address a variety of improvement proposals in order to compete in the changing global business landscape.

NOTES

1. Javalgi, R., and D. White (2002), "Strategic Challenges for the Marketing of Services Internatinonally," *International Marketing Review,* Vol. 19, No. 6, pp. 563–581.

2. Marketing News, January 17 (1994), "Going Global Requires Careful Planning, Knowing Key Factors," American Marketing Association, Chicago, IL.

3. Marketing News, August 19 (2002), *Honomichl Global Top 25,* American Marketing Association, Chicago, IL.

4. Connell, Stephen (2002), "Travel Broadens the Mind—The Case for International Research," *International Journal of Market Research,* Vol. 44, No. 1, pp. 97–106.

5. Maheswaran, Durairaj, and Sharon Shavitt (2000), "Issues and New Directions in Global Consumer Psychology," *Journal of Consumer Psychology,* Vol. 9, No. 2, pp. 59–66.

6. Bonoma, Thomas V. (1985), "Case Research in Marketing: Opportunities, Problems, and a Process," *Journal of Marketing Research,* Vol. 22, No. 3, pp. 199–208.

7. Cohen, Ronald J. (1999a), "Qualitative Research and Marketing Mysteries: An Introduction to the Special Issue," *Psychology & Marketing,* Vol. 16, No. 4, pp. 287–289.

8. Cohen, Ronald J. (1999b), "What Qualitative Research Can Be," *Psychology & Marketing,* Vol. 16, No. 4, pp. 351–368.

9. See Welch, C., R. Marschan-Piekkari, H. Penttinen, and M. Tahvanainen (2002), "Corporate Elites as Informants in Qualitative International Business Research," *International Business Review,* Vol. 11, pp. 611–628.

10. Maheswaran and Shavitt, op. cit.

11. Imms, Mike, and Gill Ereaut (2002), *An Introduction to Qualitative Market Research,* Sage Publications, Thousand Oaks, CA.

12. Polit, Denise F., and Bernadette P. Hungler (1995), *Nursing Research Principles and Methods,* J.B. Lippincott Company, Philadelphia, PA.

13. See Welch et al., 2002, op. cit.; Taylor, S.J., and R. Bogdan (1998), *Introduction to Qualitative Research Methods,* New York. John Wiley & Sons.

14. Lewis, Steve, and Misty Hathaway (1998), "International Focus Groups: Embrace the Unpredictable," *Quirk's Marketing Research Review,* Vol. 12, No. 10, pp. 36–41.

15. Nancarrow, Clive, Len Tiu Wright, and Chris Woolston (1998), "Pre-Testing International Press Advertising," *Qualitative Market Research: An International Journal,* Vol. 1, No. 1, pp. 25–38.

16. Aaker, David A., V. Kumar, and George S. Day (2004), *Marketing Research,* New York: John Wiley & Sons, Inc.

17. Maheswaran and Shavitt, op. cit.

18. Craig, C. Samuel, and Susan P. Douglas (2000), *International Marketing Research,* John Wiley & Sons, Inc., New York.

19. Nevid, Jeffrey S., and Nelly L. Sta. Maria (1999), "Multicultural Issues in Qualitative Research," *Psychology & Marketing,* Vol. 16, No. 4, pp. 305–325.

20. Czinkota, Michael R., Pietra Rivoli, and IIkka A. Ronkainen (1992), *International Business,* The Dryden Press, New York.

21. Hall, Edward T. (1976), *Beyond Culture,* Anchor Press, Garden City, NY.

22. Czinkota et al., op. cit.

23. Nevid and Sta. Maria, op. cit.

24. Ibid.

25. Zikmund, William (2000), *Exploring Marketing Research,* 6th ed. Orlando, FL: Dryden Press.

26. Ibid.

27. Hofstede, Geert (1983), "National Cultures in Four Dimensions," *International Studies of Management & Organization,* Vol. 13, No. 1/2, pp. 46–74.

28. Ball, Donald A., Wendell H. McCulloch, Jr., Paul L. Frantz, J. Michael Geringer, and Michael S. Minor (2002), *International Business,* McGraw-Hill Irwin, New York.

29. Nevid and Sta. Maria, op. cit.

30. Rydholm, Joseph (1996), "Leaping the Barriers of Time and Distance," *Quirk's Marketing Research Review,* Vol. 10, No. 10, November, pp. 10–11, 42–45; Iyer, Ravi (1997), "A Look at the Indian Market Research Industry," *Quirk's Marketing Research Review,* Vol. 11, No. 10, November, pp. 22–26.

31. Zikmund, op. cit.

32. Nash, Bruce and Allan Zullo (1988), *The Mis-Fortune 500,* Simon & Schuster, Inc., New York.

33. Lee, Barton, and Alexander Wong (1996), "An Introduction to Marketing Research in China," *Quirk's Marketing Research Review,* Vol. 10, No. 10, November, pp. 18–19, 37–38.

34. Malhotra, Naresh K. (2004), *Marketing Research—An Applied Orientation,* Prentice Hall Inc., Upper Saddle River, NJ.

35. Welch et al., 2002, op. cit.

36. Macdonald, Stuart, and B. Hellgren, "The Interview in Management Research," *Iconoclastic Papers,* Vol. 1, No. 2, 1998.

37. Welch et al., 2002, op. cit., p. 626.

38. Hamilton, Kent D. (1998), "An International Marketing Research Checklist," *Quirk's Marketing Research Review,* Vol. 12, No. 10, pp. 42–45.

REFERENCES

Aaker, David A., V. Kumar, and George S. Day (2004), *Marketing Research,* John Wiley & Sons, Inc., New York.

Arnould, Eric J., and Melanie Wallendorf (1994), "Market-Oriented Ethnography: Interpretation Building and Marketing Strategy Formulation," *Journal of Marketing Research,* Vol. 31, No. 4, pp. 484–504.

Bailey, Eric (1989), "Nissan Says Corporate Snoop Suit is Absurd," *Los Angeles Times,* December 9, 1989, p. C1.

Ball, Donald A., Wendell H. McCulloch, Jr., Paul L. Frantz, J. Michael Geringer, and Michael S. Minor (2002), *International Business,* McGraw-Hill/Irwin, New York.

Bonoma, Thomas V. (1985), "Case Research in Marketing: Opportunities, Problems, and a Process," *Journal of Marketing Research,* Vol. 22, No. 3, pp. 199–208.

Calder, Bobby J. (1977), "Focus Groups and the Nature of Qualitative Marketing Research," *Journal of Marketing Research,* Vol. 14, No. 3, pp. 353–364.

Cohen, Ronald J. (1999a), "Qualitative Research and Marketing Mysteries: An Introduction to the Special Issue," *Psychology & Marketing,* Vol. 16, No. 4, pp. 287–289.

Cohen, Ronald J. (1999b), "What Qualitative Research Can Be," *Psychology & Marketing,* Vol. 16, No. 4, pp. 351–368.

Connell, Stephen (2002), "Travel Broadens the Mind—The Case for International Research," *International Journal of Market Research,* Vol. 44, No. 1, pp. 97–106.

Craig, C. Samuel, and Susan P. Douglas (2000), *International Marketing Research*, John Wiley & Sons, Inc., New York.

Czinkota, Michael R., Pietra Rivoli, and IIkka A. Ronkainen (1992), *International Business*, The Dryden Press, New York.

Dow Jones News Service (1997), "Procter & Gamble Unveils New 'High Efficiency' Tide Detergent," March 20, 1997.

Durgee, Jeffrey F. (1986), "Depth-Interview Techniques for Creative Advertising," *Journal of Advertising Research*, Vol. 25, No. 6, pp. 29–37.

Fern, Edward F. (1982), "The Use of Focus Groups for Idea Generation: The Effects of Group Size, Acquaintanceship, and Moderator on Response Quantity and Quality," *Journal of Marketing Research*, Vol. 19, No. 1, pp. 1–13.

Gengler, Charles E., and Thomas J. Reynolds (1995), "Consumer Understanding and Advertising Strategy: Analysis and Strategic Translation of Laddering Data," *Journal of Advertising Research*, July/August, Vol. 35, No. 4, pp. 19–33.

Goldman, Alfred E. (1962), "The Group Depth Interview," *Journal of Marketing*, Vol. 26, No. 3, pp. 61–68.

Grunert, Klaus G., and Suzanne C. Grunert (1995), "Measuring Subjective Meaning Structures by the Laddering Method: Theoretical Considerations and Methodological Problems," *International Journal of Research in Marketing*, Vol. 12, pp. 209–225.

Gutman, Jonathan (1982), "A Means-End Chain Model Based on Consumer Categorization Processes," *Journal of Marketing*, Vol. 46, No. 2, pp. 60–72.

Haire, Mason (1950), "Projective Techniques in Marketing Research," *Journal of Marketing*, Vol. 14, No. 5, pp. 649–656.

Hall, Edward T. (1976), *Beyond Culture*, Anchor Press, Garden City, NY.

Hamilton, Kent D. (1998), "An International Marketing Research Checklist," *Quirk's Marketing Research Review*, Vol. 12, No. 10, pp. 42–45.

Han, C. Min, Lee Byoung-Woo, and Ro Kong-Kyun (1994), "The Choice of a Survey Mode in Country Image Studies," *Journal of Business Research*, Vol. 29 (February), pp. 151–162.

Hofstede, Geert (1983), "National Cultures in Four Dimensions," *International Studies of Management & Organization*, Vol. 13, No. 1/2, pp. 46–74.

Imms, Mike, and Gill Ereaut (2002), *An Introduction to Qualitative Market Research*, Sage Publications, Thousand Oaks, CA.

Iyer, Ravi (1997), "A Look at the Indian Market Research Industry," *Quirk's Marketing Research Review*, Vol. 11, No. 10, November, pp. 22–26.

Jastrzembski, Jim, and Barbara Leable (2002), "Unearthing the Truth—In the U.S. and Overseas, CNH Global Talks to Loader Backhoe Users to Develop New Models," *Quirk's Marketing Research Review*, Vol. 16, No. 10, pp. 20–23.

Kumar, V. (2000), *International Marketing Research*, Upper Saddle River, NJ: Prentice Hall.

Langerak, Fred, Ed Peelen, and Ed Nijssen (1999), "A Laddering Approach to the Use of Methods and Techniques to Reduce the Cycle Time of New-to-the-Firm Products," *Journal of Product Innovation Management*, Vol. 16, pp. 173–182.

Lee, Barton, and Alexander Wong (1996), "An Introduction to Marketing Research in China," *Quirk's Marketing Research Review,* Vol. 10, No. 10, November, pp. 18–19, 37–38.

Lewis, Steve, and Misty Hathaway (1998), "International Focus Groups: Embrace the Unpredictable," *Quirk's Marketing Research Review,* Vol. 12, No. 10, pp. 36–41.

Maheswaran, Durairaj, and Sharon Shavitt (2000), "Issues and New Directions in Global Consumer Psychology," *Journal of Consumer Psychology,* Vol. 9, No. 2, pp. 59–66.

Malhotra, Naresh K. (2004), *Marketing Research—An Applied Orientation,* Prentice Hall Inc., Upper Saddle River, NJ.

Mariampolski, Hy (1999), "The Power of Ethnography," *Journal of the Market Research Society,* Vol. 41, No. 1, pp. 75–87.

Marketing News, January 17 (1994), "Going Global Requires Careful Planning, Knowing Key Factors," American Marketing Association, Chicago.

Marketing News, August 19 (2002), *Honomichl Global Top 25,* American Marketing Association, Chicago.

Nancarrow, Clive, Len Tiu Wright, and Chris Woolston (1998), "Pre-Testing International Press Advertising," *Qualitative Market Research: An International Journal,* Vol. 1, No. 1, pp. 25–38.

Nash, Bruce, and Allan Zullo (1988), *The Mis-Fortune 500,* Simon & Schuster, Inc., New York.

Nason, Stephen W., and Madan M. Pillutla (1998), "Towards a Model of International Research Teams," *Journal of Managerial Psychology,* Vol. 13, Nos. 3/4, pp. 156–166.

Nevid, Jeffrey S., and Nelly L. Sta. Maria (1999), "Multicultural Issues in Qualitative Research," *Psychology & Marketing,* Vol. 16, No. 4, pp. 305–325.

Paradise, L.M., and A.B. Blankenship (1951), "Depth Questioning," *Journal of Marketing,* Vol. 15, No. 3, pp. 274–288.

Peile, Lucy (2003), "Insight Through Ethnography: Researching Children in a Different Way," *Advertising & Marketing to Children,* October–December, pp. 63–67.

Polit, Denise F., and Bernadette P. Hungler (1995), *Nursing Research Principles and Methods,* J.B. Lippincott Company, Philadelphia.

Reynolds, T., and J. Gutman (1984), "Advertising is Image Management," *Journal of Advertising Research,* Vol. 24, No. 1, pp. 27–37.

Reynolds, T., and J. Gutman (1988), "Laddering Theory, Method, Analysis, and Interpretation," *Journal of Advertising Research,* Vol. 28, No. 1, pp. 11–31.

Reynolds, T., and David B. Whitlark (1995), "Applying Laddering Data to Communications Strategy and Advertising Practice," *Journal of Advertising Research,* July/August, pp. 9–17.

Rokeach, M.J. (1968), *Beliefs, Attitudes and Values,* San Francisco: Jossey Bass.

Rydholm, Joseph (1996), "Leaping the Barriers of Time and Distance," *Quirk's Marketing Research Review,* Vol. 10, No. 10, November, pp. 10–11, 42–45.

Rydholm, Joseph (2001), "Seeking the Right Mix," Quirk's Marketing Research Review, Vol. 15, No. 10, pp. 22–25.

Song, Miri, and David Parker (1995), "Commonality, Difference and the Dynamics of Disclosure in In-Depth Interviewing," *Sociology,* Vol. 29, No. 2, pp. 241–256.

Taylor, S.J., and Bogdan, R. (1998), *Introduction to Qualitative Research Methods,* New York. John Wiley & Sons.

Wansink, Brian (2003), "Using Laddering to Understand and Leverage a Brand's Equity," *Qualitative Market Research: An International Journal,* Vol. 6, No. 2, pp. 111–118.

Weiers, Ronald M. (1988), *Marketing Research,* Prentice Hall Inc., Upper Saddle River, NJ.

Welch, C., R. Marschan-Piekkari, H. Penttinen, and M. Tahvanainen (2002), "Corporate Elites as Informants in Qualitative International Business Research," *International Business Review,* Vol. 11, pp. 611–628.

Woodward, Julian L., David Hofler, Fred Haviland, Herbert Hyman, Jack Peterman, and Harry Rosten (1950), "Depth Interviewing," *Journal of Marketing,* Vol. 14, No. 2, pp. 721–724.

Yankelovich, D. (1981), *New Rules,* New York: Random House.

Zikmund, William (2000), *Exploring Marketing Research,* 6th ed. Orlando, FL: Dryden Press.

Zimmerman, Alan S., and Michael Szenberg (2000), "Implementing International Qualitative Research: Techniques and Obstacles," *Qualitative Market Research: An International Journal,* Vol. 3, No. 3, pp. 158–164.

CHAPTER 10

NEGOTIATIONS IN INTERNATIONAL MARKETING

Allan Bird and Lynn E. Metcalf

Ernie Brown checks his watch with annoyance. As the youngest and brightest sales representative in his company, he's been sent to Telco Mfg. in Mexico City, to pitch his company's newest line of equipment. He's been waiting more than forty minutes to meet with Javier Arroyo—one of Telco's most influential managers and also the person responsible for authorizing capital purchases at the Mexico City facility—to free himself up from other appointments. Finally, Ernie is led back to Señor Arroyo's office. The conversation begins with "small talk"—mostly questions about Ernie's activities since arriving in Mexico City. Upon learning that Ernie had not seen any of the local sights, Señor Arroyo offers to take him sightseeing later that afternoon. Ernie responds with a polite, yet firm rejection, adding that this is a business trip and that his boss expects him back in Los Angeles the following day. Señor Arroyo continues to talk about famous buildings in Mexico City and the history of the architecture. Exasperated at the slow pace, Ernie interrupts him, asking for a tour of the plant so that he can get a better sense of how the new equipment might fit in and indicating his strong desire to discuss the new line he's touting. Señor Arroyo side-steps the request by asking about Ernie's family. But Ernie will not be put off and insists on moving on to the reason for his visit. At this point, Señor Arroyo gives in and begins to answer Ernie's questions. Later, while touring the plant facilities, Ernie's cell phone rings. He answers it, and as he talks he notices Señor Arroyo's irritation. Ernie terminates the call, saying, "I'll get back to you on that tomorrow; my host is giving me the evil eye." Back in Señor Arroyo's office, Ernie pulls out his laptop and presentation materials. "Now, I'd like to show you something. This is our new line of equipment. I've got some data on its performance characteristics in a plant setting like yours. Let's take a look."

Negotiating a deal can be rough sailing in one's own country. Negotiators, such as Ernie in the opening vignette, often sail uncharted waters when negotiating cross-culturally. Cultural factors can complicate, prolong, and frustrate negotiations; and finding accurate, useful information can be a challenge. Much of the information that is available to an expanding corps of international managers about negotiating behaviors in countries around the world is descriptive.[1] Negotiators may find themselves relying on very basic lists of *do's* and *don'ts,*[2] which may not always contain tips relevant to negotiating. Moreover, items included in such lists are generally not comparable across countries. Empirical work that systematically compares variations across a range of countries is scarce.[3] An example of the types of common information available to a negotiator for Mexico is presented in Table 10.1. What the table makes clear is the lack of information on many dimensions, the stereotypical nature of what is available, and the contradictions that exist—without explanation—between widely available sources. In this era of increased global cooperation, it is imperative that negotiators be equipped with a better understanding of the orientations they might expect at the negotiation table.[4]

A comprehensive framework having potential to yield comparable information across countries on 12 negotiating tendencies was proposed 20 years ago by Stephen E. Weiss and William Stripp.[5] The framework was conceptual, with loosely defined dimensions. The intent was simply to sensitize researchers and practitioners to possible culturally based differences in negotiation attitudes, behaviors, and contexts.[6] To use the framework in empirical work it was necessary to define each dimension more precisely, which led us to review the extensive bodies of negotiation and cross-cultural research that have built up over the last two decades. Based on our review, we redefined 9 of the original 12 dimensions. Figure 10.1 comprises our reinterpretation of the framework.

THE NEGOTIATION ORIENTATIONS FRAMEWORK: DEFINING THE DIMENSIONS

Refinements in the definition of the 12 dimensions in the framework are presented below. Precise definitions provide the basis of good measurement and the means by which subsequent research findings can be compared and synthesized.[7]

Basic Concept of Negotiation: Distributive versus Integrative

Basic Concept of Negotiation refers to how each party views the negotiating process. A bipolar continuum, with distributive bargaining and integrative

Table 10.1
Conventional Wisdom about Negotiation in Mexico and the United States

Dimension	Mexico	United States
Basic Concept of Negotiation: Distributive or Integrative	Mexicans have a win-win attitude. Hard bargainers. Long, vigorous discussions.	Problem solving. Look for mutual gains, whenever possible.
Most Significant Type of Issue: Task or Relationship	Mexicans are relationship oriented.	Establish rapport quickly before "getting down to business." Personal relationships are ignored when discussing issues.
Selection of Negotiators: Abilities or Status	Expertise is less important than fitting in with the group.	Negotiators have relevant skills and expertise.
Influence of Individual Aspirations: Individualist or Collectivist	Mexicans pursue individual goals, personal recognition. Interests of the group are a dominant factor.	Self-interested negotiators.
Internal Decision-Making Process: Independent or Majority Rule	Decision-making authority is vested in a few at the top. Mexicans prefer consensus.	Independent problem solvers.
Orientation toward Time: Monochronic or Polychronic	Do not expect punctuality. Easy-going business atmosphere. Quick decisions perceived as concessions. Mexicans take time to reach decisions.	Meetings begin and end promptly. Agenda driven. Action oriented. Decisions are reached by the end of the meeting.
Risk-Taking Propensity: Risk Averse or Risk Tolerant	Mexican negotiators avoid risk.	Short-term oriented; focus on immediate gains.
Basis of Trust: External or Internal	Trust based on personal relationships.	Heavy reliance on the legal system. Lawyers involved from start to finish.
Concern with Protocol: Formal or Informal	Mexicans value formality; follow established etiquette.	Do not like formality in business interaction.
Style of Communication: Low Context or High Context	Mexicans avoid direct answers.	Direct and to the point.

(continued)

Table 10.1 (continued)

Dimension	Mexico	United States
Nature of Persuasion: Factual-Inductive or Affective	Truth is based on feelings. Emotional arguments are more effective than logic.	Deals are evaluated on their technical merits.
Form of Agreement: Explicit Contract or Implicit Agreement	Words are not a binding commitment to action. Relationships ensure follow-through.	Contracts are emphasized, along with the fine points of an agreement.

Sources: Recommendations are drawn from a variety of sources including *Business Mexico,* 2002; CultureGrams World Edition 2007; Elashmawi, 2001; Fisher & Ury, 1991; Hall & Hall, 1990; Hampden-Turner & Trompenaars, 2000; *Investor's Business Daily,* 2004; Kras, 1989; Moran & Stripp, 1991; and Morrison, Conaway, & Borden, 1994.

problem solving as endpoints, is consistent with R.E. Walton and Robert B. McKersie.[8]

Distributive Perspective

The assumption underlying distributive bargaining strategies is that one party gains at the expense of the other. Negotiators fitting this profile believe that there will be one winner and one loser,[9] assume that their interests directly conflict with those of the other party,[10] seek to meet only their own goals or interests in order to maximize the benefit for their side,[11] and focus on the need for the other party to concede.[12] The prevailing belief is "what is good for the other party must be bad for us."[13]

Integrative Perspective

The assumption underlying integrative bargaining strategies is that there is opportunity for both parties to gain from a negotiated agreement because they place different values on the issues being negotiated and can find effective trade-offs by conceding less important issues to gain on more important ones. Integrative negotiation involves both cooperation to expand the pie and competition to divide the pie between the two parties.[14] Negotiators fitting this profile believe that win-win solutions can be generated,[15] employ a problem-solving approach to develop solutions that expand the size of the rewards available to everyone,[16] and attempt to understand the underlying issues and their relative importance to both parties in order to capitalize on the different interests of both parties and to find effective trade-offs.[17]

Figure 10.1
The Negotiation Orientations Framework

Dimensions	Negotiator's Profile	
1. Basic Concept of Negotiation	Distributive	Integrative
2. Most Significant Type of Issue	Task	Relationship
3. Selection of Negotiators	Abilities	Status
4. Influence of Individual Aspirations	Individualist	Collectivist
5. Internal Decision-Making Process	Independent	Majority Rule
6. Orientation toward Time	Monochronic	Polychronic
7. Risk-Taking Propensity	Risk-averse	Risk-tolerant
8. Basis of Trust	External to the Parties	Internal to the Parties
9. Concern with Protocol	Formal	Informal
10. Style of Communication	Low-context	High-context
11. Nature of Persuasion	Factual-inductive	Affective
12. Form of Agreement	Explicit	Implicit

Most Significant Type of Issue: Task versus Relationship

Most Significant Type of Issue refers to the types of issues negotiators spend more time discussing. Although negotiators may be concerned with both task and relationship in a negotiation, they are likely to emphasize one over the other.[18]

Task

Negotiators with a task frame focus on specific issues having to do with the project at hand and view these issues as being external to the relationship.[19] Negotiators who believe that task issues are more important tend to focus the entire negotiation on the deal being discussed and not so much on the people involved in the discussions.[20]

Relationship

Negotiators with a relationship frame view task-related issues as being inseparable from the relationship. They devote time to activities that build trust and friendship between the members, believing that this provides a foundation for addressing task issues.[21] Negotiators who believe that the relationship is primary tend to focus the entire negotiation on the people involved in the discussions and not so much on the deal being discussed.[22]

Selection of Negotiators: Abilities versus Status

Selection of Negotiators refers to the criteria used to select members of the negotiating team. Achievement-based people evaluate and relate to others based on what they have accomplished; status-based people evaluate and relate to others based on who they are.[23]

Abilities

People with an achievement-based view believe members of a negotiating team should be selected because they possess certain job-related skills or because they have expertise that will be useful during the course of the negotiations.[24] Examples of relevant skills or expertise include education, technical or scientific knowledge, legal training, vocational achievement, negotiating experience, or language fluency.

Status

People with a status-based view believe members of a negotiating team should be selected because of who they are and whom they know. Examples of relevant characteristics include family background, influential connections, seniority, age, or gender.[25] Negotiators from status-based cultures may be senior, high-ranking officials, who wield considerable influence in their organizations[26] and who may also command great respect in the community at large.[27]

Influence of Individual Aspirations: Individualist versus Collectivist

Influence of Individual Aspirations refers to the emphasis negotiators place on the achievement of individual goals and the need for individual recognition.

Individualist

Harry C. Triandis defines individualists as people who see themselves as loosely linked to and independent of others.[28] They are motivated primarily by their own preferences, needs, and rights, and they give priority to their personal goals. From this, we can describe individualist negotiators as being emotionally independent from the organization to which they belong and as striving to achieve outcomes that are in their own best interests. They may also keep the organization's interests and goals in mind, but will do so because they expect personal reward and recognition for their decisions.[29]

Collectivist

Triandis defines collectivists as people who see themselves as closely linked to and parts of groups of co-workers or a company, for example.[30] They give priority to the goals of the collective. From this, we can describe collectivist negotiators as strongly identifying with and being loyal to their organizations; consequently, they may strive to achieve outcomes that are in the organization's best interest and may do so with no expectation of personal recognition or gain. The negotiating team may assume joint responsibility and/or receive joint recognition for actions taken or decisions made.[31]

Internal Decision-Making Process: Independent versus Majority Rule

Internal Decision-Making Process refers to the manner in which a negotiating team reaches decisions. Jeanne M. Brett identifies a range of decision-making behaviors, where either one person on the team has the authority to make the decision or a large proportion of the team's members must agree to a particular decision.[32]

Independent

Leaders or other influential individuals on the negotiating team may make decisions independently without input from others on the team.[33]

Majority Rule

Decision-making power is delegated to the entire team. The team leader seeks input and support from team members and listens to their advice.

Orientation toward Time: Monochronic versus Polychronic

Orientation toward Time refers to the value that negotiators place on time. Edward T. Hall and Mildred Reed Hall defined two culturally derived concepts of time that are important to international business.[34]

Monochronic

People whose orientation toward time is monochronic pay attention to and handle tasks one at a time, plan and schedule their activities, and set agendas and adhere to them. Monochronic negotiators believe that issues in a negotiation should be resolved effectively within the allotted time frame. They believe that time is money.[35]

Polychronic

People whose orientation toward time is polychronic handle several tasks simultaneously rather than in scheduled succession. Polychronic people do not expect human activities to proceed like clockwork. Consequently, scheduling is approximate rather than specific, and delays do not have the negative associations found in monochronic cultures. Negotiators from polychronic cultures believe that taking the time to get to know their counterparts and building a relationship is more important than adhering to a schedule. The actual clock time spent discussing and resolving issues is of minor importance.[36]

Risk-Taking Propensity: Risk Averse versus Risk Tolerant

This dimension refers to negotiators' willingness to take risks.

Risk Averse

Risk-averse negotiators are hesitant to proceed with proposals that may have unknowns and/or contingencies associated with them.[37] Risk-averse negotiators will take steps to avoid the risk of failing to come to an agreement.[38] Consequently, they may be more likely to make concessions in order to avoid the risk of failing to come to an agreement.[39]

Risk Tolerant

Risk-tolerant negotiators adopt a perspective that there is a level of acceptable risk that should be taken in a negotiation. They are interested in reducing risk, rather than avoiding it altogether. Risk-tolerant negotiators are willing to proceed with proposals that may have unknowns and/or contingencies associated with them.[40] Risk-tolerant negotiators show greater willingness to run the risk of failing to come to an agreement.[41] They accept the possibility that they may need to walk away from the table without a deal; hence, they are less likely to make concessions.[42]

Basis of Trust: External to the Parties versus Internal to the Relationship

Trust is one party's belief that the other party will take action to honor agreements that have been reached.[43] In all countries, trust provides the foundation upon which both parties to a negotiation can work together; however, negotiators from some countries trust that the other party will fulfill its obligations because there is a signed contract and the sanction of law to back it up, while negotiators from other countries trust that the other party will fulfill its obligations because of the relationship that exists between them.

External to the Parties

Negotiators with this viewpoint trust the other party because a contract has been negotiated and agreed to, which can be litigated and enforced.[44] The legal system and governmental agencies are viewed as providing an adequate, reliable, and effective underpinning for commercial transactions. A partner will honor the terms of the contract because the legal system will impose sanctions otherwise. The written word is binding; a deal is a deal.[45] In this context, a trustworthy partner is one who complies with the law.

Internal to the Relationship

Negotiators with this frame trust the other party because they have invested in a relationship that has been built up over time, and they believe that the other party is committed to it. The relationship between the parties is what matters; the contract is simply a symbol of the bond between the parties who drafted it.[46] A trustworthy partner is one who strives to maintain the relationship, possibly by modifying an existing contract to reflect new developments.[47]

Concern with Protocol: Formal versus Informal

Concern with Protocol has to do with the importance placed on rules for acceptable self-presentation and social behavior. It corresponds to Pertti J. Pelto's[48] characterization of tight and loose cultures, which we use to define the dimension more fully.

Formal

Negotiators with a high concern for protocol will adhere to strict and detailed rules that govern personal and professional conduct, negotiating procedures, as well as the hospitality extended to negotiators from the other side. Rules governing acceptable behavior might include dress codes, use of titles, and seating arrangements.[49] Negotiators believe that there is a limited range of appropriate behaviors, and there is strong agreement on the team about what constitutes correct action.

Informal

Negotiators with a relatively low concern for protocol adhere to a much smaller, more loosely defined set of rules. Team members may believe there are multiple ways to behave appropriately in a particular situation and may even have conflicting ideas about what is appropriate.

Style of Communication: High Context versus Low Context

This dimension refers to the degree to which people rely on verbal statements to communicate their primary message. Two culturally derived styles of communication are important to international business.[50]

Low Context

Low-context communicators believe that clarity is critical for effective communication, and they perceive direct requests to be the *most* effective strategy for accomplishing their goals.[51] The onus is on the communicator to make sure that the other party understands what is being said.[52] Low-context communicators are less likely to pick up on hints, particularly if the parties do not know each other well. Frank, open communication is perceived as the best way to resolve differences.[53] It is possible to offer criticism without having the other person take offense.

High Context

High-context communicators perceive direct requests to be the *least* effective strategy for accomplishing their goals. Directness is often considered rude and offensive; hence high-context communicators tend to be tactful, use qualifying words, and listen carefully. High-context communicators often hide their true feelings in order to maintain harmony in a relationship.[54] It is very difficult to offer criticism without having the other person take offense.[55] Importantly, people cannot be separated from the message, which means that reaching agreement with someone is completely dependent on liking that person.

Nature of Persuasion: Factual-Inductive versus Affective

This dimension refers to the type of evidence negotiators use to develop persuasive arguments. After an extensive review of the literature on philosophy, culture, and argumentation, we synthesized the variety of persuasive arguments in a bipolar dimension, with factual-inductive and affective as endpoints.

Factual-Inductive

Factual-inductive negotiators base their arguments on empirical facts and use linear logic (if-then statements) to persuade the other party.[56] Proof used to support persuasive arguments includes such things as scientific evidence, professional standards, expert opinion, costs, market value, and other hard data.[57] Moreover, factual-inductive negotiators believe the strongest case is made by presenting their best arguments first.

Affective

Affective negotiators may base their arguments on abstract theory, ideals,[58] references to status and relationships, and/or appeals to sympathy.[59] Evidence used to support persuasive arguments includes such things as moral standards, equal treatment, tradition, and reciprocity.[60] Affective negotiators develop their arguments indirectly. They may start with peripheral arguments and present their best arguments last, after the other party has reacted.[61]

Form of Agreement: Explicit Contract versus Implicit Agreement

This dimension refers to the preferred form of agreement between the parties: either formal written contracts or informal oral agreements. Formal written contracts clearly specify desired partner actions, the degree to which both parties of the agreement will cooperate and conform to each other's expectations, as well as the penalties that one party can extract should the other party fail to perform. Informal agreements often consider the historical and social context of a relationship and acknowledge that the performance and enforcement of obligations are an outcome of mutual interest between parties.[62]

Explicit Contract

Negotiators with this frame favor and expect written, legally binding contracts.[63] A written contract records the agreement and definitively specifies what each party has agreed to do.[64] Consequently, negotiators believe that written agreements provide the stability that allows their organization to make investments and minimize the risk of business loss.[65]

Implicit Agreement

Negotiators with this viewpoint favor broad or vague language in a contract because they feel that definitive contract terms are too rigid to allow a good working relationship to evolve. Particularly with new relationships, negotiators may feel that it is impossible to anticipate and document every conceivable contingency. They may also believe that contracts inhibit the parties from exploring unexpected or unusual opportunities for improvement and success. Negotiators view the contract as a rough guideline, not because they want to evade responsibility, but because the relationship, not the contract, is primary.[66]

USING THE FRAMEWORK IN RESEARCH AND PRACTICE

Now we return to our opening vignette and consider how the Negotiation Orientations Framework can help us understand the difficulties that Mr. Brown and Señor Arroyo are having. Even before the parties enter into discussions, the Selection of Negotiators emerges as an important factor in understanding possible tensions in their discussion. Señor Arroyo has been selected because of his influence in the company (status), while Mr. Brown has been chosen because of his proven performance (ability). Mr. Brown arrives punctually for the meeting and becomes impatient at having to wait (monochronic Orientation toward Time); meanwhile Señor Arroyo seems unconcerned with the delay (polychronic). Once Mr. Brown finally gets a chance to speak with Señor Arroyo, he finds that the conversation focuses on nonbusiness matters. For Señor Arroyo the Most Significant Type of Issue to be addressed is whether or not the two parties can develop a good *relationship*—something he signals by seeking to get to know Mr. Brown on a more personal level. In contrast, Mr. Brown focuses on the *task*, that is, the details of the negotiation. The two also have different orientations regarding Style of Communication, with Mr. Brown talking directly and somewhat informally (low context) while Señor Arroyo adopts a more circumspect and subtle approach (high context).

Within the space of just a few hours, tension points along 4 of the 12 dimensions have already been identified. It is likely that more will surface as the two proceed more deeply into the negotiation process. Whether these tension points become minor irritants or major stumbling blocks will depend on several factors, including the desire of both negotiators to achieve an agreement, the skill of both negotiators at reducing, rather than amplifying tensions, and the ability of both negotiators to discriminate between differences in negotiating positions and differences in negotiation orientations. The Negotiation Orientations Framework is a useful tool in helping negotiators identify tension points that may arise as a consequence of cultural differences in orientations.

Linking Hofstede's Dimensions of National Culture to Negotiation Orientations

What accounts for these differences in negotiation tendencies? One of the most widely explored explanations is culture; differences in cultural values lead to different negotiating orientations.[67] Geert Hofstede identified four work-related dimensions of national culture that have been used extensively in cross-cultural research, training, and management: Power Distance, Uncertainty Avoidance, Individualism-Collectivism, and Masculinity-Femininity. While research supporting the validity of Hofstede's dimensions is extensive, surprisingly few of these studies link them to negotiating orientations. The notion that cultural values may explain differences in negotiating tendencies led us to explore linkages between Hofstede's dimensions and the negotiation orientations in the Weiss and Stripp framework.[68] First, we reviewed the research relating Hofstede's dimensions to negotiating behaviors and developed hypotheses (Table 10.2) based on this review. Next, we conducted a systematic review of prior work on the negotiating tendencies found in Brazil, China, Germany, Japan, Mexico, and the United States and identified the "typical" orientation of negotiators from each country on each of the 12 dimensions in the Negotiation Orientations Framework. As an example, prior work indicates that U.S. and German negotiators would be selected on the basis of their abilities and that status considerations would figure in more heavily in Brazil, Mexico, China, and Japan. Then, we developed an ordered ranking of the countries on each negotiating dimension and correlated those rankings with country rankings on Hofstede's dimensions.

Our analysis showed strong correlations for countries with high UAI scores and a majority-rule orientation on the Internal Decision Making Process, as well as

Table 10.2

Hypotheses Linking Hofstede's Dimensions of National Culture to Negotiation Orientations

Negotiation Orientation	Hofstede Dimension	Support for Hypothesis
1. Basic Concept of Negotiation	MAS*	None
2. Most Significant Type of Issue	IDV	Moderate
3. Selection of Negotiators	PDI	None
4. Influence of Individual Aspirations	IDV	Moderate
5. Internal Decision-Making Process	UAI	Strong
6. Orientation toward Time	UAI	Strong
7. Risk-Taking Propensity	UAI	Moderate
8. Basis of Trust	UAI	Moderate
9. Concern with Protocol	UAI	Moderate
10. Style of Communication	IDV	Strong
11. Nature of Persuasion	UAI	Strong
12. Form of Agreement	UAI	Moderate

*MAS = Masculinity; IDV = Individualism; PDI = Power Distance Index; UAI = Uncertainty Avoidance.

monochronic tendencies on Orientation toward Time. Low UAI scores were strongly correlated with a factual-inductive orientation on Nature of Persuasion. High scores on IDV were strongly correlated with a low-context Style of Communication. Results for the linkages between the other eight negotiation orientations in the framework and Hofstede's cultural values were less clear (Table 10.2).

While theoretical links between cultural values and negotiation orientations can be found, our findings suggest that researchers ought to be wary of making inferences about negotiating tendencies on the basis of work-related cultural values. Even though managers from countries with high masculinity scores may be more competitive,[69] this does not necessarily translate to a distributive orientation on the Basic Concept of Negotiation.

Although it may be reasonable to expect a connection between negotiation and culture, it is clear from the extensive body of empirical research that national culture does not account in whole, or even in large part, for differences in negotiation orientations. A number of models have been proposed that (1) attempt to capture the myriad influences on international negotiating behavior and (2) permit comparisons between countries on a set of dimensions.[70] These models focus on what individuals do and how culture influences negotiating behavior.[71] When supported by empirical findings, the use of a dimensional framework or model enables meaningful cross-national comparison. Such comparisons are useful to negotiators; possible areas of tension can be systematically identified and adjustments in expectations and negotiation behaviors can be made, which increases the likelihood of positive outcomes.[72] The Salacuse framework, which includes ten negotiating tendencies, is the only one of these models that has been empirically investigated in full.

The Salacuse Framework: An Alternative Approach that Supports the Negotiation Orientations Framework

To measure the ten negotiating tendencies in his framework, Jeswald W. Salacuse developed a survey instrument, which included his ten bipolar dimensions, measured on five-point scales. Respondents were instructed to indicate where their own negotiating style and approach in business negotiations fell along each of the ten continua. In his 1998 study, Salacuse reported results from a survey of 191 respondents from 12 countries, finding that nationality did account for differences in negotiating tendencies.[73]

In a five-country study, which included nearly 1,200 business people and university students with business experience from Finland, India, Mexico, Turkey, and the United States, we confirmed the utility of the Salacuse framework (Figure 10.2) in identifying country differences in negotiating tendencies.[74] Specific country differences in mean scores were identified using pair-wise tests. For

Figure 10.2
Salacuse Dimensions of Cultural Variation in Negotiation

Negotiation Factors	Range of Cultural Responses		
1. Goal	Contract	← →	Relationship
2. Attitudes	Win/Lose	← →	Win/Win
3. Personal Styles	Informal	← →	Formal
4. Communications	Direct	← →	Indirect
5. Time Sensitivity	High	← →	Low
6. Emotionalism	High	← →	Low
7. Agreement Form	Specific	← →	General
8. Agreement Building	Bottom Up	← →	Top Down
9. Team Organization	One Leader	← →	Consensus
10. Risk Taking	High	← →	Low

five of the dimensions—Goal, Attitudes, Personal Styles, Time Sensitivity, and Agreement Building—we found significant differences in mean scores on seven of the ten paired comparisons. In only one case—Agreement Form—did we find no significant differences in mean scores among the five countries. In addition to reporting mean scores, we looked at the dispersion of responses (intracultural variation) within each country. Intracultural variation (ICV), measured by the standard deviation, can help capture critical cross-cultural differences. Our results showed that ICV for India was consistently larger than the other four countries across all ten negotiating tendencies, indicating that widely varying tendencies on a given dimension can be found among individual negotiators within India. In contrast, ICV for the United States was the smallest among the five countries for seven of the ten negotiating tendencies, indicating relatively consistent tendencies among individual U.S. negotiators on the majority of dimensions. Although each country presented a unique pattern of negotiation orientations, not surprisingly, countries were found to be similar on some dimensions. For example, no significant differences were found between pairs of countries on agreement form, despite the fact that ICV varied widely. In sum, the findings from this study confirmed that cross-national variation in negotiation tendencies could be identified using the Salacuse framework. Equally important, if not more so, the findings revealed that individuals and groups within cultures may be united on some dimensions, deeply divided or split on others, and uncommitted on others.

While the Salacuse framework was effective in revealing the varied and complex nature of negotiation tendencies between and within cultures for several dimensions, it was also useful in revealing tendencies that are contrary to conventional wisdom with respect to typical negotiating behaviors in the countries studied. For example, most sources indicate that Mexican and Indian negotiators do not expect punctuality and tend to follow a slower pace; Turkish negotiators are punctual, yet also follow a slower pace; and "time is money" for U.S. negotiators.[75] Yet respondents from Finland, India, Mexico, and Turkey reported a higher sensitivity toward time than U.S. respondents. Similarly, based on conventional wisdom, one would expect Turkish, Indian, and Mexican negotiators to show a tendency to communicate indirectly and to prefer relationships over contract. This was not the case. Conventional wisdom also did not hold for emotionalism, with Finnish and U.S. respondents preferring neither to act emotionally nor to keep their emotions under wraps. These findings suggest that negotiators should be wary of conventional thinking and prepare differently than "conventional wisdom" might suggest.

Despite the utility of the Salacuse framework, several of the dimensions in the framework are not clearly defined. For example, in his discussion of time sensitivity, Salacuse[76] refers to two different concepts: whether negotiators from a given country are punctual or late and whether negotiators are quick to make a deal or proceed slowly. To the extent that these are conceptually separable, they should be treated as such. The 12 dimensions in the Negotiation Orientations Framework are consistent with the Salacuse dimensions and offer improvements in conceptualization.

The Negotiation Orientations Framework: Not 12 but 24 Dimensions

With the dimensions of the Negotiation Orientations Framework defined in terms of extant bodies of research, we sought to develop measurement scales that could be used to assess tendencies in negotiating behaviors across countries and to gather data that would allow comparisons between countries. Descriptions of the behaviors exemplifying each pole of each dimension in the Negotiation Orientations Framework were converted to statements, yielding 71 items, which were scored on a five-point Likert scale, with endpoints "strongly agree" and "strongly disagree." The resulting Negotiation Orientations Inventory was administered to a sample of 1,000 business persons and university students with business experience from Finland, Mexico, Turkey, and the United States. The majority of our measures simply did not work as intended. In developing items, we followed the literature and carefully included items that reflected both poles of each dimension. The assumption was that we could reverse code items representing the opposing end of a given pole and include them in a scale. Doing so resulted in reliabilities well below the criterion we had set. This led us to examine the possibility that, while the Negotiation Orientations Framework suggested that the ends of a dimension (for example, explicit contract versus implicit agreement) could be viewed as polar opposites, in practice, people may not think of them as such (for example, explicitness and implicitness are independent constructs). Similar to the results of individual-level research about individualism and collectivism,[77] most constructs that the negotiation literature treats as bipolar appear to be better understood as distinct dimensions. Consequently, we began to think in terms of 24 negotiating tendencies, rather than 12 dimensions each with two poles, and we redefined our indicators and scales accordingly.

We used the resulting scales and also several single-item indicators to look at differences in negotiation orientations across the four countries on the dimensions in the Negotiation Orientations Framework.[78] We did, indeed, find significant differences in negotiating orientations for Finland, Mexico, Turkey, and the United States. Moreover, the results revealed that constructs frequently presented as bipolar may not be. Rather than demonstrating an orientation toward one pole of a continuum to the exclusion of the other, respondents from all four countries were often oriented toward both. Similar to our work with the Salacuse dimensions, we found significantly different patterns of response for all four countries on most negotiating tendencies. And, once again, we found surprising results on a number of dimensions, given the orientations commonly cited in negotiation guides,[79] providing additional evidence that conventional wisdom on negotiating tendencies may be misleading.

CONCLUSION

Cultural differences can complicate, prolong, and even frustrate international negotiations. In an ideal world, skilled negotiators would come to the table with deep knowledge and familiarity with the culture and negotiation orientations of their counterparts; however, the pace and pressures of global business make this highly unlikely. Consequently, a framework that focuses on key dimensions of the international negotiation context and process can serve as a valuable tool in assisting negotiators and researchers alike in identifying potential points of conflict. The Negotiation Orientations Framework provides perhaps the most comprehensive approach to date for systematic comparison of national cultural differences in negotiations.

Our empirical analyses point to several important conclusions and implications. First, the results of our work confirm that a dimensional framework is useful for identifying meaningful cross-national comparison. Negotiators can use the dimensions in a framework to systematically identify possible areas of tension, thereby making it possible to appropriately adjust their expectations and negotiation practices accordingly.

Second, our work demonstrates that, while cultural values may account for some differences in negotiation orientations, it does not wholly account for the observed differences between negotiators from different countries. As Weiss notes, just as multiple values are most likely to determine behavior, multiple behaviors are likely to result from one value.[80] Our findings suggest that negotiators ought to be wary of making inferences about negotiating tendencies on the basis of cultural values alone, because measurements of cultural values are often too general and not sufficiently context specific.

Third, our experience with designing measures for the Negotiation Orientations Framework reveals that constructs frequently presented as polar opposites should be treated as separate dimensions. Researchers need to think in terms of 24 separate constructs rather than 12 bipolar dimensions. This suggests a very different approach to measure design than we had anticipated. It also suggests that understanding intercultural negotiation is considerably more complex than is appreciated in the current intercultural negotiation literature. Thinking in terms of 24 separate constructs rather than 12 bipolar dimensions also has equally interesting implications for negotiators. Taking Basis of Trust as an example, negotiators should realize that the goals of a signed contract and of building a relationship are not necessarily mutually exclusive and that the achievement of one can lead to the other. Moreover, a negotiator who becomes aware of being personally oriented toward both contracts and relationships develops a more fine-grained appreciation of self-awareness, as well as an appreciation that the party across the table may hold a similarly complex perspective.

Finally, and perhaps most importantly, although information on country-specific negotiating styles may be available, international negotiators ought to question conventional wisdom about negotiation stereotypes. Simply stated, conventional wisdom may not be accurate. Again, using Basis of Trust as an example, it is no longer accurate or useful—if it ever was—for a U.S. negotiator to expect a Mexican counterpart to be solely relationship oriented or a U.S. compatriot to be solely contract oriented.

NOTES

1. *CultureGrams World Edition 2007;* Farid Elashmawi, *Competing Globally: Mastering Multicultural Management and Negotiations* (Boston: Butterworth Heinemann, 2001); Dean Allen Foster, *Bargaining Across Borders: How to Negotiate Business Successfully Anywhere in the World* (New York: McGraw-Hill, 1992); Richard R. Gesteland, *Cross Cultural Business Behavior* (Copenhagen: Munksgaard International Publishers, Ltd., 1997); Robert T. Moran and William G. Stripp, *Dynamics of Successful International Business Negotiations* (Houston: Gulf Publishing Company, 1991); Terri Morrison, Wayne A. Conaway, and George A. Borden, *Kiss, Bow, or Shake Hands: How to Do Business in Sixty Countries* (Holbrook, MA: Bob Adams, Inc., 1994); Jeswald W. Salacuse, *The Global Negotiator: Making, Managing, and Mending Deals around the World in the Twenty-First Century* (New York: Palgrave Macmillan, 2003).

2. For example, Roger E. Axtell, ed., *Do's and Taboos Around the World* (New York: John Wiley & Sons, Inc., 1993).

3. Lynn Metcalf and Allan Bird, "Integrating the Hofstede Dimensions and Twelve Aspects of Negotiating Behavior: A Six Country Comparison," in *Comparing Cultures: Dimensions of Culture in a Comparative Perspective,* ed. Henk Vinken, Joseph Soeters, and Peter Ester (Leiden, The Netherlands: Koninklijke Brill B.V., 2004), 251–69.

4. Lynn Metcalf, Allan Bird, Mahesh Shankarmahesh, Zeynep Aycan, Jorma Larimo, and Dídimo Dewar Valdelamar, "Cultural Tendencies in Negotiation: A Comparison of Finland, India, Mexico, Turkey, and the United States," *Journal of World Business* (forthcoming).

5. Stephen E. Weiss and William Stripp, "Negotiating with Foreign Businesspersons: An Introduction for Americans with Propositions on Six Cultures" (#85-6, New York University Graduate School of Business Administration, 1985).

6. Stephen E. Weiss and William Stripp, "Negotiating with Foreign Businesspersons: An Introduction for Americans with Propositions on Six Cultures," in *The Cultural Context in Business Communication,* ed. Susanne Niemeier, Charles P. Campbell, and Rene Dirven (Amsterdam: John Benjamins Publishing Company, 1998), 51–118.

7. Gilbert A. Churchill, Jr., "A Paradigm for Developing Better Measures of Marketing Constructs," *Journal of Marketing Research* 16, no. 1 (1979): 64–74.

8. R.E. Walton and Robert B. McKersie, *A Behavioral Theory of Labor Negotiations* (New York: McGraw-Hill, 1965).

9. Alma Mintu-Wimsatt and Julie B. Gassenheimer, "The Moderating Effects of Cultural Context in Buyer-Seller Negotiation," *The Journal of Personal Selling and Sales Management* 20, no. 1 (2000): 1–9.

10. Max H. Bazerman and Margaret A. Neale, *Negotiating Rationally* (New York: The Free Press, 1992), 16–22.

11. Ji Li and Chalmer E. Labig, Jr., "Creative Relationship-Focused Negotiations in International Business," *Creativity and Innovation Management* 5, no. 2 (1996): 99–106.

12. Michele Gelfand, Marianne Higgins, Lisa H. Nishii, Jana L. Raver, Alexandria Dominguez, Fumio Murakami, Susumu Yamaguchi, and Midori Toyama, "Culture and Egocentric Perceptions of Fairness in Conflict and Negotiation," *Journal of Applied Psychology* 87, no. 5 (2002): 833–45.

13. Bazerman and Neale, *Negotiating Rationally,* 16.

14. Wendi Adair and Jeanne Brett, "Time Culture and Behavioral Sequences in Negotiations," Working paper #268 (Dispute Resolution Research Center, Northwestern University, Evanston, IL 2001), 6.

15. Mintu-Wimsatt and Gassenheimer, "The Moderating Effects of Cultural Context in Buyer-Seller Negotiation."

16. Linda L. Putnam and Majia Holmer, "Framing, Reframing, and Issue Development," in *Communication and Negotiation,* ed. Linda L. Putnam and Michael E. Roloff (Newbury Park, CA: Sage Publications, 1992), 128–55.

17. Bazerman and Neale, *Negotiating Rationally,* 16–18.

18. Robin L. Pinkley, "Dimensions of Conflict Frame: Disputants' Interpretations of Conflict," *Journal of Applied Psychology* 75, no. 2 (1990): 117–27

19. Michele Gelfand, Lisa H. Nishii, Karen M. Holcombe, Naomi Dyer, Ken-Ichi Ohbuchi, and Mitsuteru Fukuno, "Cultural Influences on Cognitive Representations of Conflict: Interpretations of Conflict Episodes in the United States and Japan," *Journal of Applied Psychology* 86, no. 6 (2001): 1060.

20. Fons Trompenaars, *Riding the Waves of Culture: Understanding Diversity in Global Business* (Burr Ridge, IL: Irwin Professional Publishing, 1993), 78.

21. David Victor, *International Business Communication* (New York: HarperCollins Publishers, 1992), 145.

22. Trompenaars, *Riding the Waves of Culture,* 78.

23. Ibid., 11.

24. Ibid., 115.

25. Ibid., 11.

26. Ibid., 115.

27. Eva S. Kras, *Management in Two Cultures: Bridging the Gap Between U.S. and Mexican Managers* (Yarmouth, ME: Intercultural Press, 1989), 40.

28. Harry C. Triandis, *Individualism and Collectivism* (Boulder, CO: Westview Press, 1995), 2.

29. Trompenaars, *Riding the Waves of Culture,* 67.

30. Triandis, *Individualism and Collectivism,* 2.

31. Trompenaars, *Riding the Waves of Culture,* 67.

32. Jeanne M. Brett, *Negotiating Globally: How to Negotiate Deals, Resolve Disputes, and Make Decisions Across Cultural Boundaries* (San Francisco: Jossey-Bass, 2001), 154.

33. Trompenaars, *Riding the Waves of Culture,* 63.

34. Edward T. Hall and Mildred Reed Hall, *Understanding Cultural Differences: Germans, French, and Americans* (Yarmouth, ME: Intercultural Press, Inc., 1990), 13.

35. David Victor, *International Business Communication* (New York: HarperCollins, 1992), 234–36.

36. Victor, *International Business Communication,* 237–241.

37. Weiss and Stripp, "Negotiating with Foreign Businesspersons: An Introduction for Americans with Propositions on Six Cultures" (#85-6, New York University Graduate School of Business Administration, 1985), 9.

38. Bazerman and Neale, *Negotiating Rationally,* 34.

39. Dipankar Ghosh, "Tolerance for Ambiguity, Risk Preference, and Negotiator Effectiveness," *Decision Sciences* 25, no. 2 (1994): 263.

40. Weiss and Stripp, "Negotiating with Foreign Businesspersons: An Introduction for Americans with Propositions on Six Cultures," in *The Cultural Context in Business Communication,* ed. Susanne Niemeier, Charles P. Campbell, and Rene Dirven (Amsterdam: John Benjamins Publishing Company, 1998), 9.

41. Bazerman and Neale, *Negotiating Rationally,* 41.

42 Ghosh, "Tolerance for Ambiguity, Risk Preference, and Negotiator Effectiveness," 264.

43. David T. Wilson and K.E. Kristan Moller, "Buyer-Seller Relationships: Alternative Conceptualizations," in *New Perspectives on International Marketing,* ed. Stanley J. Paliwoda (New York: Routledge, 1991), 87–107.

44. Francis Fukuyama, *Trust: The Social Virtues and the Creation of Prosperity* (New York: The Free Press, 1995), 27.

45. Trompenaars, *Riding the Waves of Culture,* 49.

46. Victor, *International Business Communication,* 150.

47. Trompenaars, *Riding the Waves of Culture,* 49.

48. Pertti J. Pelto, "The Difference Between 'Tight' and 'Loose' Societies," *Transaction* April (1968): 37–40.

49. Weiss and Stripp, "Negotiating with Foreign Businesspersons: An Introduction for Americans with Propositions on Six Cultures" (#85-6, New York University Graduate School of Business Administration, 1985), 7.

50. Victor, *International Business Communication,* 148.

51. William B. Gudykunst, Yuko Matsumoto, Stella Ting-Toomey, Tsukasa Nishida, Kwangsu Kim, and Sam Heyman, "The Influence of Cultural Individualism-Collectivism, Self-Construals, and Individual Values on Communication Styles Across Cultures," *Human Communication Research* 22, no. 4 (1996): 518.

52. Harry C. Triandis, *Culture and Social Behavior* (New York: McGraw-Hill, Inc., 1994), 184.

53. Gudykunst et al., "The Influence of Cultural Individualism-Collectivism," 525; Trompenaars, *Riding the Waves of Culture,* 98.

54. Gudykunst et al., "The Influence of Cultural Individualism-Collectivism," 525.

55. Triandis, *Culture and Social Behavior,* 185, 196.

56. Barbara Johnstone, "Linguistic Strategies and Cultural Styles for Persuasive Discourse," in *Language, Communication, and Culture: Current Directions,* ed. Stella

Ting-Toomey and Felipe Korzenny (Newbury Park, CA: Sage Publications, 1989), 145.

57. Roger Fisher and William Ury, *Getting to Yes: Negotiating Agreement without Giving In* (New York: Penguin, 1991), 85.

58. E.S. Glenn, D. Witmeyer, and K.A. Stevenson, "Cultural Styles of Persuasion," *International Journal of Intercultural Relations* 1, no. 3 (1977): 57.

59. Wendi L. Adair and Jeanne M. Brett, "Culture and Negotiation Processes," in *The Handbook of Negotiation and Culture,* ed. Michele J. Gelfand and Jeanne M. Brett (Stanford, CA: Stanford University Press, 2004), 162.

60. Fisher and Ury, *Getting to Yes,* 85.

61. Triandis, *Culture and Social Behavior,* 185.

62. Robert Frankel, Judith Schmitz Whipple, and David J. Frayer, "Formal versus Informal Contracts: Achieving Alliance Success," *International Journal of Physical Distribution & Logistics Management* 26, no. 3 (1996): 49.

63. Weiss and Stripp, "Negotiating with Foreign Businesspersons: An Introduction for Americans with Propositions on Six Cultures," (#85-6, New York University Graduate School of Business Administration, 1985), 9.

64. Trompenaars, *Riding the Waves of Culture,* 43.

65. Frankel et al., "Formal versus Informal Contracts," 49.

66. Trompenaars, *Riding the Waves of Culture,* 43.

67. See, for example, Adair and Brett, "Culture and Negotiation Processes"; Michele J. Gelfand and Deborah A. Cai, "Cultural Structuring of the Social Context of Negotiation," in *The Handbook of Negotiation and Culture,* ed. Michele J. Gelfand and Jeanne M. Brett (Stanford, CA: Stanford University Press, 2004); Rajesh Kumar, "Culture and Emotions in Intercultural Negotiations: An Overview," ed. Michele J. Gelfand and Jeanne M. Brett (Stanford, CA: Stanford University Press, 2004); Michael W. Morris and Michele J. Gelfand, "Cultural Differences and Cognitive Dynamics: Expanding the Cognitive Perspective on Negotiation," ed. Michele J. Gelfand and Jeanne M. Brett (Stanford, CA: Stanford University Press, 2004).

68. Metcalf and Bird, "Integrating the Hofstede Dimensions."

69. G. Hofstede, *Culture's Consequences: Comparing Values, Behaviors, Institutions, and Organizations Across Nations,*. 2nd ed. (Thousand Oaks, CA: Sage Publications, 2001).

70. See, for example, Raymond Cohen, *Negotiating Across Cultures* (Washington, DC: United States Institute of Peace, 1997); Claude Cellich and Subhash C. Jain, *Global Business Negotiations: A Practical Guide* (Mason, OH: Thomson South-Western, 2004), 3; Jeswald W. Salacuse, *Making Global Deals: Negotiating in the International Marketplace* (Boston: Houghton-Mifflin, 1991); Weiss and Stripp, "Negotiating with Foreign Businesspersons: An Introduction for Americans with Propositions on Six Cultures," (#85-6, New York University Graduate School of Business Administration, 1985); Adair and Brett, "Culture and Negotiation Processes."

71. Stephen E. Weiss, "International Business Negotiations Research: Revisiting 'Bricks, Mortar, and Prospects,'" in *The Handbook of International Management Research,* ed. Betty Jane Punnett and Oded Shenkar (Ann Arbor, MI: University of Michigan Press, 2004), 421.

72. Metcalf et al., "Cultural Tendencies in Negotiation."

73. Jeswald W. Salacuse, "Ten Ways that Culture Affects Negotiating Style: Some Survey Results," *Negotiation Journal* 14, no. 3 (1998): 221–35.

74. Metcalf et al., "Cultural Tendencies in Negotiation."

75. Foster, *Bargaining Across Borders;* Kras, *Management in Two Cultures*; Morrison, Conaway, and Borden, *Kiss, Bow, or Shake Hands;* Salacuse, *The Global Negotiator;* and Victor, *International Business Communication.*

76. Salacuse, *The Global Negotiator.*

77. Daphna Oyserman, Heather M. Coon, and Markus Kemmelmeier, "Rethinking Individualism and Collectivism: Evaluation of Theoretical Assumptions and Meta-Analyses." *Psychological Bulletin,* 128, no. 1 (2002): 3–72.

78. Lynn Metcalf, Allan Bird, Mark Peterson, Terri Lituchy, and Mahesh Shankar-mahesh, "Cultural Tendencies in Negotiation: A Comparison of Finland, Mexico, Turkey, and the United States," Academy of International Business, 2006.

79. See, for example, Morrison, Conaway, and Borden, *Kiss, Bow, or Shake Hands.*

80. Weiss, "International Business Negotiations Research," 437.

CHAPTER 11

IT IS THE DISTRIBUTION, STUPID!

Andrew R. Thomas and Timothy J. Wilkinson

SCENARIO: DECISIONS, DECISIONS

Not long ago, an American export management company that had a joint venture in China manufacturing motorcycles went looking for new distributors in Central America. For several years previously, the U.S. firm had been highly successful in South America and Africa, locating distributors for its line of basic transportation motorcycles. Using Honda technology, the Chinese motorcycles were proven to be of high quality and reliability. Most importantly, they sold for less than a third of the cost of competing Japanese models.

The first stop in the search for Central American distributors was Costa Rica, the most prosperous country in the region. A growing economy and political stability had created an optimal market for successful sales: a rising lower middle class that could now afford dependable motorcycles for its transportation needs. Such a formula had worked very well in Colombia, Ethiopia, Venezuela, Burkina Faso, Argentina, South Africa, Brazil, Nigeria, Peru, and Cameroon. Like most others seeking to gain entry into high-growth emerging markets, the U.S. firm's key to success was selecting and recruiting the right kind of distributors for its products.

The executive in charge of developing entry strategy was able to locate two possible distributors in Costa Rica. Based on his previous successes in the above-mentioned markets and others, the executive believed himself invincible when it came to identifying who would best represent his company's products.

The first candidate for the Costa Rican distributorship was a young entrepreneur who had begun his career in the agriculture business, importing farm implements and fertilizers. He had built a nice network that covered the entire country's market and was interested in the Chinese motorcycles because he felt they would complement his existing product lines.

However, the second candidate seemed to be the better fit. One of the richest men in the country, he had made his fortune as the exclusive distributor of Honda cars, Scania trucks, and Komatsu heavy equipment. Having sold Honda motorcycles in the past, the second candidate was interested in getting back into the low-end transportation business. In the eyes of the U.S. executive, this man appeared to be the more logical choice for distributorship.

When it came time to travel to San Jose to interview the two prospects, the American had a sales goal of 250 motorcycles per year for each of the first three years. According to his research, the annual sales of motorcycles for the entire country was approximately 2,700 units and growing nicely at a rate of 10 percent per year. The sale of 250 units annually would establish a foundation that could be leveraged later on to ultimately build market share to 20–25 percent.

The first interview held was at the agriculture entrepreneur's office. Although it was clear to the American that the first candidate was wildly enthusiastic about the opportunity to offer the Chinese motorcycles throughout his network, the two individuals never connected on a personal level. Furthermore, any positive feelings on the American's part soon evaporated when the young man showed projections that the annual sales would be no greater than 100 units for the first couple of years. The Costa Rican said it would take a long while for the marketplace to adjust to a Chinese-branded product, but once it did, the potential would be tremendous. At this point, the American coolly ended the conversation and told his counterpart that he would take his plan under advisement. Twenty minutes later, the American was dropped off by taxi in front of the sparkling offices of the Honda/Scania/Komatsu distributor.

Within an hour of their meeting, it was agreed that the Honda dealer would become the exclusive distributor of the Chinese motorcycles. It was clear that he had the sales staff, service capability, financial resources, and knowledge of distribution to handle the motorcycles. And, much to the delight of the U.S. businessman, the first order was to be for 1,000 units: four times what the American thought it would be. Dinner that night was a celebration of the new relationship at San Jose's most prestigious private club. All that was needed was an exclusive distribution agreement giving the Costa Rican sole rights to the Chinese motorcycles for five years. Then, once the agreement was in place, a revolving Letter of Credit would be opened to begin shipping the motorcycles in 125-unit increments over the first year.

After the exclusive agreement was consularized and notarized, the first 125 units were shipped from China to Costa Rica without incident. The Letter of Credit went smoothly, and communication between the two firms was regular and efficient. However, everything changed when it came time to ship the next 125 units. To reinitiate the revolving Letter of Credit, a document was required from the distributor to the confirming bank. For more than a month, the U.S. firm's employees called, e-mailed, and faxed its exclusive distributor. The only individuals they could get in touch with were administrative assistants, who generated the same pat answers: "he's away on a trip...in a meeting...away from his desk." With the second lot of motorcycles languishing on a dock in Shanghai and the other 700 units ready for production, pressure was building.

Unannounced, the American executive boarded a plane and flew to San Jose to see what was going on. He took a taxi at the airport and went right to his new distributor's office. Not surprisingly, his new distributor was unavailable. Nor were any of the motorcycles or promotional materials anywhere to be found on the showroom floor.

Distraught, the American caught a cab to his hotel. During the 30-minute trip, he was startled to see many small motorcycles on the streets of San Jose: something that was not the case during his last visit a few months earlier. Many of the motorcycles were the models of one of his leading competitors from Taiwan.

After a couple of stiff drinks at the hotel bar, the American swallowed his pride and called the young entrepreneur whom he had rejected earlier as exclusive distributor. Half expecting to be hung up on, the American was shocked when the young man agreed to join him for dinner to discuss what was happening with the motorcycles. Not gloating too much, the young Costa Rican showed pictures of the American's motorcycles still sitting in a bonded warehouse at the port of Limon. He further showed photos of a brand new motorcycle distribution company located in the heart of San Jose that was importing small motorcycles from Taiwan. Due to lack of competition, newspaper articles stated that sales of the Taiwanese products might exceed 500 units that year. In scanning the articles, the American recognized the last name of the successful distributor: the same surname as his chosen distributor. In the end, the two turned out to be brothers.

THE DYSFUNCTIONAL DISTRIBUTION MODEL

The most common way for manufacturers to expand into international markets is by using independent agents and distributors. Yet, a glance through almost any international business or international marketing textbook reveals a glaring omission: almost no one tackles the question of distribution. When the subject is addressed, it is often conceptualized as a transportation issue,[1] a question of logistics,[2] or rolled into an analysis of international networks and market entry.[3] The central issues of how to select, bargain with, and maintain a viable working relationship with a distributor is relegated to a few paragraphs. Moreover, much of what has been written on international distribution covers topics relevant only up to the point where an agreement has been signed, to the neglect of ensuing monitoring and compliance issues. This is ironic given the emphasis on relationship building in the field of international business.

Distributors have become powerful in the industrialized, Western world. Consider the vast majority of products that are sold and distributed by entities other than the actual manufacturers. Wal-Mart's ability to squeeze its suppliers is legendary and of little wonder, with 30 percent of the U.S. market for household staples such as toothpaste, shampoo, and paper products, and 15–20 percent of all CD, DVD, and video sales. As a result of its market power, Wal-Mart "homes in on every aspect of a supplier's operation—which products get developed, what they are made of, [and] how to price them."[4] Vlasic Pickles allowed its market position to be completely undermined by permitting Wal-Mart to sell its product for only $2.97 per gallon jar. This proved to be a "devastating success" for Vlasic, as sales and growth numbers increased even as profit margins shriveled.[5]

Wal-Mart is not an exception to the rule; it is merely the most visible example. Detroit has struggled for years to produce automobiles that could compete against Japanese products and has recently made great strides in engineering. Nevertheless, when it comes to the sales of those same cars, U.S. automobile manufacturers have turned over control of distribution to existing dealer networks. In home electronics, medical equipment, chemicals, do-it-yourself, and nearly every other industry imaginable in the developed world, megadistributors have emerged to dominate the sales and distribution of most products.

According to ComputerWeekly.com,[6] even Dell Inc., the poster child of direct distribution, is starting to partner with malls and airports to sell its products through in-store kiosks. The control that manufacturers in industrialized countries once had over their products has been given away, and manufacturers have come to a place where they have learned to live with it. They know that the control over the sales and distribution of their products no longer lies in their hands, but in the hands of megadistributors.

In our opinion, giving up control to distributors is a poor way to conduct business, and over time, this dysfunctional system has become the norm. As a result, when American firms internationalize, they are likely to take this faulty model with them to the great delight of overseas distributors. Control is automatically given away without thought or negotiation.

Blue Sky Beverage Company illustrates how and why many firms cede control of their products. A $1.8 million natural juice drinks firm, Blue Sky decided to expand beyond its small Santa Fe–based market by taking its product international. After expending a great deal of effort in attempting to locate a distributor at trade shows in Germany and Japan, Blue Sky president Richard Becker settled on Kansai Cheerio, an Osaka-based soft-drink manufacturer. Like so many U.S. firms, Blue Sky naturally and without thought gave total control of the marketing, sales, and distribution of its product in Japan over to Cheerio. And again, like so many other U.S. companies, Blue Sky also agreed to sell its product to the Japanese distributor at 33 percent less than it does to its American distributors.

Cheerio redesigned Blue Sky's cans, ran ads that the manufacturer did not understand, and adopted only two of the company's flavors, discarding the rest. President Becker tried to justify his decision by reasoning that he could not afford an office in Japan, his international expansion had cost little, and that an 8-percent increase in total sales had resulted from Cheerio's first order. Within two years of international expansion, 10 percent of Blue Sky's product was exported to Japan. In 2000, the company was acquired by Hansen Beverage Company.[7]

In the case above, Becker's willingness to forgo control, select a distributor with products similar to his own, and sell his product at a deep discount did not turn out to be a fatal decision. However, it reflects the seductive nature of the power relationship of distribution systems in the developed world. In countries that are less economically and politically advanced, such an abrogation of control can easily lead to disaster.

For the foreseeable future, the chance that American manufacturers will regain control over the sales and distribution of their products at home is negligible. The megadistributors in nearly every industry are blocking the entrance and getting stronger every day. Although such a scenario appears bleak and is so for most manufacturers operating in the United States, there is hope. There does exist an opportunity for manufacturers to regain control over the sales and distribution of their products in developing countries overseas. In high-growth emerging markets around the world, manufacturers still possess the ability to directly influence what happens to their products once they enter the distribution chain. The malleability and newness of these markets have not allowed the megadistributors to become entrenched. For sure, the Wal-Marts and Home Depots are trying to make their mark in Mexico, China, and eastern Europe; however, their inroads do not yet reach very far. The window of opportunity is open for manufacturers to shape and mold the way distribution gets done in these markets. The questions are, will they do it and how can it be done the right way? Figure 11.1 illustrates an approach that exporters should pursue if they want to build an effective international distribution system. Each element of this system is described below.

See It from the Distributor's Perspective

Scholars who have studied culture and international business warn of the subconscious influence of self-reference criteria (SRC) upon our behavior and actions. SRC has been defined as the unconscious tendency to interpret a particular business situation through the lens of one's own cultural experience and value system.[8] There are many examples of SRC cited in business literature. For example, an American who equates niceness with agreement and is disconcerted by "unnecessary" formalities is experiencing the effects of SRC. Similarly, SRC would be at play for a German who is appalled by the cutting and systematic humor of a British counterpart at a sales meeting.

SRC plays an important albeit subtle role in the selection of international distributors. In the case introduced above, the second candidate was the exclusive distributor of Honda cars, Scania trucks, and Komatsu heavy equipment and

Figure 11.1
Building Successful Distribution

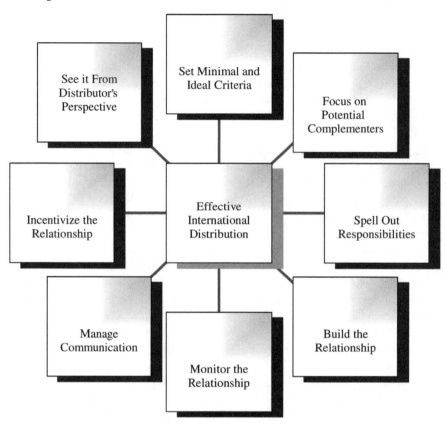

stated that he had also sold some Honda motorcycles in the past. In reality, through family connections, he was involved in a directly competing venture in Costa Rica. This information was withheld from the American executive because the distributor saw the arrival of the American not as an opportunity to be grasped, but as a threat that needed to be eliminated.

The Costa Rican distributor, like most business persons in emerging markets, operates in an environment characterized by risk and uncertainty. In this world, opportunity is bounded by turbulent events that could destabilize a life's work in a short period of time. In such a setting, control and predictability are of the utmost importance. Rather than seeing the entrance of low-end motorcycles from China as a way to increase market share, the distributor saw it as a threat that needed to be dealt with. For him and for other host country distributors in the developing world, the environment is already uncertain enough. The solution to the threat of increased uncertainty is to lock any potential destabilizers out of the market. By entering into a contract to become the exclusive distributor in Costa Rica, this individual was able to deftly eliminate what he perceived to be a potential problem.

Set Minimal and Ideal criteria

To ensure the success of a distribution arrangement, both parties must bring something of value to the table.[9] The initial question for the manufacturer is what kind of distributor it wants, and the answer depends upon the circumstances and what needs to be achieved. In emerging markets, distributor selection criteria should include consideration of distribution outreach, functionality, appropriateness for products, cultural context, consumer/distributor interaction, and past performance.[10] Figure 11.2 provides a list of attributes that have been successfully used to evaluate potential partners.

It is important to determine the qualities needed before undertaking the screening and selection process. Once the criteria have been established, you must adhere to those criteria while examining potential candidates. A new environment, the uncertainty that accompanies exporting, and the increased risk of operating in international markets all conspire to convince new exporters to find an easy way out. In this scenario, it would be easy to fall into the trap of turning over merchandise control to the most confident sounding individual. This is a temptation, and to ignore your carefully crafted criteria is a mistake.

Once the criteria are decided upon, assess potential partners in terms of minimal and maximal characteristics. One element we strongly suggest for consideration is whether or not a potential distributor is involved with directly competitive products. In emerging markets, the selection of such a distributor is almost always a mistake for small to medium-sized businesses. To understand why, it is necessary to consider the perspective of the would-be partner.

Equally important, the manufacturer needs to bring to the table such things as exclusivity, patent and trademark protection, quality, favorable pricing, training, new and improved products, and periodic visits. The most critical element that the exporter contributes is his or her commitment to exporting the product to a particular market. The inspiration, motivation, and vision for the venture must come from the exporter.[11]

Focus on Potential Complementers

Far too many American companies have been cheated when they chose an international distributor who sold products similar to their own. Their flawed logic goes something like this: in an attempt to capture maximum market share, the manufacturer chooses a distributor who has a history of handling products and services similar to its own rather than mentoring one that does not have that

Figure 11.2
Distributor Profile Evaluation Worksheet

Distributor Profile Evaluation Worksheet

Distributor name: _____ Date of evaluation: _____

Distributor Attributes	Ideal	Good	Minimal	Less than minimal	Does not exist
Market knowledge	5	4	3	2	1
Distribution knowledge	5	4	3	2	1
No competing products	5	4	3	2	1
Ability to cover territory	5	4	3	2	1
Payment history	5	4	3	2	1
Sales organization	5	4	3	2	1
Administrative support	5	4	3	2	1
Inventory maintenance	5	4	3	2	1
Sales records	5	4	3	2	1
Forecasts of purchases	5	4	3	2	1
Marketing plans	5	4	3	2	1
Competitive research	5	4	3	2	1
Advertising support	5	4	3	2	1
Manufacturer relationships	5	4	3	2	1
Product specific	5	4	3	2	1
Product specific	5	4	3	2	1
Product specific	5	4	3	2	1
Product specific	5	4	3	2	1
Product specific	5	4	3	2	1
Product specific	5	4	3	2	1
Total Each Column					
EVALUATION SCORE (Total of all columns)					

*NOTE: Minimally acceptable distributors should have an evaluation score of 3 times the total number of distributor attributes. For example, if a manufacturer decides there are 20 distributor attributes, a prospective distributor must score a minimum of 60 to be considered acceptable. Anything below that number and the prospect must be discarded.

shared experience. In doing so, the manufacturer anticipates that training will require a much shorter amount of time and that all that will need to be done is place its product in the distributor's pipeline. While this is a fast, efficient solution and the rationale might initially seem logical, it is a flawed line of thinking.

In the vast majority of cases, the best choice of distributor for a manufacturer's product in a given market is a potential complementer, that is, a company that sells and distributes goods that will enhance the image and perception of the manufacturer's products. In the Costa Rican example, the best candidate was clearly the young man who sold agricultural products, as these lines complemented the image of the motorcycle as a basic transportation vehicle for workers and farmers.

A different example comes from Trinidad and Tobago, where barbeques and related activities are a way of life. With more than 25 national holidays per year and six weeks of vacation for the average worker, residents make full use of their abundant free time to host massive gatherings where outdoor grilling is the principal activity. Seeing an opportunity, a Midwest manufacturer of natural gas and propane grills decided to explore the Trinidad and Tobago market for its products. At first glance, the most logical choice for a distributor seemed to be Choice Mart, a San Diego–based megaretailer that rivals Wal-Mart in Central America and the Caribbean. Choice Mart has points of sale around the country and was the largest vendor of grills in the market; however, Choice Mart was also the exclusive distributor of seven other brands in Trinidad and Tobago.

The Midwest manufacturer decided it did not want its products thrown onto shelves next to direct competitors; instead, they sought out a complementer. In Trinidad and Tobago, natural gas and propane are sold primarily at gas stations. Three main companies controlled the service station market in Trinidad and Tobago, and the U.S. manufacturer decided that such a company would be the kind of distributor it was looking for. Six months after the decision, the U.S. manufacturer was number two in the marketplace and still rising.

Spell out Responsibilities

All responsibilities need to be defined and explained so that both parties are completely clear as to who needs to do what to ensure that the relationship remains mutually beneficial. A well-written distribution contract can ensure, at least on paper, that manufacturers have as much control as possible.[12] However, business people repeatedly fall into the trap of ascribing a higher value to a document than they should. This is natural, given the detail and complexity of most agreements, as well as the time and energy required for their production. Therefore, it is important to understand the limitations of these legal instruments.

Distributor agreements seemingly create the impression that the document itself has generated business. If a manufacturer wants to successfully sell and distribute its products, it needs to realize that a document prepared and agreed to by lawyers will not accomplish this task. A distributor will be successful only if he or she is properly motivated; in other words, the key to selling and distributing products in global markets is not rooted in a legal document but in the development of strong relationships and a sound, cogent business strategy.

Nevertheless, a carefully defined distributor agreement can provide a degree of security against badly intentioned individuals who are seeking to hurt the manufacturer and impede market entry. Years ago, John Deere, like so many major U.S. manufacturers attempting to enter the Middle East, was being wooed into signing a blanket agreement that would allow a local distributor to operate with impunity. As is often the case, large initial purchase orders were dangled out as a motivation to sign. John Deere, however, saw through the histrionics and presented a 30-page distribution agreement that was so comprehensive and thorough that it scared off the potential distributor. In this case, the agreement served as a tool to better qualify and assess the credibility of a potential distributor.

Build the Relationship

An international distributor agreement should be viewed as a starting point in an ongoing and evolving relationship. Unlike the United States, where a robust legal system ensures the integrity of impersonal and arm's-length business transactions, the legal infrastructure of emerging markets is often both unstable and unpredictable. In Eastern Europe, for example, contracts are often written with clever phrases, small print, and all manner of trickery. Such contractual aggression is made possible by poorly developed legal and regulatory regimes and court proceedings that require a great deal of time and money.[13]

Control or governance of foreign distributors is most effective when it is the result of relational norms developed and implemented by the manufacturer. There are three aspects to relational norms. First, both parties need to exhibit flexibility in their dealings with one another. If practices prescribed by the distributor agreement prove to be unworkable or detrimental to either side, then the appropriate adaptations should be made. Second, both sides should actively engage in an information exchange. Manufacturers and distributors have the right to expect that information involving operations will be shared. Finally, both parties need to exhibit an approach that demonstrates solidarity, placing a high value on the relationship. Solidarity deters behavior that might jeopardize the relationship and improves efficiency. One study found that firms that governed their foreign distributors through relational norms enhanced their competitive position in foreign markets.[14]

Monitor the Relationship

There exist a number of standards that manufacturers can bring into play as a means of assessing distributor performance, including distributor sales performance, distributor inventory management, distributor selling capabilities, distributor attitudes, competition facing distributors, and general growth potential of the distributor.

Again, it may seem foreign to a U.S. manufacturer, but it is actually possible to exert positive control over the sales and distribution of products in global markets. This is accomplished by a process that proactively stays informed of the distributor performance in a number of areas. Doing so allows the manufacturer and its distributor to clearly identify areas of weakness so that appropriate adjustments can be made in a timely manner. Dishearteningly, the opposite is usually the case; that is, little or no monitoring of the distributor is done, and when things go bad (and they often do), it is simply too late to do anything about it. Distributor activities that should be monitored and controlled include functional reports, customer reports, financial ratios, and sales analyses.

In the mid-1990s, R.J. Reynolds International (RJR) sought to reconfigure the company's sales and distribution strategy in Central and Eastern Europe. In 1996, RJR was the fourth largest manufacturer of fast-moving consumer products in its industry. Yet, after establishing performance standards for its distributors, it achieved a number one market position. RJR's success resulted from the introduction of a DSS, or distributor sales/service supervisor, into the mix. The DSS, a Reynolds employee, was either on-site at the distributor's facility or spent a couple of days a week with the distributor. He or she performed an operations checklist to ensure that the distributor fulfilled every aspect of the distribution function in accordance with the performance standards set by the manufacturer. In essence, this checklist served as a monitoring and controlling function of the distributor's operation that surrounded the manufacturer's products.

If RJR decided to install full-time staff at a given location, at least two individuals were sent from the company. Even the most well-intentioned employee, if alone, can fall prey to an unscrupulous distributor who might offer a "gift" to have the employee help it get more control over the relationship. Furthermore, RJR's offices inside its distributor's facilities had its own separate telecommunications systems and secured areas for all files, documents, correspondence, and the like.

The DSS managed the manufacturer's interests within the distributor's business by placing orders on behalf of the distributor, ensuring that the product remained within the distributor's territory and keeping levels of pricing and distributor credit to its customers in accordance with preset agreements with the manufacturer. In fully developed distribution systems, the DSS had budgetary responsibilities for the manufacturer within the distributor's business; however, at no time did he or she ever have access to managing the distributor's money.

Manage Communication

It is the responsibility of the manufacturers to develop and implement a communication strategy that enhances the quality and quantity of interaction between themselves and the distributors. Successful manufacturers implement a two-pronged approach in their communication strategy: the first track is designed to satisfy operational requirements such as purchase orders, delivery, inventory, payments, and pricing; the second communication avenue exists to influence distributor behavior. Personal selling, advertising, sales promotions, and so forth are used to persuade, inform, and educate the distributor in the ways of the manufacturer whose products it represents.

Inherent challenges will arise between manufacturer and distributor when it comes to effective communication. Physical separation, differences in size, organization type, operating procedures, and native languages will prove to be challenges at some point. This is further compounded because most emerging market distributors forge their business relationships on a foundation of inherent distrust of even their closest associates.

Another issue that is often overlooked is that of confidentiality in communications. Stories abound involving executives who, traveling overseas, have been offered by enterprising hotel clerks the opportunity to purchase faxes or e-mails to or from their competitors. In many markets, it is not uncommon for meeting rooms, mobile phones, cars, and hotel suites to be bugged by local distributors.

Incentivize the Relationship

In addition to monitoring, exporters can influence the behavior of distributors by offering appropriate incentives. Rather than providing standard operating procedures to control the behavior of the distributor, a better approach focuses on outcomes using a "carrot and stick" policy: the distributor is compensated when and if sales occur. The advantage of this approach is that it provides maximal autonomy for the distributor while placing the responsibility for results squarely on his or her shoulders.[15]

PC Globe, a Tempe, Arizona-based software company, initially offered distributors exclusivity without establishing any standards of performance. Not surprisingly, their overseas sales were disappointing. Eventually, the firm changed its approach. In exchange for exclusivity, a distributor must now order and prepay for 20 percent of what it thinks it can sell in the first year, with exclusivity guaranteed as long as it continues to order the same amount each quarter. According to company executives, these distributors "do not get exclusivity as much as the opportunity for exclusivity."[16]

Incentivizing the relationship would not have solved the opportunistic behavior of the Honda dealer described in the opening scenario; however, incentivization plus monitoring should help partners to effectively co-align their goals.

From the outset in Romania, RJR pursued a direct sales and distribution strategy, with its employees in control of operations in the four largest national cities. This was done to demonstrate to the then-unconvinced national wholesalers that RJR was serious about controlling and monitoring the distribution process of its own products. Slowly, local distributors were set up in the outlying areas of

Romania, with RJR keeping control over the biggest markets. After a year all Romanian cities, except Bucharest, were turned over to local distributor operations. Forty DSSs from RJR were now working among local distributors across the country. Control in Bucharest was maintained to ensure that the capital, which represented 20 percent of the entire market, would not fall under the influence of a single distributor and disrupt the delicate equilibrium that had been achieved. When RJR employed a direct sales and distribution strategy, its return on investment was 97 percent. Upon switching to a monitor and control approach, however, RJR's return on investment skyrocketed to nearly 500 percent.

CONCLUSION

Although its critical importance cannot be overstated, distribution is generally the most globally differentiated and least understood of all marketing mix components. It is also the component most likely to hinder success in foreign markets, especially for small and mid-sized companies. Proper distribution planning can ensure that the best available channels and distribution methods are in place to efficiently and economically move products and services to customers.

The process for establishing successful sales and distribution strategies in high-growth emerging markets is formidable. We recommend that managers analyze the situation from the perspective of the distributor, set clear criteria for distributor selection, search out and work with firms marketing complementary products, make sure that expectations are explicit and clear, build a long-term relationship with the distributor, monitor the relationship, and provide appropriate incentives to keep the relationship on track. Through the application of these strategies, manufacturers will be better able to maximize opportunities found in global markets.

In the case of the motorcycle manufacturer that was utterly deceived in Costa Rica, the lessons from that experience slowly found their way into the corporate culture of the organization. Although many mistakes continued to be made in recruiting and selecting foreign distributors, the American firm gradually has begun to realize the critical importance of breaking out of the dysfunctional domestic distribution model and establishing something new and much more dynamic.

Immediately after the Costa Rica debacle, mental checklists and queries among the staff preceded most discussions about new business. As the organization began to adjust its culture to the realities of global distribution, processes for distribution selection were formalized. Ultimately, minimally acceptable criteria were decided upon. Three years later, the achieved distributor retention rate was well over 80 percent, and not surprisingly, sales and revenues were up over 60 percent.

The end product was a series of mutually beneficial relationships in which the manufacturer was firmly in control of the sales and distribution of its products.

NOTES

1. David M. Neipert, *A Tour of International Trade* (Upper Saddle River, NJ: Prentice Hall, Inc., 2000).

2. Gerald Albaum, Jesper Strandskov, and Edwin Duerr, *International Marketing and Export Management,* 3rd ed. (Harlow, England: Addison Wesley Longman Publishing Company, 1998).

3. Paul Ellis, "Social Ties and Foreign Market Entry," *Journal of International Business Studies* 31, no. 3 (2000): 443–69.

4. Anthony Bianco and Wendy Zellner, "Is Wal-Mart Too Powerful?" *Business Week Online,* October 6, 2003, www.businessweek.com.

5. Charles Fishman, "The Wal-Mart You Don't Know," *Fast Company* 77 (December 2003).

6. Ibid.

7. Paul B. Brown, "Beverage Maker Bypassed the Problems of U.S. Expansion by Marketing Overseas," *Inc. Magazine,* April 1990, www.inc.com/magazine/19900401/5138.html.

8. James S. Lee, "Cultural Analysis in Overseas Operations," *Harvard Business Review* (March–April 1966): 106–14.

9. Steven E. Harbour, "Five Rules of Distribution Management," *Business Horizons* 40, no. 3 (1997): 53–59.

10. A. Coskun Samli, *Entering and Succeeding in Emerging Countries* 1st ed. (Mason, OH: South-Western Educational & Professional Publishing, 2004).

11. Tamer S. Cavusgil and Shaoming Zou, "Marketing Strategy-Performance Relationship: An Investigation of the Empirical Link in Export," *Journal of Marketing* 58, no. 1 (January 1994): 1–21.

12. Harbour, "Five Rules of Distribution Management," 53–59.

13. Balazs Hamori, "Dog Strategies in the Transition Economies," *Business Horizons* 42, no. 5 (September 1999).

14. C. Zhang, S.T. Cavusgil, and A.S. Roath, "Manufacturer Governance of Foreign Distributor Relationships: Do Relational Norms Enhance Competitiveness in the Export Market?" *Journal of International Business Studies* 34, no. 6 (2003): 550–56.

15. Charles Pahud de Mortanges and Joost Vossen, "Mechanisms to Control the Marketing Activities of Foreign Distributors," *International Business Review* 9 (1999): 75–97.

16. Inc.com, "Exclusivity vs. Temporary Monopoly," January 1995, http://pf.inc.com/articles/1995/01/11160.html.

CHAPTER 12

GLOBAL CUSTOMER SERVICE

Calin Veghes

The days are long gone when a company can rest on its past laurels with the relative assurance that its customers will not stray to "the other side." A lot of money and resources are spent each year to obtain faithful customers; it would be a shame to risk losing them as a result of poor customer service. Inventory shortages, back orders, and long delivery times can quickly eat up profits with returns and canceled orders. This has been true for some time now, whether a company is doing business only domestically or starting to venture into the new global marketplace. The challenges are certainly compounded, sometimes exponentially, when dealing at the global level.

To maintain and cultivate relationships with existing customers or initiate business with new ones, companies are compelled to constantly and consistently provide the best products, at competitive prices, that give the most value and the highest levels of service possible. Only now, companies must find ways to do all of this on a global level.

As a result of this new decree from the global marketplace, companies need to focus more and more on providing the best service to their customers. But a problem arises, because every company, in every industry, wants to delivery quality customer service. Therefore, the real question before global business leaders is not, "How do I offer and deliver stronger customer service?" Instead, the fundamental questions are, first, "How do I develop a global customer-service strategy?" and second, "What must I actually do to deliver high-quality customer service globally?"

DEVELOPING A GLOBAL CUSTOMER-SERVICE STRATEGY

For most companies doing global business, it is likely that the only thing their customers share is the fact that they buy the same products and services. Beyond basic product requirements, however, each global customer is as unique as the culture and nation from which they come. In addition, global customers can differ in terms of product application, geographic area, market mix, and target markets.

A successful global customer-service strategy must recognize customers' differences and then address these differences as fundamental parts of the global customer-service strategy. This is best accomplished by the following:

Customer-focused mind-set: Learning what is most important to your customers,

Overdelivering: Exceeding customer expectations,

Flexibility: Respond quickly and appropriately,

Adaptability: Embracing changes continuously to spur growth,

Delivering value: Differentiating the company's offerings in a commoditized world,

Empathy: Getting into the customer's thinking,

Spotting trends: Listening for the future, and

Reinforcing your message: Reminding customers of how the company serves them.

Customer-Focused Mind-Set: Learning What Is Most Important to Your Customers

Global customer service should be far more than a department title or a promotional slogan; it should be an integral part of the global strategic plan. Partnering with key suppliers to deliver recognized and measurable global customer service should be as much a part of the corporate culture as achieving sales goals, increasing inventory turns, or improving return on investment.

For the proper execution of a global customer strategy, a company must clearly understand the expectations and needs of its key customers. To best do this, many global firms learn as much as they can about the top 20 percent of their customers, who probably represent about 80 percent of their business according to Pareto's Rule of 80/20. Some of the ways they investigate include the following:

- Holding regular meetings with a key customer's functional management groups;
- Meeting routinely with key distribution partners in each market where the company employs independent distributors or agents to market, sell, or service your company's products and services;
- Conducting local market customer focus groups for the smaller customers (nonglobal account customers), consumers, and so forth;
- Engaging in discussions with end users of the company's products and services;

- Observing first-hand selected customers' business and work processes and procedures in selected key markets (or all of their individual markets if necessary), especially as it relates to how customers use your products or services;

- Documenting each key customer's or customer segment's, industry segment's, unique traits and capabilities by individual market; and

- Sharing all relevant information with your company's own sales, marketing, manufacturing, and customer-service personnel, which will help to enhance customer service globally and locally.

Overdelivering: Exceeding Customer Expectations

Implementing successful global customer service requires carefully analyzing customers individually, the major customers' groups, and specific markets to find specific areas where a company can excel in terms of product and service offerings and the accompanying customer service to be provided, with the ultimate objective being to consistently exceed the customer's expectations. Some of the ways this can be accomplished include the following:

- Making it easy for customers to do business with the company;

- Developing a Web site and pursuing e-commerce for product information, order entry, project status, and so forth;

- Demanding accurate and reliable shipping dates from vendors, and handling field installation and quality issues in a priority manner; and

- Keeping customers apprised of current codes and regulations, and sharing new product information from key suppliers.

Flexibility: The Ability to Respond Quickly and Appropriately

The ability to be flexible and change quickly is fundamental to global business success. The great distances and dimensions that affect the normal conduct of global business demand that leaders maintain a high degree of flexibility. In addition to the routine customer-service issues facing those who do business beyond their own domestic markets, things can get off track quickly and in a big way when a company elevates business to a multicontinental and global level, perhaps due to weather, material supply problems, or a myriad of other reasons. It can happen quite quickly and with little or no warning.

To constantly improve their level of global customer service, leaders align themselves with manufacturers and other suppliers who are also flexible. They also develop delivery programs unilaterally or with their suppliers that use their own warehouse facilities as a resource to always be best positioned to meet their global customers' service requirements.

Adaptability: Growth Requires Continuous Ability to Embrace Changes

In global markets, customer groups and market segments will most likely differ in terms of product requirements and service requirements from one market to another in each newly entered market. As with any new experience, bringing new product and service offerings will require certain amounts of adaptation to each local market's needs and wants, especially as experience in these markets grows and evolves.

Not only will your company's product and service offerings need to be adapted to each local market over time, so too will the customer-service organization itself have to adapt to the changes in each market. Very often this will require that specific groups within the customer-service organization assemble and become market or regional experts to ensure that the proper level of localization and regionalization is brought to each market and region. These experts greatly assist in maintaining high-quality market and culturally sensitive customer service.

Unlike adapting to changes in a domestic market, global customer-service organizations will need either to develop their own internal expertise or to develop trusted alliances with local enterprises to serve as a channel of customer and consumer information and competitive product and service information. Such information is essential for the successful global company to identify trends in these faraway markets, which then enables the company to maintain and enhance the company's customer service, keeping it competitive.

Delivering Value: Differentiating the Company's Offerings in a Commoditized World

It is often said that "value is total benefits delivered minus price." If price is the only measurement for products and services, then there is usually no differentiating characteristic to the buyer in today's world of commoditized products and services. If there is no perceived value, product and service together becomes a commodity. Thus, there is no measurable way to differentiate one supplier from another.

To assure value, global firms must partner to provide clear, consistent, and reliable product and service features that deliver measurable benefits to customers and end users. A few obvious (but often overlooked) traits of extraordinary customer service include quality products, complete and on-time deliveries, unexpected product and service features at no extra cost, professional and knowledgeable support staff, problem solving, and attention to detail.

Empathy: Getting into the Customer's Thinking

Global firms consider what they want from manufacturing partners; they certainly want more than a competitive price point. They want reliability, effective promotions, market intelligence, specification interpretation, loyalty, unique sales features, and polite and courteous personal attention. This list is basic, but it is not negotiable. All items must be present all the time to ensure satisfaction. A global customer-service strategy makes sure that a firm is giving its customers the same consideration.

Spotting Trends: Listening for the Future

Global firms continually ask their customers what they want and what they expect. They try to spot trends before their competitors, and they carefully listen for subtle ways to improve their customer service. They also search for what their competitor is doing well, not doing, or is doing poorly. Moreover, besides the salesperson selling the actual product or service, it is the customer-service person that has ongoing contact and communication with customers and consumers using the product or service. In fact, even more than the salesperson, it is the customer-service representative, whose primary responsibility is only servicing the customer, that is in the better position to probe customers and consumers in a nonthreatening manner, under the guise of servicing versus selling.

As the founder of Sony Corporation was once quoted as saying when he spotted a new emerging trend, "We do not create products, we create markets." His new company's initial success was launched with the development of the Sony Walkman to capitalize on the trends he saw with the emerging generation that embraced music as a new religion, that is, members of the Woodstock Generation who needed to have music with them everywhere they went. So it is with a global company's customer-service organization; they will need to work very closely with global marketing, sales, and product and service development groups to communicate the new trend information they receive from the customers. Additionally, the global customer-service organization serves a vital role as a key conduit for these departments to initiate discussions with customers and consumers alike to elicit perceptions, opinions, experiences, and other needed information. With such invaluable information, the global company is in the best position to spot and confirm trends and then to capitalize on these trends with new and enhanced product and service offerings.

Reinforcing Your Message: Reminding Customers of How the Company Serves Them

How customers view their suppliers may be directly related to how often they are reminded of how they are being supported. Global firms let their customers know what is done for them on a regular basis, both in terms of products delivered and customer-service support.

KEY AREAS TO FOCUS UPON

To help you go further in delivering excellent customer service to customers globally, here are a few key areas upon which to focus.

Making Ordering Easy

Superior global customer service starts from the first customer contact; make it especially easy for your customers to order from you and order in many different ways to suit their own needs. This requires spending time adapting your company's ordering processes right down to the forms that you ask customers to fill out. A few key areas to pay close attention to are as follows:

1. *Customer name and address:* Make sure you leave plenty of space for the name and address; foreign addresses tend to be a lot longer than U.S. addresses.
2. *Instructions:* If you are selling clothing or shoes, reduce the number of potential customer returns by providing easy access to easy-to-read size conversions. By adapting your product and service descriptions and order forms into the local language and preferred color schemes, you will also reduce any possible confusion by the customer when ordering from you.
3. *Mailings:* If you are mailing anything directly to the customer, consider a multilingual format with ordering instructions in both English and all local languages. Also, be sure to specify that the customer should complete the information in printed Roman characters. If you do not, you may need to have your orders deciphered or translated. This will take a lot more time than you think, and the costs are high.
4. *Customer responses:* Provide your customers alternative and convenient ways to respond back to you, such as telephone, fax, mail, or the Web. Most orders taken today in the United States still are done by telephone. This is not necessarily the case in other markets where the cost of a telephone call is much higher as compared to the United States, so most orders are placed via fax or through the mail. If you are selling business to business, you need to include an Internet option as well as a fax option. Despite the seemingly ubiquitous use of the Internet, many business-to-business orders are still received via fax.

Handling Customer Orders

If your company offers a telephone ordering option, carefully consider how your company will handle incoming calls from customers in foreign markets. How will your company route these calls to its domestic operation? Will your company set up facilities in Europe, in Asia, and so forth? Differing cultures, multiple languages, time, and operating costs are key reasons why it often makes sense to set up an overseas call center. While many people living outside of North America comprehend and speak English to varying degrees, they typically feel more comfortable talking in their native language when placing orders and requesting service.

A foreign-based customer call center may make financial sense, too. It is generally less costly to have a large volume of calls that originate in Europe also terminate in Europe at a European call center versus a U.S.-based call center. Also, if foreign calls are being routed to the U.S.-based call center, make sure your company considers time zone changes when it schedules its customer call center hours.

One aspect of handling customer orders to particularly consider is payment alternatives. Be sure your company understands the preferred methods of payment in each local market, and then offer a variety of market-appropriate payment options. The United States and Canada are still largely check-based economies, whereas most of the rest of the world (industrialized or developing markets) are transaction-based economies that use either direct debit or bank transfer. Also, cash on delivery, check, and payment by invoice may be other options to consider.

It would be a mistake to assume that customers will pay by credit card as is usually done in the United States and Canada. In much of Europe and especially in Germany, the payment for most mail-order goods is done on open account; in other words, customers are billed only after the product is received and in good order.

Product Fulfillment

Product fulfillment depends on the products your company is shipping, your company's acceptable turnaround time, and its investment in its global markets, including its global customer service. If your company is in the early stages of developing its global business or if it has products with relatively low rates of return, it should generally consider using your current domestic fulfillment operation. If your company's strategy is committed to establishing a fully globalized business or it has products that have high rates of return, it may be better to set up foreign product fulfillment operations or hire a local market firm to handle local order fulfillment.

How your company ships products will impact delivery time. It will be a lot cheaper to ship products via ocean freight, but your company will definitely save more time by sending your products by airfreight.

Also, if you are shipping products as individual orders and the U.S. Postal Service (USPS) or your company's freight consolidator uses the USPS as its delivery agent, the order travels as mail from your company to the customer. This can be quite expensive. Alternatively, if the package is being shipped from the United States for delivery by a foreign postal administration, the package travels to the destination country as cargo and then it becomes mail upon entering the postal system of the destination country, a process that is typically at lower cost to the shipping company, your company.

If your company is distributing from a foreign fulfillment location, products usually leave the United States in bulk. Then the products are usually delivered to your company's overseas operation or a contracted operation in the local market. The local fulfillment operation then separates the merchandise, packages, and addresses the orders. Packages then enter the local market postal distribution system via an optimized and cost-effective fulfillment scheme.

Customer Returns and Refunds

To provide superior customer service, companies should not allow currency fluctuations to impact a customer's refund. Customers around the world should be reimbursed at the same conversion rate as when the sale was processed. Companies and customers should not seek to make or lose money on returns or refunds.

Decisions to reimburse customers for postage spent to return an item usually depend on your company's profit margin on that product or that specific order or order type. If margins are substantial, companies may want to refund the customer for any shipping costs incurred to demonstrate its dedication to superior customer service and to motivate the customer for future purchases.

CREATING GLOBAL CUSTOMER SERVICE STANDARDS

When creating standards for global customer service, global firms make certain that they are measurable. For example, one objective may be 100 percent packing accuracy. Packing inspection of 100 percent is not an objective. It is one possible solution. Packing inspection is only one task of many that could achieve the objective. Other tasks or alternatives may be more effective for accomplishing the objective.

How will you measure the objective on an ongoing basis? If you cannot measure an objective, you will never know whether it was achieved. For example, 100 percent shipping accuracy may be measured using statistical sampling after final packing but prior to shipment.

Establish Global Customer Service Rules and Constraints

Identify key restrictions (hard rules) and guidelines (soft rules) that will form the boundaries around the customer-service strategy. These rules include company policies, expected return on investment, project organization, personnel availability, computer system development/support constraints, and internal operations procedures.

The rules represent key compromises between revenue producers (customer support, marketing, and sales personnel) with operations, engineering, management information system, and other project resources. Only upper management can change the rules and guidelines after the project starts. These rules are the foundation for effective communication and timely decision making.

Disassemble Each Objective into Unique Tasks

A task identifies what must be accomplished, not how. After analyzing the objectives, clearly identify what tasks are within the scope of the global customer-service team and prioritize the tasks to optimize dependencies and return on investment. The task definition and sequence is very critical to the effectiveness of the program.

It is important to establish minimum customer-service standards, make sure everyone understands them, and have a way to recognize superior performance. As procedures are developed, be sure that all three criteria are satisfied. Use creative problem-solving techniques to develop a list of feasible solutions for the task. Select a combination of possible solutions that will accomplish the objective with minimal ongoing effort.

MAINTAINING GLOBAL CUSTOMER-SERVICE STANDARDS

Beyond developing a global customer-service strategy, a global firm must maintain customer-service standards for its employees, suppliers, and, ultimately, its customers. Unfortunately, some companies have been unwilling to enhance their customer-service functions and create standards because they assumed it was not required, or the benefits did not appear tangible. Historically, it was wiser to wait until external circumstances (for example, economic conditions, product trends, and so forth) appeared imminent and then react. In today's global economy, however, such thinking is clearly contradictory to the proactive global customer-service approach demanded if a company is to transform itself into a truly successful global company competing in the new global marketplace.

What Are the Standards We Are Maintaining?

Maintaining standards may involve the weekly or monthly analysis of the measurement of a company's global customer-service standards. Such questions as "Can we offer additional services that the customer may not be aware that we offer?" or "What would it take to have the customer use only our services?" make this process more fluid and responsive to customer needs.

Handling Complaints

Companies must maintain standards for the handling of complaints. One study by the Technical Assistance Research Program Institute shows 70 percent of unhappy global customers will not make another purchase from the offending firm. On the other hand, 95 percent of customers will return if their complaint is resolved quickly. It goes without saying that effective, speedy resolution of complaints keeps customers happy.

SUMMARY

Successful global customer service does not just happen. It must be planned, implemented, monitored, and then continually refined. The creation of a global customer-service strategy and the organization to deliver it successfully requires fine-tuning new management processes to bring about exceptional customer service on a global scale. Shifting an organization's central focus from primarily domestic customers to customers in markets in the four corners of the world means that extraordinary multicultural customer relations and service will need to become a natural operating procedure for the aspiring global customer-service organization. When customers from markets around the world feel that they are the central and primary concern of a company, they buy more and repeatedly from that company regardless of where that company may be located, whether it is around the corner or around the world.

Making the shift from a domestically focused customer-service approach to a global customer-service approach requires a complete change of mind-set of how a company does business. Such new thinking will undoubtedly require customer-service executives to concentrate on the critical success factors of people, process, technology, and environment, and all of these at a global level. Ultimately, a tight focus on these critical factors leads to the creation of an environment that supports the acquisition and maintenance of the right people, the right processes, and the right technology to compete on a global basis.

In the exploding borderless economy, a long-term dedication to not only developing a full global customer-service strategy but also evolving such a strategy when implemented as a comprehensive approach to building the total global company will undoubtedly produce a true, sustainable competitive advantage.

CHAPTER 13

GLOBAL MARKETING AND ETHICS

Andrew R. Thomas and Timothy J. Wilkinson

If you are going to be involved in international marketing, especially marketing in developing countries, you will see things that you have never imagined possible and you will be challenged with ethical dilemmas that will leave you perplexed, exhausted, and potentially, if you are not prepared, debased and corrupted. The people you meet will often appear as poseurs, pretending to be what they are not. You will often find yourself in social circumstances where behavior that would be considered illegal or unethical in the United States or Europe will be viewed as normal and beneficial. It is also likely that you will end up in situations that are so ambiguous that the moral compass that has thus far directed your life will be inadequate, even if you are a straitlaced moralist who has strong opinions on what is right and what is wrong. Because ethical challenges can be so great in international marketing, a prepared businessperson cannot afford to neglect his or her ethical and moral development before launching out into overseas markets. In this chapter we describe several possible scenarios that you may face and give some suggestions about how to deal with ethical decision making in the international business environment.

In many situations, the best customer to represent your product in a global market does not always appear on the surface to be the most desirable candidate. While visiting his distributor in Nairobi a few years ago, Thomas was introduced to a man from eastern Congo who came in to discuss buying some motorcycles. Thomas was most anxious for the meeting because he had no representation in that part of the country. His enthusiasm waned when he saw the man from Congo for the first time. The man looked like he had arrived right out of the bush. He wore old plastic sandals, a stained, torn, and dirty shirt, and a ripped pair of pants. Most disturbing was the smell; the potential business partner could be smelled from two kilometers away. Meeting this man defied the logic stated in the timeless expression, "You never get a second chance to make a good first impression."

When Thomas and the Congolese businessman were formally introduced and exchanged the traditional three-kiss, French greeting, Thomas proceeded to do the most typical of all American business practices and offered the African his business card. The man from Congo asked for a sheet of paper and wrote his name and country on the paper and presented it as his.

After the formalities, Thomas began his standard sales pitch, not wanting to offend this poor man who obviously did not have the resources to do business with him. As one of the motorcycles was sitting on the showroom floor, they stared at the unit, discussed all of its wonderful features, and then took a spin around the block. Upon returning to the office, Thomas gave the man from Congo a baseball cap and key chain. A smile covered his entire face, and he once again gave Thomas the three-kiss, French greeting.

The man sat down and a long conversation ensued about the Congo, the weather, and all manner of trivial local topics. After three hours boredom was beginning to set in. Still, Thomas did not want to offend this "wanna-be" businessman. He thought, "When in Africa, do what the Africans do. If he wants to play big shot, go along with him." So, when the man from Congo began to ask what appeared to be irrelevant questions about Thomas's business, Thomas suggested they get a Coke. The caffeine rush would permit him to stay awake long enough to make the poor African feel important. After an hour had passed, the African leaned forward, looked Thomas in the eye, and began to ask clear, informed, and important questions.

"What is the unit price?"

"$1,500 delivered to Nairobi."

The man from Congo asked for another sheet of paper and wrote down $1,500.

"How many motorcycles could be loaded into a 20-foot ocean container?"

"Forty."

For the next ten minutes the man from Congo proceeded to multiply by longhand 1,500 by 40. Thomas was tempted to offer his calculator but reckoned it might be better to let him play big shot for a little longer. After the African successfully completed the equation, the man from Congo looked up and stared at the ceiling for ten minutes. Finally he announced, "I'll take 40 units."

Thomas was not shocked. He was certain the man from Congo believed he would ship the motorcycles and let him pay later. Still trying not to offend him, Thomas told him as politely as possible that it would be necessary to pay the entire amount prior to shipment. Thomas figured this would quietly end the meeting so they could get on to the more pressing matter of lunch.

Without saying a word, the man from Congo reached into his large backpack and pulled out an old cardboard box that was wrapped in worn-out tape and smelled almost as bad as he did. The African then opened up the box and proceeded to count out U.S.$60,000 in one-hundred dollar bills. As he counted, Thomas peered unbelievably into the box and roughly calculated there was at least 3 million dollars inside, all in U.S. currency. At that moment, this poor, wanna-be businessman was transformed into Thomas's new distributor for eastern Congo and his new best friend.

Any astute international business traveler will tell you that it is not smart to ask someone from where they have accumulated their wealth. In any airport waiting lounge anywhere in the world it is possible to find an American who will tell you his life story in 20 minutes. An African, Latin, Asian, or Russian man, however, will never *tell* you how he became rich. If you have his confidence, he may eventually *show* you how he obtained his wealth. In emerging markets local distributors and other business people live by the expression, "You can ask me how I made my millions, but do not ask me how I made my *first* million."

Some months later, Thomas ventured to eastern Congo to see his new best friend—call him Samuni. The Democratic Republic of the Congo is one of the great paradoxes of the world. Underneath its soil are some of the largest gold, diamond, copper, and platinum deposits on earth. If properly exploited, Congo's 44 million people could live healthy and prosperous lives. Instead, because of rampant corruption and perennial governmental mismanagement of these assets, the average life expectancy for both men and women is less than 50 years of age and the average annual income is less than $250. It is within this environment, however, that some tremendous personal fortunes have been amassed. Everyone knows of the $5 billion that Mobutu Sese Seko, the former president, accumulated during the reign of his kleptocracy for over 30 years. What people may not know is how Samuni and many like him also became rich. They did not steal from the government. They did it the old-fashioned way: they *earned* it. Admittedly, at the same time, favorable relationships with key government officials usually serve as an essential "enabler" for the owners of such successful businesses.

Because of the severe lack of infrastructure, many of the minerals in Congo are being extracted by individuals in search of instant wealth—like the forty-niners of California's gold rush in the nineteenth century. The gold or diamonds are sold for the most universal of currencies, the U.S. dollar. It was recently concluded by the Federal Reserve that over 70 percent of all U.S. currency bills in the world are held outside of the United States. A significant portion of these bills seem to have ended up in eastern Congo. Dollars are everywhere, as they are in almost all emerging markets. In a former Belgian colony where French is the official language and English is rarely spoken, the universal communicator is the U.S. dollar.

Samuni goes into the mining areas with his old box and buys gold and diamonds with his U.S. dollars—at a high margin for himself. Next he travels to

Nairobi or Kampala where he exchanges the metals for consumer goods like cups, plates, knives, clothes, radios, Coca-Cola, televisions, and spare parts with Asian middlemen—again at a high margin for himself.

Using his connections in customs—connections that are supported as just another cost of doing his business—Samuni transports the goods from Kenya or Uganda to eastern Congo and imports with little or no duties. He then sells the goods back to the miners in exchange for the same U.S. dollars that started the process—at a high margin for himself.

The goods are sold from two tractor-trailers that move slowly down the road like a portable shopping mall. Whenever the trucks approach a small village, people come from miles around to see the latest goods: Indian kitchen utensils, American soft drinks, Korean televisions, Chinese radios. It is the Central African version of a suburban shopping center.

It is hard to calculate the net worth of Samuni's business since there are no bankers, accountants, lawyers, insurance brokers, tax collectors, or dry cleaners for hundreds of miles. A close friend estimates it is at least U.S.$300 million. Thomas's business with Samuni alone averaged over U.S.$2.4 million each year for more than four years, especially high for such a small, impoverished market such as Congo.

It goes without saying that Samuni's business empire was built in the middle of the worst genocide since the Killing Fields of Cambodia. The conflict between the Hutu majority and the Tutsi minority in Central Africa has led to untold human atrocities throughout the region. In April 1994, Rwanda, Burundi, and Eastern Zaire erupted into a tribal bloodbath that claimed the lives of at least 1.5 million men, women, and children. The violence continues unabated today with absolutely no end in sight.

On one of Thomas's visits to the region, he found Samuni operating near Goma—site of Africa's largest refugee camp—where more than 200,000 Hutu were still living under the pseudoprotection of the United Nations. After the traditional three-kiss, French greeting, Samuni took Thomas and one of his brothers by foot deep into the bush. They walked for almost an hour until coming upon a clearing where a 40-foot ocean container was resting. The box, surrounded as it was by the green of the jungle, looked disconcertingly out of place. As they approached a terrible stench met them. It was so overwhelming that it caused Thomas to vomit. To the right of the container were two local men throwing lime on the newly dug ground. After regaining his composure, Thomas approached one of the men and asked him what was going on:

"Two days ago, a local bushman discovered the container. The doors were locked and it smelled real bad. The bushman opened the doors and discovered, piled up at the entrance to the container, the corpses of several small children."

Right before Thomas vomited for the second time he asked, "How many bodies were in the container?"

"We counted 206," he said calmly. "There wasn't a child over the age of five inside."

Thomas vomited again and then tears began to pour out of his eyes. The man with the shovel continued to throw down the lime. As Thomas tried to recompose himself and began to stagger away, the man whispered to him, "God has left here."

When Thomas rejoined Samuni and his brother on the other end of the clearing, he found them talking on his global system for mobile communications phone to a London commodity house. They were asking for the closing price of gold on the London Exchange, completely oblivious to the massacre of the children. When Thomas asked them their feelings about what had happened here, they brightly smiled and exclaimed, "Gold is up U.S.$2 per ounce," and started back to the trail.

LEAVING IT AT HOME...

Such atrocities as mass genocide can never be accepted by any of us, while at the same time, to consider Samuni an evil or dispassionate man is merely to acknowledge our own naiveté and ignorance about the lives of many people living in developing countries. Simply put, there are a lot of men in the world like Samuni who would make wonderful customers or suppliers for Western companies. Often these individuals have been either ignored or rejected by Western businesspeople.

In the developing world high-end goods are readily available through what, for lack of a better term, we call contraband markets. If you ask international business managers to name the number one place in the world for the point of purchase of commercial goods, many will say Hong Kong, Miami, or Dubai. In actuality most goods are purchased at Ciudad del Este in eastern Paraguay. It is estimated that more than about U.S.$50 billion a year in consumer goods move in and out of this city in the eastern part of Paraguay on the border with Argentina and Brazil. The reason is simple. Ciudad del Este presents, few, if any, market barriers. There are two bridges that connect Ciudad del Este to Brazil, and those bridges get filled with tour buses of Brazilians coming in to shop and avoid the very high import taxes on many consumer goods that are charged in Brazil. When people get off these buses in Paraguay they are met by young children selling them duffle bags and plastic shopping bags. The Brazilian shoppers then spend six or eight or even ten hours moving through the city, buying every possible item they can from the major manufacturers and distributors of consumer goods.

According to retired colonel William W. Mendel, Ciudad del Este is "a town of a quarter million inhabitants and an international trading center where the admixture of drug runners, terrorists, and pinstriped bankers trespasses on the sovereignty and safety of democratic countries and their citizens, thereby representing a threat to the United States and the region."[1] On the other hand, Cuidad del Este is crowded with legitimate businesses. You can get an Armani suit from the official Armani retailer. You can buy Dom Pérignon champagne. You can buy original equipment manufacturer parts for your General Motors car that is made in Brazil. Legitimate retail exists side-by-side with the contraband market. Companies operating in this corner of Paraguay realize that even though this is a contraband market, in order to succeed in the South American environment, they have to have a presence in a place like Ciudad del Este.

From an ethical perspective, companies have to make a decision whether they want to do business in ethically challenged environments. Corruption is not an isolated feature of one city or a small number of countries. It is a fact of life in the major emerging markets of the global economy.

In Russia, every business that operates there, whether an international firm or a local one, is required to have a *kriesha*. *Kriesha* means a roof in Russian. That essentially is what protects you as a business from the things that are falling down all around you. If you do not have a *kriesha*, which can be obtained through regularly monthly payments to the local mafia or to the former government officials, many of them KGB, you are left in a situation without a roof and things can really fall down on you quickly.

China offers its own challenges. Because of its size and growth many people are now excited about the consumer market in China. The big issue confronting companies there is the huge number of goods that come across China from the West to the East, much of it tax-free. Since little or no duties are paid, these products are able to be sold in the stores in Guangzhou, Shenzhen, Shanghai, or Beijing a lot more easily because they are cheap. To what extent should international marketers play by local rules, especially when to apply American standards overseas can lead to a real loss of competitive advantage?

WHAT TO DO

When attempting to formulate ethical standards or an ethical approach to business a major problem quickly becomes apparent: People disagree about what is right and what is wrong. The moral consensus that used to exist in the West has been under assault since the Enlightenment of the 18th century. During the second half of the 20th century, moral relativism, tempered by legal sanction, became the "standard" by which moral dilemmas were addressed. One need only listen to the equivocations and hairsplitting of medical ethicists to see how once universally held presuppositions are now dismissed, forgotten, or ignored. In his book *After Virture*, Alasdair MacIntyre describes the process of moral decline. He states that moral theory was initially linked to objective and impersonal standards that provided a rational justification for subsequent policies, judgments, and actions. In other words, conduct was at one time premised upon rationally justifiable standards that were external to the personal preferences of individuals in a particular set of circumstances. This has been displaced by emotivism, wherein all evaluative judgments are nothing but expressions of preference, attitude, or feeling. Emotivism is an illusive protagonist because its engagers assert principles that "function as a mask for expressions of personal preference."[2] The rationale proceeds as follows: My profit margins are greater because my Chinese joint venture partner is subcontracting out to Chinese Laogai (slave labor) camps. These camps have nothing to do with me. This is a decision of my joint venture partner. Besides, economic growth in China will eventually result in democratization and human rights.

We believe that a world in which "social identity can then be anything, can assume any role or take any point of view, because it *is* in itself nothing"[3] results in what Alexandr Solzhenitzyn asserts in his classic work *The Gulag Archipelago* as an intolerable society that oscillates between a lack of individual self-regulation and collectivist control.[4] International marketing conducted within an emotive context is likely to be tainted by individual self-interest at the expense of other people. In this chapter we have addressed some of the ethical challenges faced by managers engaged in international marketing.

Rather than providing a full-fledged discussion of ethical theory, our goal is to present a practical approach to operating in an ethical manner in international business situations. Therefore we are the first to admit that moral theorists could legitimately criticize our approach as a simplistic series of assertions. However, given the widespread acceptance of moral relativism and its cousin, emotivism, our approach is to appeal to the classical traditional and Christian traditions, tempered by several contemporary analytical tools intended to guide ethical decision making. Thus, our approach is pragmatic and is not intended as an argument in favor of any particular ethical system. We suggest that international marketers take the following steps.

Consider Legalities

While ethics is broader than law, legal considerations are necessarily encompassed by moral concerns. Firms operating in international markets are constrained by home and host country laws, as well as the regulations of supranational organizations (for example, the European Union) as well as applicable international laws and treaties. For American firms the Foreign Corrupt Practices Act (FCPA) is of particular concern. Passed by Congress in 1977, the FCPA stipulates that Americans may not bribe the officials of foreign governments in order to obtain business or favorable regulatory decisions. These "officials" include not only individuals directly employed by foreign governments, but also employees of state-owned (or controlled) enterprises as well as individuals working for governments on a contractual basis. Payment to a third party for the purpose of bribing an official is also prohibited, even when "willful blindness" is employed. An American businessperson may be in violation of the FCPA even if he or she does not make reasonable inquiries as to how the money turned over to the third party will be used.

Figure out Your Ethical Values before You Enter the Market

Epitomized by Aristotle, the classical tradition consists of varying catalogs of virtues characterized by *practice* ("cooperative human activity through which goods internal to that form of activity are realized in the course of trying to achieve those standards of excellence which are appropriate. . .with the result that human powers to achieve excellence, and human conceptions of the ends and goods involved, are systematically extended"), the narrative order and wholeness of an individual's life and moral tradition. Each of these characteristics must be present in order for a human quality to be considered a virtue.[5] Lists of virtues are provided by Homer (physical strength or excellence), Aristotle (friendship), the New Testament (faith, hope, love, and humility), Jane Austen (constancy), and Benjamin Franklin (cleanliness, silence, and industry). These lists of virtues vary, are sometimes in conflict (Aristotle/Homer, Aristotle/Jesus Christ and St. Paul), and are sometimes synthesized as in the case of Jane Austen's combination of seemingly disparate virtues. However, despite the differences in these accounts, they are similar in that they all claim some form of institutional hegemony.[6]

We suggest that firms incorporate virtue ethics into their company mission statements or operating documents. An explicate statement and understanding of what is considered to be unethical can be used to guide competitive and strategic decisions. For example, Fred Tipson, the senior policy counsel of Microsoft Corporation, made the following statement while speaking at the first Internet Governance Forum held in Athens:

> Things are getting bad. . .and perhaps we have to look again at our presence there. . . We have to decide if the persecuting of bloggers reaches a point that it's unacceptable to do business there. We try to define those levels and the trends are not good there at the moment. It's a moving target.[7]

Clearly embarrassed by Tipson's remark, the giant software firm went into defensive operational mode with a quick official statement that read, "Microsoft is not considering the suspension of the company's internet services in China."[8] Clearly the executives at Microsoft have yet to think through the ethical challenges posed by doing business in the world's largest totalitarian state. By carefully setting limits and forming policy before moving into markets with high levels of moral hazard, firms are better able to cope with the kinds of fluid ethical dilemmas that they are likely to face.

Think about Your Stakeholders

Some questions might be, Would any of our company's stakeholders—employees, shareholders, upper management, suppliers, customers, and so forth—be embarrassed if they found out what we were doing from a marketing perspective? Would they immediately disapprove of the behavior? It is one thing to be embarrassed, but would they also think that the behavior is simply wrong?

While solely relying on the subjective impressions of others as a guide to ethical behavior is dubious, the prospect of disapproval by those who are concerned about the organization and/or its products should give pause to a company's managers. If you think that what you are about to do will appear to others as wrong, unusual, or embarrassing, it probably is an activity that is best avoided. Managers should consider how they would view a situation if they or organizational stakeholders were the recipients of the behavior in question. If a misleading ad or a promise of customer service was not adhered to, or a quality product that was advertised turned out to be a less than quality product, you can be sure that you and other participants would be unhappy with the situation.

Finally, in your organization do you see anybody concerned that there might be something going on that might not be completely right? Is there a culture within the organization that allows questionable things to take place? Do employees and others have the freedom to speak up if they perceive unethical behavior within the company. Certainly it is better to invite stakeholders to critique the actions of the firm than it is to read those critiques in a newspaper, Web site, or somebody's blog.

Ultimately for international marketers, business ethics cannot be divorced from one's sense of morality in *all* spheres of life. Dualism, in the sense that one's personal life (and personal sense of morality) is somehow a separate sphere from one's professional life (and professional ethics), is one of the unfortunate consequences of the post-Enlightenment Age. Given this reality, we recommend that people engaged in international marketing think through their moral beliefs carefully and steer a conservative, ethical course as they take advantage of profitable overseas opportunities.

NOTES

1. William W. Mendel, "Paraguay's Ciudad del Este and the New Centers of Gravity," *Military Review* (March–April 2002): 51.

2. Alisdair MacIntyre, *After Virtue,* 2nd ed. Notre Dame, IN: University of Notre Dame Press, 1984), 19.

3. Ibid., 34.

4. Alexandr Solzhenitzyn, *The Gulag Archipelago* (New York: Harper & Row, 1973).

5. MacIntyre, *After Virtue,* 275.

6. Ibid, 186.

7. "Microsoft Considers China Policy," BBC News, http://newsvote.bbc.co.uk/mpapps/pagetools/print/news.bbc.co.uk/2/hi/technology/610218.

8. "Microsoft Restates China Policy," BBC News, November 3, 2006, http://news.bbc.co.uk /2/hi/technology/6114846.stm.

INDEX

About the Editors and Contributors

GENERAL EDITOR

BRUCE D. KEILLOR is coordinator of the American Marketing Association's Office for Applied Research-Direct Marketing and Professor of Marketing and International Business at The University of Akron. He is also a research fellow at Michigan State University. Dr. Keillor specializes in international marketing strategy and direct multi-channel marketing and has authored more than 60 articles published in journals worldwide. He has also contributed to numerous books. In addition to his academic credentials, Dr. Keillor has also been an active entrepreneur as co-owner of a direct-marketing software company he helped found in 1994. Dr. Keillor also has extensive executive education and consulting experience as a copartner in BBA Associates, a global marketing consulting firm.

EDITORS

TIMOTHY J. WILKINSON is Associate Professor of Marketing at Montana State University, Billings, where he teaches courses in international marketing, consumer behavior, and marketing research. Previously, he served as Associate Director of the Institute for Global Business and Associate Professor of Marketing and International Business at The University of Akron. With a primary research interest in export promotion and international entrepreneurship, his papers have been presented at national and international conferences and published in a variety of academic and applied business journals, including *Long Range Planning, Business Horizons, MIT Sloan Management Review, Journal of Small Business Management,* and the *Journal of International Business Studies.*

ANDREW R. THOMAS is Assistant Professor of Marketing and International Business and Director of the Center for Organizational Development at The University of Akron. A successful global entrepreneur, he has conducted business in more than 120 countries. He is a *New York Times* best-selling author; his books include *Global Manifest Destiny* and *Aviation Insecurity,* and, with M. David Dealy, *Defining the Really Great Boss* (Praeger, 2004), *Change or Die* (Praeger, 2005), and *Managing by Accountability* (Praeger, 2006). He is also coeditor of *Direct Marketing in Action* (Praeger, 2006).

CONTRIBUTORS

YEQING BAO is Assistant Professor of Marketing at the University of Alabama in Huntsville, where he teaches courses in buyer behavior, promotional strategy, and international business. His research interests are consumer socialization, advertising, and international marketing. He has published in leading academic journals, such as the *International Journal of Research in Marketing, Journal of Business Research, Journal of Advertising Research,* and others.

ALLAN BIRD is the Eiichi Shibusawa-Seigo Arai Professor of Japanese Studies and Director of the International Business Institute in the College of Business Administration, University of Missouri–St. Louis. He previously held positions at California Polytechnic State University and New York University and has been a visiting professor/researcher at Columbia University, Monterey Institute of International Studies, Osaka International University, and the National Self-Defense Academy in Japan. He has received numerous grants and fellowships, including a Fulbright Research Fellowship and an NEC Faculty Research Fellowship. His work has appeared in the *Academy of Management Journal,* the *Strategic Management Journal,* the *Journal of Organizational Behavior,* the *Journal of International Business Studies,* and other academic and practitioner journals. He is the author/editor of several books, including *The Encyclopedia of Japanese Business and Management, Japanese Multinationals Abroad: Individual and Organizational Learning,* and *Ekuzekuchibu no Kenkyuu.* With Roger Dunbar and Tom Mullen he published *Bridging Cultures,* an award-winning CD-ROM and workbook for expatriates and their families.

LANCE ELIOT BROUTHERS is Professor of Western Hemispheric Trade and Director of the Ph.D. program in International Business at the University of Texas at El Paso. Professor Brouthers has been consistently ranked among the top international business scholars in the world. He has won or been a finalist for numerous research and teaching awards, including the Igor Ansoff Award for business strategy, an international award sponsored by Coopers & Lybrand and given only once every two years. Professor Brouthers has published about

70 refereed articles and book chapters relating to international business in top journals, including *The Journal of Management Studies, The Journal of Management, Strategic Management Journal,* and *The Journal of International Business Studies.*

JOHN CASLIONE is Founder, President, and CEO of GCS Business Capital, Inc., a middle-market mergers-and-acquisitions advisory firm with offices worldwide. He is highly sought after as an expert on the global economy, global business development, and doing business in China. A frequent guest on CNBC Europe's *Squawk Box* and *Morning Exchange* programs, he has personally implemented business strategies for companies in almost 90 countries on six continents. He also serves as director and advisor for a number of companies in the United States, Europe, and Asia. He is an adjunct professor at the Edwin L. Cox School of Business at Southern Methodist University, where he teaches marketing strategy in the Executive Education Program. The author of *Global Manifest Destiny: Growing Your Business in a Borderless Economy* and *Growing Your Business in Emerging Markets: Promise and Peril,* Caslione earned his B.S. and MBA from the University of New York and his J.D. from the Illinois Institute of Technology.

ASHUTOSH DIXIT is Assistant Professor of Marketing at Cleveland State University. While undertaking his Ph.D. at the Georgia Institute of Technology, he was awarded a CIBER Fellowship to study in Japan and was also selected to be AMA-Sheth Doctoral Consortium Fellow. He received the Terry Sanford Award (twice) and the Coca-Cola Center Award (twice) for his research in 2002 and 2003. Prior to joining the Cleveland State University faculty in 2004, he was a faculty member of the University of Georgia at Athens and held a senior executive position in the information technology industry. His research interests are in market evolution, competition and pricing issues, electronic commerce, international business, and marketing education. He has authored numerous papers, and his research has appeared/or is forthcoming in the *Journal of Marketing, Journal of Public Policy and Marketing, Business Horizons, Journal of Business Research, Marketing Education Review,* and *Neural Networks for Business Forecasting.* His most recent book is *Upheaval in the Airline Industry* (coauthored with Jagdish N. Sheth, Fred C. Allvine, and Can Uslay).

RAJSHEKHAR (RAJ) G. JAVALGI is Professor of Marketing and International Business in the Nance College of Business Administration, Cleveland State University. He is also Associate Dean for Strategic Initiatives and Research and the Director of Doctor of Business Administration. He teaches courses in the areas of international marketing, international business, marketing research, multivariate statistical methods, and marketing management, and he has received numerous research and teaching awards, including the Gold Medal Award. He has had broad experience working with international business professionals, for example, assisting small and medium enterprises (SMEs) in developing international marketing plans, export plans, country analyses, and in cultural issues of doing business in the developed and emerging economies. He has received two Business International Education grants to build and sustain international business programming at Nance. Javalgi has published over 100 scholarly and professional journal articles, conference papers, and book chapters in the field of international business/marketing, with an emphasis on foreign direct investment, international trade, internationalization of services, cross-cultural analysis, global e-commerce, and entrepreneurship.

GARY A. KNIGHT is Associate Professor and Director of the International Business Program at Florida State University. His research focus is the internationalization of SMEs, born-global firms, international business strategy, and the effect of terrorism on international firms. He has written some 90 articles, published in academic journals and conference proceedings. He is coauthor of the textbook *International Business*. He serves on the editorial review boards of the *Journal of International Business Studies, Journal of International Marketing,* and *Journal of International Entrepreneurship.* He obtained his MBA from the University of Washington and his Ph.D. from Michigan State University and was an executive in industry before joining academia. He was a Fulbright Scholar to Quebec, Canada. He speaks fluent Japanese and fluent French.

MASAAKI (MIKE) KOTABE holds the Washburn Chair Professorship in International Business and Marketing and is Director of Research at the Institute of Global Management Studies at the Fox School of Business and Management at Temple University. Prior to joining Temple University in 1998, he was Ambassador Edward Clark Centennial Endowed Fellow and Professor of Marketing and International Business at The University of Texas at Austin. Dr. Kotabe served as the Vice President of the Academy of International Business in 1997–1998. In 1998, he was elected a Fellow of the Academy of International Business for his significant contribution to international business research and education. Dr. Kotabe has written many scholarly publications, including the following books: *Global Sourcing Strategy: R&D, Manufacturing, Marketing Interfaces* (1992), *Anticompetitive Practices in Japan* (1996), *Market Revolution in Latin America: Beyond Mexico* (2001), *Global Supply Chain Management* (2006), and *Global Marketing Management,* 4th ed. (2007).

DANA-NICOLETA LASCU is Chair of the Marketing Department at the Robins School of Business, University of Richmond, in Virginia, where she teaches courses in international marketing and marketing research. She was the 2006

Fulbright Distinguished Chair in International Business at the Johannes Kepler University in Linz, Austria. She is also the author of *International Marketing* and coauthor of *Essentials of Marketing* (Thompson), and she has published in the area of emerging marketing strategies in *International Marketing Review, International Business Review, Multinational Business Review, Journal of Business Research, Journal of Global Marketing,* and *Journal of Business Ethics,* among others. She has conducted research for a number of international firms, including Ford Motor Company, Albright & Wilson, and IDV North America.

JASON MCNICOL is an international business doctoral student at the University of Texas at El Paso. He is actively researching topics on international entrepreneurship and international risk.

LYNN E. METCALF is Professor of Marketing in the Orfalea College of Business at California Polytechnic State University. Dr. Metcalf's research interests are focused on cross-cultural negotiation and new product development.

JULIE MO is an International Business Specialist with academic and work experience on three continents; she has used her MBA and multilingual knowledge (she is fluent in Chinese, English, and Spanish) in a variety of organizations ranging from giant Chinese state-owned enterprises to American private firms to the INS courts and, more recently, a federally funded nonprofit organization.

ROBERT F. SCHERER is Dean and Professor of Management in the Nance College of Business Administration, Cleveland State University. He has published in the areas of global business, occupational safety, workplace stress, and entrepreneurship. He has served as a Fulbright Senior Scholar in Chile and has taught in the Caribbean, Spain, and France. Prior to his academic career he worked in the insurance and magazine publishing fields.

VERN TERPSTRA is Emeritus Professor of International Business at the University of Michigan. He is the author of ten books, including *International Marketing,* currently in its 9th edition and printed in several languages. He has written many articles and serves on the editorial board of nine journals. He has lectured in China and had visiting professorships in Hong Kong, Indonesia, Taiwan, the Netherlands, and England. He received the Global Marketing Award from the American Marketing Association, served as president of the Academy of International Business (AIB), and has been elected a Fellow of the AIB.

CALIN VEGHES is Senior Lecturer, Department of Marketing, Faculty of Marketing, Academy of Economic Studies, in Bucharest, Romania.

GEORGE O. WHITE III is an instructor and doctoral candidate of international business in the College of Business Administration, University of Texas at El Paso. He is also an honorary professor of global commerce at Hebei Normal University (People's Republic of China). Prior to attending the University of Texas at El Paso, he was a government-appointed economic adviser to the Shijiazhuang National Hi-Tech Industry Development Zone in the People's Republic of China. His research concentrates on multinational enterprise strategies in East Asian emerging markets.

GERHARD A. WÜHRER is Chaired Professor of Marketing and Director of the Institute of Retailing, Sales and Marketing at Johannes Kepler University (JKU) in Linz, Austria. He studied Management Science and Engineering at the University of Stuttgart, Germany, and worked as a project manager in the consulting industry in Germany and Austria. His research interests cover theoretical and methodological issues, including networks and marketing in emerging markets. He is also heading the department of Marketing for Emerging Markets (M4EM) at the Institute. He has published numerous books and articles dealing with the topics of his research interests. His most recent book is *Drivers of Global Business Success: Lessons from Emerging Markets* (coeditors F. Zeynep Bilgin and Ven Sriram, 2004). He has close connections to industry as a consultant and adviser and teaches strategic marketing management and international marketing at JKU.

ROBERT B. YOUNG has been Dean of the Business Division at Lorain County Community College since 2002. He has published papers in scholarly journals, including *Business Horizons, Journal of Services Marketing,* and *Services Marketing Quarterly.* He has also presented papers at the Academy of International Business, Cleveland State University, the Association for Global Business, and the Academy of Marketing Joint Biennial Conference at Aston University, Birmingham, England. Robert's academic interests include marketing, consumer behavior, marketing research, management, and business strategy. Prior to joining Lorain County Community College, he spent almost 20 years in corporate business positions encompassing both small entrepreneurial businesses and large Cleveland-based corporations. Robert's small-business experience includes ownership positions in two family-owned enterprises. Additionally, Robert has held Director- and Vice President–level positions at Griswold Advertising (a large advertising agency), KeyCorp (the 14th largest bank holding company in the United States), and ICI Glidden Paints (the world's largest coatings company). Robert has also been involved with higher education for the past 20 years as an adjunct faculty member at a variety of area colleges, including Baldwin-Wallace College, Cleveland State University, John Carroll University, Capital University, and David N. Myers University.